The Complete Guide to Your Real Estate Closing

Answers to All Your Questions—From Opening Escrow, to Negotiating Fees, to Signing the Closing Papers

---

Sandy Gadow

McGraw-Hill

New York Chicago San Francisco Lisbon London
Madrid Mexico City Milan New Delhi San Juan
Seoul Singapore Sydney Toronto

5 6 7 8 9 0 PBT/PBT 0 9 8 7 6 5 4

ISBN 0-07-140035-4

Library of Congress Cataloging-in-Publication Data applied for.

This publication is designed to provide accurate and authoritative information in regard to the subject matter covered. It is sold with the understanding that neither the author nor the publisher is engaged in rendering legal, accounting, or other professional service. If legal advice or other expert assistance is required, the services of a competent professional person should be sought.

—From a Declaration of Principles jointly
adopted by a Committee of the American Bar
Association and a Committee of Publishers

 This book is printed on recycled, acid-free paper containing a minimum of 50% recycled de-inked fiber.

McGraw-Hill books are available at special quantity discounts to use as premiums and sales promotions, or for use in corporate training programs. For more information, please write to the Director of Special Sales, McGraw-Hill, 2 Penn Plaza, New York, NY 10121. Or contact your local bookstore.

Contents

Introduction

"Closing" or "escrow" is listed as one of the top 10 problem areas that occur in a real estate transaction. This final step in purchasing property can go smoothly—if you take a few precautions beforehand. Knowing what questions to ask, whom to ask, and when to ask will prepare you for a hassle-free and smooth closing. Asking the right questions will also save you money.

After years of working as an escrow officer, guiding confused buyers and anxious sellers through their various closing and escrow documents, I realized that there wasn't a single book available that explained the subject of escrow and closing all by itself.

Normally the subject of escrow and closing is buried within a few pages of a real estate book or a how-to-make-a-million-in-real-estate guide. Your real estate agent, your banker, your attorney, and even your friends will all give you piecemeal advice about buying or selling a home.

The goal of this book is to give you a comprehensive, step-by-step guide to the process of closing on a property. *The Complete Guide to Your Real Estate Closing* is written by a title and escrow professional. You will benefit from my 25 years' experience as an escrow and closing officer, closing thousands of transactions. *The Complete Guide to Your Real Estate Closing* is based on firsthand, real-life situations. You will learn insider information and helpful tips found nowhere else. I will also share with you the knowledge I have gained as a mortgage broker, closing loans for clients ranging from first-time homebuyers to seasoned real estate investors. Homebuyers, real estate agents, lawyers, and title professionals will find this book a useful resource.

How and When Does Escrow Begin?

This question baffles the most seasoned of investors and leaves the first-time homebuyer confused and even scared. Will my interests be protected? Who will watch out for me and my new investment? Who will tell me when and how I should perform certain closing and escrow tasks?

We will begin this book at the point where the buyer has finally come to an agreement with the seller. The buyer has taken a lot of time and gone to a lot of trouble to find the perfect property. Many hours have been spent talking price and terms with the seller. Finally, the parties have agreed upon a purchase price and the buyer has even agreed to put up a deposit to confirm the contract.

Now what happens? How does this property, this real estate, actually change hands? And what do you need to do to ensure that the transaction will occur precisely according to the terms both parties have negotiated? Who will see that all the terms of the purchase agreement are abided by and that the monies will be distributed properly? How can you be sure you are not paying one penny more than you have to?

Well, the very next thing you need to do is "open escrow," a procedure known variously in some parts of the country as the "closing," "title closing," or "settlement." To accomplish this task, you simply give your entire deposit and all your instructions regarding the transaction to an impartial third party, most likely a title company, but it may be an escrow company, an abstract company, an abstract attorney, or a real estate attorney.

This third party then has the responsibility of handling all the details necessary for the property to change hands. A title search will be ordered, loan applications will be processed, any inspections will be performed and work cleared, and money will change hands when a deed is recorded and title is transferred from seller to buyer.

When you do go ahead and open escrow, you will most likely be told that everything is in good hands and will be taken care of for you. Don't worry, people say. Everything will be OK. Besides, the closing and escrow process is so complicated that only the most experienced professionals will understand what is going on.

But wait a minute! Don't you have any questions about this mysterious closing procedure? Would you like to know how you can be assured that your purchase or sale closes on time? Don't you wonder if any of the fees are negotiable and how you can arrange to pay less at the closing? Are you sure you are taking title in the best manner to provide for the future? After all, you are entrusting some very important papers and some very large sums of money to perfect strangers, not to mention the responsibility you're giving them. Are you doing it all blindly? Wouldn't you feel better if you knew what in the world was about to happen in escrow and at your closing? Wouldn't you like to be in control of which decisions are made?

The Complete Guide to Your Real Estate Closing will provide you with all the tools and tips you need to know to answer your questions and put you in control.

All right, then, let's proceed to determine how much you already know about escrow and closing. Let's figure out your "closing IQ." Do your best to answer these representative questions:

- What do I need to know about my purchase contract?
- Why are the contingencies written into the contract so important?
- Why do I really need an attorney?
- What information is needed to open escrow?
- Why should my deposit check be held in escrow rather than given directly to the seller?
- What does the closing agent do with my deposits?
- Who do I ask each of my specific questions?
- What papers will I be asked to sign and how will these papers be prepared?
- How will my loan be processed?
- What closing costs will I be required to pay?
- What costs and fees will be negotiable? When should I start negotiating these fees?
- What is title insurance and why do I need it?
- Why does it matter how I take title to the property?
- What problems might arise in my closing to prevent my purchase from coming to a close?
- How can I be certain that the papers I sign are correct?
- Who decides when the closing will occur?
- Can I change the way I hold title after escrow closes?
- What happens if my closing has to be canceled?

OK, how did you do? If you were able to answer all of these questions to your own satisfaction, your closing and escrow IQ is probably high enough for you to figure nothing can go wrong and you're excused from reading this book. But if you were unsure about some of your answers, your closing and escrow IQ, whatever it is, could most certainly be raised by reading this book. You most certainly will benefit from money-saving tips and insider closing, title, and loan information.

This book will provide the answers to these questions and others about escrow and closing.

We'll go step by step, clearly and simply, through ordinary closing instructions and common loan documents. We'll check for completeness and accuracy. We'll find out what problems to watch out for. We'll determine if you are being charged the correct amounts for each expense. You'll learn how to feel confident that your closing will take place promptly.

I will tell you how to find out the true cost of your title insurance and how you can cut down this large expense. I will lead you through the maze of paperwork involved in a closing and answer your questions at each step along the way. I will point out common mistakes and real-life solutions. I will help you remove any obstacle that stands in the way of your successful property purchase or sale. I will give you the basic strategies for a successful closing, in addition to valuable insider tips. I will show you how to make the contingencies written in the purchase contract work to your advantage. I will guide you to a successful closing with ease and hopefully save you money in the process.

I will give you resources to verify and look up information on your own, including various Internet Web sites which may give you sample forms which you can print out in the convenience of your home. I will give you a complete state-by-state procedures guide, which outlines closing and lending practices for whichever state you are located in. This guide will tell you where you can go to file a complaint against your lender, real estate agent, or title company. It will tell you how a closing is handled and how property taxes are paid in your area.

I have compiled information together in one place for you, often only found scattered over hundreds of sources. I will continue to post updates to this chart as they become available at my Web site, **www.escrowhelp.com**.

By the time you have finished reading this book, you should have the closing IQ of a genius, and what's more, you'll even be able to communicate knowledgeably with your closing and title officer. You'll be speaking his or her language, "escrowese." It's easy. Really it is!

This book is designed to give you a good understanding of what all parties involved in your closing should be doing for you. It provides you with all the information you need to ask questions about your transaction. I will point out questions you may forget to ask and ones that you were not aware you should ask. Perhaps after reading this book, you'll even be able to inform the closing agent of some things the agent didn't know about before or had forgotten. Title and closing agents are not infallible, you know.

Most important of all, with what you learn from reading this book, you should feel confident enough to follow your purchase or sale all the way through closing and know what's happening at each step. You will be in control of your closing and you will be sure you're being treated fairly and not paying one penny more than is required.

Following your closing is easier than you may think, and it is well worth the small investment of your time. This book is your guide; saving money and executing legal documents that benefit you is your reward.

No matter whether you are buying a house for shelter for yourself and family or as an income property and as a nest egg for your retirement, that property is an important investment. Just as you wouldn't really want to trust someone else to take your money and buy a car or some jewelry, neither should you leave your real estate affairs wholly in the hands of someone else.

Your real estate investment is bound to be the largest financial commitment you will make during your entire lifetime. It's very important to you and you should be satisfied that it's handled correctly. Because no one else has your best interests in mind more than you do, you should know how to prepare, understand, and control your closing yourself. You may even want to direct your own closing yourself and, with this guidebook in hand, you will have the tools to do that.

By the way, I will refer to *escrow instructions* as *closing instructions* or *closing statements*, although these terms may be used interchangeably to refer to the same document. Your money is "in escrow" and the process to complete your real estate transaction will be referred to as "the closing." Keep in mind that those transactions in the Western part of the United States will refer to the closing as "escrow" and the closing agent as the "escrow officer."

Best of luck with your home purchase or sale.

—Sandy Gadow
April 2004

Please feel free to e-mail me with your individual questions at: sandygadow@ escrowhelp.com. If you would like to write me with questions or comments about this book or your escrow questions, please write to me at: P.O. Box 2165, Palm Beach, FL 33480.

Acknowledgments

I wish to acknowledge my Aunt Evy, from whose advice grew my "real estate mentality" and to whom I owe my inspiration for staying in the real estate profession; Jackie Boccabella at California Land Title Company, who started me in the escrow business many years ago; my family and friends, who waited patiently and always gave me encouragement; and my mother for sending me weekly newspaper clippings and articles and keeping me abreast of the latest developments in the real estate industry. A special thanks to Brad Gadow for his support and patience while eating many a meal on a dining table strewn with escrow and closing papers.

About the Author

Sandy Gadow is a title and closing officer with more than 25 years' experience in escrow, title, and real estate. She is a noted authority on escrow and the author of the book *All About Escrow and Real Estate Closings* and the continuing education textbook *The Nuts and Bolts of Escrow*. Sandy has written articles for *Realty Times*, the largest real estate news service on the Internet, and has provided content for hundreds of consumer and industry real estate Web sites.

Sandy is a licensed mortgage broker and real estate sales agent, a member of the American Land Title Association, the California Escrow Association, the National Association of Real Estate Editors, and the California Association of Realtors. She has helped thousands of people buy their homes and is often consulted as an expert on escrow and real estate closing topics.

Chapter One

An Overview of the Closing Process

Many books have been written about how to find a home or rental property, negotiate a purchase price, and arrive at mutually acceptable terms. This book starts where most other real estate books end—when the contract for the sale of the property is signed, but the money hasn't yet been transferred and most of the paperwork hasn't been signed.

Signing the contract on a house is the first step in a complex process that ends when you close on the house and receive the deed to the property. The purpose of this book is to make this complex process simpler for you.

In this first chapter, I'll summarize the steps involved in a real estate closing. I'll assume you have no prior knowledge or experience of escrow and closing, and I'll review each of the parties involved and the roles and responsibilities each one has.

Remember: I'm beginning at the point when you have negotiated a price and signed a contract to buy or sell a property. You've taken a deep breath and are ready to make the sale final. So let's get started.

What Is Escrow?

Escrow is a means for enabling ownership transfers to occur fairly and squarely. It involves bringing an impartial third party into a transaction to see that the buyer and seller perform as they have agreed they would. Escrow enables a buyer and seller to do business with minimum risk, because the responsibility for handling the funds and documents is placed in the hands of someone who is not the least bit affected by the outcome. The escrow holder is a disinterested go-between for the parties involved in the transaction, one whose legal obligation is to safeguard the interests of everyone who is affected by the outcome.

In more technical terms, escrow ensures that something called "concurrent performance" takes place. "Concurrent performance" means that the deed that transfers title on the property from seller to buyer will be recorded at the same time or on the same day on which the buyer's money is released to the seller and other parties to the escrow transaction. The deed will be recorded only after all obligations—such as loans, inspection fees, monies for termite clearance, title fees, and the like—have been paid. Escrow closing guarantees that your money is taken care of properly and legally and that your real estate transaction will occur with concurrent performance.

An escrow closing also assures you that your money and important papers are safely in the hands of a disinterested third party who has the legal responsibility to protect them. In essence, escrow and closing provides a clearinghouse for funds and documents and a means for seeing that all the conditions of your real estate transaction are met before the property changes hands. All parties to the closing have legal protection during the period of closing, and everything is managed by the disinterested escrow holder, which minimizes the possibility of fraud or violation of any terms of the agreement.

Although there may be an escrow involved in many different kinds of transactions, such as refinancing, sales of notes, sales of businesses, sales of business assets, transfers of liquor licenses, and even the purchase and sale of personal property items over the Internet—from fishing poles to Barbie dolls—escrow is used most extensively in the sale of real estate. In this context, escrow may assist in the transfer of real estate, in the transfer of personal property included with real estate, or in the processing of a loan. In short, an escrow is useful whenever a third party is needed to ensire impartiality, to keep or hold any funds or documents safely until all the details have been settled. This third party handles all of the details necessary to complete the transaction and then, after the details have all been taken care of, disburses the documents and monies to the proper parties at the proper time.

You may wish at times that there were some kind of escrow or closing arrangement available when you sent off your cash, check, or money order for some mail-order merchandise because you never know whether you'll receive your order or not and you never know whether you'll be satisfied once you do receive it. Unfortunately, there is no such arrangement available. You just have to hope that the mail-order company is honest enough to send you the merchandise after it receives your money and that it will handle promptly any complaint you might have.

The amount of money involved in any single mail-order transaction is generally insignificant, however, when compared with the amounts of money involved in real estate transactions. That's why escrow is so important to your real estate purchase, sale, or trade. It enables the transfer to take place with the fewest problems possible and ensures full satisfaction of the contract.

What Are the Requirements for an Escrow Closing?

A contract involving an escrow must comply with the four basic requirements for any valid contract, namely, that there must be competent parties, a valid consideration (usually money but can be anything offered by one party and accepted by another), a property, and mutual agreement as to the terms and conditions. The buyer and seller then become the primary parties or "principals" in the escrow, and when there is a lender involved, the lender becomes a primary party in need of escrow protection, too.

The written contract used to initiate most real estate closings is called a real estate purchase agreement and receipt for deposit. Later, this contract is accompanied by written escrow and closing instructions. When properly written and signed by the principal parties, these instruments become binding contracts fully enforceable in a court of law. Just as the principals have to comply with the terms of the contracts they have signed, so, too, must the closing agent comply with the terms of the closing instructions.

How Does Escrow Start?

The person representing you in your purchase or sale, whether it be a real estate agent or an attorney, will usually open escrow for you. However, you can directly hire a title or escrow company to handle escrow for your transaction if no attorneys or agents are involved and if the lender involved in the transaction does not require a particular escrow company.

What Does the Escrow/Closing Officer Do and for Whom Does the Officer Work?

Your escrow will be assigned to an escrow or closing officer and given an escrow or file number. Your realtor or attorney may be the person opening escrow on your behalf, so you will want to check with him or her for your file number, the name of the title or escrow company, and the name of the closing officer in charge of your file. The officer assigned to your escrow closing acts as your personal secretary, no matter whether you are the buyer or the seller. The officer may be called an "escrow officer," "closer," "closing agent," "title officer," or "settlement agent." By law the officer must comply with the terms and conditions of your instructions and must keep your funds safely deposited in a separate escrow account. The officer will also strive to be as confidential as possible.

The closing officer acts as the impartial party in the transaction and performs all the necessary clerical duties involved in order to close your escrow. Among these duties are the following:

■ Ordering the title search showing the current status of the property. This will later be compiled into a title report.

■ Securing payoff amounts and/or beneficiary statements from existing lenders of all amounts owing on the property and requesting releases from the lender, called *full reconveyances*, of any mortgages or deeds of trust to be paid off in escrow.

■ Obtaining instructions and loan documents from the new lender (buyer's lender).

■ Obtaining documents to clear any outstanding liens against the property.

■ Issuing receipts for deposits of documents and funds and holding funds in a separate account. (If a deposit of, say $1,000 or more, is to be held in escrow for more than a few days, you should request that it be deposited into an interest-bearing savings account; any interest accumulated is then credited to you at the close of escrow.)

■ Prorating taxes, interest, rents, etc.

■ Preparing buyer's and seller's escrow instructions and seeing that all documents are properly executed, determining when everything's going to be completed so the transaction can close.

■ Obtaining title insurance for the buyer and/or the lender.

- Arranging timely transfer of the fire insurance policy or seeing that the buyer secures a new policy.

- Recording the necessary documents, such as grant deeds, deeds of trust, powers of attorney, substitutions of liability, and reconveyances, when all the conditions of the transaction have been met.

- Disbursing all funds to the proper parties, delivering documents, and preparing the final closing statements.

Note that closing officers have quite a responsibility. They are supposed to be as impartial as a bench-sitting judge and as secretive as a mother confessor. They are supposed to know whose eyes should see which documents and to keep one party's prying eyes from seeing the other party's private papers. Above all, they are supposed to preserve the confidentiality of every escrow closing they handle. Theirs is not an easy job.

What Does the Title Company Do?

Depending on where you live, your title company may be an attorney, an independent title company, or a large national title company. Whoever performs the title search and issues the policy of title insurance will be responsible for searching the title and determining if the seller has legal right to convey title to the new buyer. The title company will list all the items relevant to your parcel of land and report them to you. (Please refer to Chapter 3, "The Title Search," to learn precisely how a title search is performed and what items it will reveal.)

Remember that one of the many extra services that escrow companies offer is information. Your escrow or closing officer will be happy to answer your questions about escrow in general and your own escrow in particular, so long as your questions are not, strictly speaking, the kind of legal questions you ought to be asking an attorney. You will find that your closing officer frequently knows the answers to closing questions or knows where the answers can be found. Indeed, she should be the first person you call whenever a question arises. The officer knows the status of your closing at any given moment and will be happy to discuss it with you. Be frank and open, because only if the officer has all of the pertinent facts available can she make sure that your title and escrow questions are answered and that your escrow will close on time. The escrow officer really is a personal secretary for you. Don't be afraid to ask your questions. Don't let yourself be rushed into signing anything you don't understand. Ask your questions first. Sign your papers second.

What Does the Attorney Do?

In many states, especially in the East, attorneys handle the closing. The attorney may order the title search and issue the title insurance policy. Your attorney will be responsible for reviewing the documents and coordinating the closing with your lender. In states where escrow or title companies handle the closing, the escrow or closing officer will perform many of the duties performed by an attorney. Even if you are in a state that uses title and escrow companies to handle the closing, you may still want to hire your own attorney to review your documents and attend the closing with you. An attorney often brings peace of mind to buyers and sellers, who may be hesitant about negotiating contracts, signing important legal documents, and making important decisions relating to holding title.

The following list summarizes typical attorney duties:

- Place buyer's good faith deposit into an escrow account.
- Order title search.
- Review title report to be certain seller has marketable title to convey to buyer.
- Review the title commitment and survey together and make sure the two documents when read together make sense.
- Review the survey to be certain that it is recent (six months or less), has the original seal, and correct legal description. Determine if there are any building line violations, based on encroachments of improvements over the building lines. Look for evidence of any unrecorded easements, such as a neighbor's walkway traversing the land, or joint driveways. Be certain that the property has access to a street.
- Investigate any liens found in the title report. (Perhaps the lien was paid off years ago. Perhaps client is planning to pay the lien with the proceeds from the closing.) Obtain a release of lien if necessary.

- If a lien cannot be cleared at the time of closing, determine if a title indemnity is an option. The title indemnity will be an agreement between the party responsible for clearing the lien and the title company.
- Evaluate the type of title insurance coverage that buyer is obtaining.
- Distribute title commitment or preliminary title report to all appropriate parties.
- Get title work to lender according to the buyer's loan instructions.
- Follow all stipulations of the purchase contract between buyer and seller.
- Prepare any addendums as necessary or make changes to the original contract. Obtain signatures from buyer and seller to any new agreement or changes in the terms and conditions.
- Clear up any discrepancies quickly by contacting buyer, seller, and realtor.
- Be available to answer questions and concerns by hesitant buyers and sellers.
- Coordinate the closing date with buyer, seller, and lender.
- Receive the closing package from the lender, reviewing all loan documents for accuracy of title description and buyer's name and address.
- Prepare or obtain a power of attorney form for any party who may be unavailable to attend the closing. Have the power of attorney form approved by the lender.
- Attend the closing and explain documents.
- Record deed, mortgage or deed of trust, satisfaction of mortgage, or any other recordable documents pertaining to the transaction.
- Return loan package to the lender with signatures.
- Deposit the lender's loan proceeds check into the attorney's escrow account.
- Distribute sales proceeds check to seller and any refund check due to buyer.
- Pay parties as necessary, such as the appraiser, credit report company, tax collector, hazard insurance agent, and water or other utility company as per final HUD-1 statement of closing costs.

What Does the Real Estate Agent Do?

If a real estate agent is involved in your purchase or sale, the agent will have specific duties to perform. Among the duties of your realtor will be the following:

- Be sure the contract is signed and initialed by all parties on all pages.
- Verify that all necessary disclosures have been given to the buyer and the seller.

- Be sure the legal description of the property is correct in the purchase agreement.

- Be sure contingencies in the contract are worded correctly.

- Contact the attorney or escrow/title company as soon as the property is under contract.

- Get deposit or "good faith money" to the closing agent or have it deposited into the broker's escrow account.

- Be clear with the attorney about who will take care of what responsibilities.

- Communicate as much information as possible to the attorney or closing agent to avoid any ambiguity.

- Follow the time limit for home and termite inspections, getting signed approval from the buyer.

- Assist the buyer in finding financing and be certain the buyer has applied within the time limit set in the contract.

- Work with the escrow/closing officer to get the title commitment or title report distributed to all parties.

- Obtain the seller's existing mortgage account number and lender information as soon as possible and give this information to the escrow/closing officer.

- Fax the closing information to the attorney or closing agent as soon as it is available. (When contacting the attorney or escrow officer to ask questions or supply information, ask to speak to their assistant or secretary if they are busy. The secretary is often very useful in conveying information about the closing to the attorney and can respond to questions promptly.)

- Obtain previous title insurance policy information as soon as contract is signed. Convey this information to the closing agent or attorney. Previous title policies save the attorney title search time and may save the buyer money on the new policy.

- Obtain previous survey information as soon as contract is signed to convey to the attorney. (Updating an existing survey can save time and money.)

- Explain to the buyer that hazard/homeowner's insurance will be required at closing. Determine which insurance company buyer intends to use.

- If the lender will be collecting escrow funds for insurance, it is necessary to provide this information to the escrow/closing officer.

- Follow up so that the insurance agent gets the binder or policy to the escrow/closing officer or attorney prior to closing.

- Deal with all issues regarding the closing as soon as they are raised. This will avoid delays at closing.

- Perform final walk-through with the buyer. Write down any concerns or items needing repair.

- Reconfirm closing day and time with the closing agent and with the buyer and the seller.

- Review the final HUD-1 statement with the buyer and the seller before the closing.

- Be sure the buyer has a certified check for closing funds or has made arrangements to wire money to the title company or closing agent.

Who Are the Other Parties to the Closing and What Do They Do?

In addition to the closing agent, title company, attorney, and real estate agent, there will probably be a lender involved in your closing. The lender will provide the financing for the property and work with your closing agent to be certain that all the conditions required to fund your loan will take place prior to closing. There will be an appraiser involved, who will examine the property and issue an appraisal report. There may be a surveyor, who will issue a survey, which may be required by your lender.

There may be a pest inspection company and a building inspection company involved in your closing. These inspectors will be responsible for performing a detailed inspection of your house and issuing a report as to their findings. There will be an insurance agent involved, as a new insurance policy will need to be issued on the property.

How Does the Escrow/Closing Officer Get Paid?

A single escrow closing fee, determined by the amount of money involved in the transaction, covers all of the usual escrow closing services except for the title insurance fees.

Customs unique to a particular geographical area generally dictate who will pay the fees (see Appendix B). In some areas, the buyer customarily pays the title and the escrow fees, whereas in other areas, the seller customarily pays half of the fees and the buyer half. In still other areas, for some unknown reason, the seller pays all of the escrow closing fees.

Just as real estate sales commissions are negotiable, so, too, is the responsibility for paying these fees. Before signing the purchase agreement, though, the buyer and the seller ought to determine who will pay the fees so there won't be any argument later about who is supposed to be paying them.

What Happens at the Closing?

After the contingencies of the purchase agreement have been met, the buyer's loan has been approved and processed, and any agreed-upon repairs and inspections have been made, you will be notified that it is time to appear at the closing agent's office. The buyer will be asked to bring in a certified or cashier's check for the down payment money and the seller will be asked to bring in proper identification for notary purposes.

At the closing, an exchange of money for the deed to the property will take place. The buyer will sign closing documents and release any remaining money owing to the seller. This payment is usually in the form of a combination of cash together with a mortgage provided by an outside lender. The seller in turn will sign a deed transferring legal title to the property to the new buyer. The actual possession of the property may occur at a later date, depending on the local custom in your area. The release of the money to the seller may occur a few days after the closing, depending on the closing agent's requirements for clearing funds.

Once completed, the deed will be recorded in the county recorder's office, together with any mortgage documents, and the buyer will receive a policy of title insurance, guaranteeing the title to the property is valid as of the date of the closing. The seller will receive the balance of the funds necessary for the sale to take place.

What Is the Timetable for a Typical Closing?

Each closing is different, but there are enough similarities that it is possible to create a timetable for a so-called "typical" closing. Take a look at the table below. It shows how long you might expect the various escrow closing activities to take (continued on next page).

TYPICAL ESCROW TIMETABLE	
Week	**Activity**
1	Open escrow.
1-2	Order preliminary title report. Shop for a loan.
3-4	Complete the loan application. Check the preliminary title report for liens, judgments, problems, etc. Review the termite report.
5-6	Prepare escrow instructions. Sign the loan documents. Buyer: deposit balance of money due. Seller: sign the deed and escrow instructions.

TYPICAL ESCROW TIMETABLE	
Week	**Activity**
6-8	Close escrow. Record the documents. Release seller's money. Pay off old loans and miscellaneous charges. Deliver the grant deed to the buyer. Prepare the closing statements.

Chapter Two

Opening Escrow

So now that we know who all the parties to the closing are and what roles they play, let's get down to the nitty gritty and walk through the opening of escrow, which is the beginning of the closing process.

What's Involved in Opening Escrow and Starting the Closing Process?

Opening escrow involves simply visiting the office of any firm that handles escrows and closings, then handing over the deposit monies and giving instructions for the transaction. Both the buyer and the seller submit escrow closing instructions, and so does the lender, if there is one.

That's all there is to opening escrow. It's something that anyone who's involved in the transaction may do—the buyer, the seller, the lender, or the real estate agent. It doesn't matter who opens the escrow, just so long as those involved in the transaction have designated someone to do it when they sign the final purchase agreement. Generally, the real estate agent, being the one most familiar with closing procedures, takes the initiative and opens the escrow, but the agent doesn't have to be the one to do it. Anyone may.

A Typical Misunderstanding: Mike and Liz like a certain house that's for sale, but because it's for sale by its owner, they decide to pass it up. After all, without a real estate agent involved, who would protect their deposit money and who would take care of all the closing details?

The Way Things Really Are: Mike and Liz could make an offer on this house with complete confidence that their interests would be protected. All they need to do is select a reputable escrow company and a knowledgeable escrow officer. In for-sale-by-owner transactions, which involve no agent at all, either the buyer or the seller or both together may open escrow. How should I select my closing agent?

In selecting a closing agent to handle your transaction, consider the following criteria:

■ *Reputation of the company in the community*—-Because you want to protect yourself and your property with a dependable closing agent, you would be wise to ask your friends and acquaintances who have had experience with real estate transactions to recommend a company they have been pleased with, one that met their expectations.

■ *Managerial experience*—-The closing agent you select should be professional and reliable and should employ skilled closing officers. Your escrow and closing officer should be knowledgeable, efficient, friendly, and confidential. After reading this book, you'll be prepared to ask questions of closing officers to determine which one you want to handle your transaction.

■ *Office location*—-Since you will have to visit the closing agent's office in person at least once and perhaps several times to prove your identity and sign numerous papers, try to select an agent with an office conveniently located near your home or work, so you can reach it during normal business hours in just a few minutes. The closing office should be neat and orderly and it should provide you and your escrow officer with quiet, dignified surroundings.

■ *Fees*—-The fees charged by escrow and closing agents vary. Whenever possible, try to select the most reputable and professional one you can find, one that also charges reasonable fees. In certain circumstances, you may have no choice when selecting a closing agent, for some institutional lenders have their own escrow closing departments and prefer to use them exclusively for their own loans. You can find out by asking lenders when you apply for a loan whether they handle their own closings.

You will always have a choice of title insurance companies, however, and you may want to shop around for one, for they vary in both rates and coverage.

The most commonly used closing agents are title insurance companies, trust companies, banks, savings and loan associations, real estate companies, and independent escrow companies, all of which are strictly regulated by the government. Lawyers, too, sometimes serve as closing agents. No matter who acts as the closing agent, though, the function of the agent is basically the same. Only the specific procedures that they follow will vary somewhat.

Be aware that the entire practice of handling a closing varies from place to place, just as the party responsible for paying the fees varies. Even within a state it varies from county to county. In Northern California, for instance, title insurance companies usually process the closing and the issuance of a title insurance policy together, whereas in Southern California, independent escrow agents handle most of the escrows, and title companies issue the title insurance separately.

In some parts of the country, particularly in the East, the buyer and the seller hire different lawyers, who, in turn, see that their clients fulfill every obligation

necessary to complete the transaction. There is some consultation between the lawyers and then, at closing, there is an exchange, an examination, and a signing of the documents. This is a more casual closing procedure, but it still involves a third party (or parties) entrusted to carry out the desires of buyer and seller.

What Information Will I Need to Open Escrow?

To open escrow, you will need to provide the closing company with the following information regarding your transaction:

- Purchase price, address, and description of property
- Seller's name and address
- Buyer's name and address
- Name of real estate agent, if any, his or her address, and the commission agreed upon
- Parties to whom preliminary reports are to be sent (generally buyer, seller, lender, and real estate agent)
- Termite report information
- Amount of deposit to be held in escrow (if your deposit is $1,000 or more, stipulate that it be put into a high-yielding interest-bearing account)
- Buyer's fire insurance agent
- Financing information

- Personal property involved in the sale, if any (e.g., washer, dryer, refrigerator, stove, window coverings, chandeliers, etc.)
- Rents, if any, including due dates and refundable deposits
- Miscellaneous information peculiar to your purchase
- Closing date
- Current tax bills and most recent title policy (helpful but not absolutely necessary)

Whether you select a closing officer yourself or have one assigned to you by the closing company, he or she must have all of this information available in order to prepare your escrow instructions properly. The better informed the officer is, the faster he or she can process your escrow closing. Chart 2-1 on the next page gives you a worksheet designed to help you organize all of this information for your closing officer. There's a blank copy in the back of this book for you to use.

What Should a Real Estate Purchase Agreement Include?

Often buyers and sellers have questions about making up a written purchase agreement of their own, especially when they come to terms without the aid of a real estate agent. Their agreement may take any number of forms, but it should spell out the basic plan for their real estate transaction, and it must be dated and signed by both the buyer and the seller. The agreement must state clearly the terms of the sale and what must occur before the property can change hands.

Although either the buyer or the seller may draw up an agreement of their own using a model that includes the standard safeguards, they would be wise to buy a standard purchase agreement form at an office supplies store or from a publisher that sells these agreements to real estate agents. Forms are available over the Internet, and you may want to review and download a form from your computer. One such site to find sample forms would be: **www.kaktus.com**.

Having a lawyer draw up the agreement is another alternative, of course, one that may be necessary for more complicated transactions. Typically, on the West Coast, lawyers do not become involved in drafting purchase, sale, or exchange agreements unless circumstances, such as a pending probate, a lawsuit, or divorce proceedings, complicate the matter. The real estate agent, the buyer, or the seller normally draws up the agreement. On the East Coast, however, lawyers play a large part in real estate transactions, in some areas drawing up the purchase agreement, examining the title, and preparing the necessary legal documents, such as the deed, mortgage document or deeds of trust, promissory notes, and so forth. (See sample purchase agreement in Chart 2-2 and Appendix A.)

Worksheet for Opening Escrow

Date July 2, 20xx

Person opening escrow Donald Duncan, agent

   Address 312 3rd St., Boonville, CA 91002

   Telephone (123) 987-4567

Property Address 12 Allendale Ct., Boonville, CA 91002

Owner Samuel P. Seller, a married man

   Address 12 Allendale Ct., Boonville, CA 91002

   Telephone (123) 456-7890

Buyer Bruce B. Buyer and Barbara A. Buyer, his wife

   Address 525 Mesa Drive, Targaret City, CA 91004

   Telephone (123) 109-8765

Sales Price $100,000   Deposit $1,000

Total down payment (including deposit) $10,000

Commission

      6% Paid to Valley Real Estate

      Paid to

1st deed of trust—lender First Federal Trust

   Amount $80,000   Terms Best available interest rate—30 years

2nd deed of trust—lender Samuel P. Seller

   Amount $10,000   Terms 10%, $212, 48 monthly pmts, due in 5 yrs

Termite Report Company Gettem Termite Control Co.

   Termite report copies sent to Buyer, Seller, Agent

Bill of Sale (personal property) washer/dryer, stove, refrigerator, some window

coverings, chandelier in dining room

Closing date August 10, 20xx

Closing costs

   Title insurance paid by Buyer

   Escrow fees paid by Buyer

   Transfer taxes paid by Seller

Title

   Purchaser to take title as Joint tenants

Miscellaneous Seller to pay up to $250 for termite work

Chart 2-1. Example of worksheet for opening escrow

RESIDENTIAL PURCHASE AGREEMENT AND DEPOSIT RECEIPT

RECEIVED FROM _Bruce B. Buyer and Barbara A. Buyer, his wife_
hereinafter designated as BUYER, the sum of $ _1,000.00 (One Thousand and no/100ths----------------_ (DOLLARS)
evidenced by ☐ Cash, ☒ Other _Pers Chk_ to be deposited one day after acceptance with: _Secure Title Company_
on account of the PURCHASE PRICE of $ _100,000.00_ (_One Hundred Thousand and No/100ths---------_ DOLLARS)
for the real property situated in the City of _Boonville_, County of _Barrett_, California.
described as: _12 Allendale Ct. A.P. #184-162-21_ upon the following TERMS and CONDITIONS:

1. **DEPOSIT INCREASE.** The deposit shall be increased to $ _N/A_ within ___ days from acceptance, evidenced by Cash.
2. **PRORATIONS.** Rents, taxes, interest and other expenses of the property to be prorated as of the date of recordation of the deed. Security deposits, advance rentals, or considerations involving future lease credits shall be credited to Buyer.
3. **CLOSING.** On or before _8/10/XX_ or within _30_ days from acceptance, whichever is later, both parties shall deposit with an authorized escrow holder all funds and instruments necessary to complete the sale in accordance with the terms hereof. Thereafter any party, including Agent, may disclose the terms of sale. The representations and warranties herein shall not be terminated by conveyance of the property. Escrow fee to be paid by _Buyer_.
4. **PHYSICAL POSSESSION.** Physical possession, with all keys and garage door openers, shall be delivered to Buyer (check either item (1) or (2)):
   ☒ 1. Upon recordation of the deed.
   ☐ 2. After recordation, but not later than midnight of _____ Unless Seller has vacated the premises prior to recordation, Seller shall pay Buyer ___ per day from recordation to date of possession and leave in escrow a sum equal to the above per diem amount multiplied by the number of days from date of closing to date allowed for delivery of possession. Said sum to be disbursed to the persons entitled thereto on the date possession is delivered.
5. **EVIDENCE OF TITLE.** In the form of ☒ a policy of title insurance, ☐ other: _____ to be paid for by _Buyer_.
6. **EXAMINATION OF TITLE.** Fifteen (15) days from date of acceptance hereof are allowed the Buyer to examine the title to the property and to report in writing any valid objections thereto. Any exceptions to the title which would be disclosed by examination of the records shall be deemed to have been accepted unless reported in writing within said fifteen (15) days. If Buyer objects to any exceptions to the title, Seller shall use due diligence to remove such exceptions at his own expense before close of escrow. But if such exceptions cannot be removed before close of escrow, all rights and obligations hereunder may, at the election of the Buyer, terminate and end, and the deposit shall be returned to Buyer, unless he elects to purchase the property subject to such exceptions.
7. **ENCUMBRANCES.** In addition to any encumbrances referred to herein, Buyer shall take title to the property subject to: (1) Real Estate Taxes not yet due, and (2) Covenants, conditions, restrictions, rights-of-way and easements of record, if any, which do not materially affect the value or intended use of the property. The amount of any bond or assessment which is a lien shall be ☒ paid, ☐ assumed, by _SELLER_. If assumed, the outstanding principal balance of such obligation ☐ shall, ☐ shall not be credited to Buyer at close of escrow.
8. **FIXTURES.** All items permanently attached to the property including attached floor coverings, draperies with hardware, shades, blinds, window and door screens, storm sash, combination doors, awnings, light fixtures, TV antenna, electric garage door openers, outdoor plants, and trees, are included free of liens.
9. **PERSONAL PROPERTY.** The following personal property, on the premises when inspected by Buyer, is included in the purchase price and shall be transferred to Buyer free of liens by a Bill of Sale at close of escrow. No warranty is implied as to the condition of said property: _Washer/Dryer, Refrigerator Stove, Window Coverings, Chandelier in Living Room._
10. **MAINTENANCE.** Seller covenants that the heating, air-conditioning (if any), electrical, sewer, septic system, drainage, sprinkler (if any) and plumbing systems including the water heater, as well as built-in appliances and other mechanical apparatus shall be in working order on the date occupancy is delivered. Seller shall replace any cracked or broken glass including windows, mirrors, shower and tub enclosures. Until occupancy is delivered, Seller shall maintain landscaping, grounds and pool (if any). Seller agrees to deliver the property in a neat and clean condition with all debris removed. The following items are specifically excluded from the above: _None_

Buyer and Seller understand and acknowledge that Broker shall not in any circumstances be liable for any breach in this clause.
11. **NOTICES.** By acceptance hereof, Seller warrants that he has no notice of violations relating to the property, from City, County, or State agencies.
12. **PROVISIONS ON THE REVERSE SIDE.** The provisions marked ☒ below, printed in full on the reverse side, are included in this agreement.
   ☒ A. Pest Control Inspection, paid by: ☒ Buyer, ☐ Seller
   Other structure: _____
   Section (2) work to be paid by: ☒ Buyer, ☐ Seller
   ☐ B. Existing Pest Control Report Dated: _____
   By _____
   ☐ C. "As is." but Subject to Buyer's Approval
   ☐ D. Waiver of Pest Control Inspection
   ☐ E. City and County Inspection within ___ days of acceptance
   ☐ F. Condominium Disclosure
   ☐ G. Home Protect Ctr. ☐ paid by ___ ☒ waived by _Buyer_
   ☐ H. Special Studies Zone Disclosure
   ☒ I. Inspections of Physical Condition of Property, to be approved or disapproved within _5_ days of acceptance
   ☐ J. VA Appraisal Clause
   ☐ K. FHA Appraisal Clause
   ☒ L. Smoke Detectors provided by Seller
   ☐ M. Flood Hazard Zone
   ☐ N. Contingent upon the sale of _____
13. **ACCESS TO PROPERTY.** Seller agrees to provide reasonable access to the property to Buyer, inspectors and appraisers representing Buyer.
14. **REAL ESTATE TRANSFER DISCLOSURE STATEMENT.** Seller shall comply with Sec. 1102 of the California Civil Code by providing Buyer "as soon as practicable before the transfer of title" a completed Real Estate Transfer Disclosure Statement (Statutory PPC Form 110.21/22 CAL)
15. **BUYER'S APPROVAL.** If the Real Estate Transfer Disclosure Statement (PPC Form 110.21/22CAL) is delivered after the execution of an offer to purchase, the Buyer is allowed to terminate the transaction by written notice delivered to Seller or Seller's agent within the time limit provided by Sec. 1102 of the California Civil Code and have all deposits returned less expenses incurred by Buyer to date of termination. Nothing disclosed by the Seller shall require Seller to correct or improve the condition disclosed except as otherwise agreed to in writing.
16. **DEFAULT.** In the event that Buyer shall default in the performance of this agreement, unless the parties have agreed to a provision for liquidated damages, Seller may, subject to any rights of the agent herein, retain Buyer's deposit on account of damages sustained and may take such action as he deems appropriate to collect such additional damages as may have been actually sustained, and Buyer shall have the right to take such action as he deems appropriate to recover such portion of the deposit as may be allowed by law. In the event that Buyer shall so default, unless Buyer and Seller have agreed to liquidated damages, Buyer agrees to pay to the brokers entitled thereto such commissions as would be payable by Seller in the absence of such default. Buyer's obligation to said brokers shall be in addition to any rights which said brokers may have against Seller in the event of default. In the event legal action is instituted by the broker or any party to this agreement to enforce the terms of this agreement, or arising out of the execution of the agreement or the sale, or to collect commissions, the prevailing party shall be entitled to receive from the other party a reasonable attorney fee to be determined by the court in which such action is brought.
17. **EXPIRATION.** This offer shall expire unless a copy hereof with Seller's written acceptance is delivered to Buyer or his Agent within ___ days.
18. **TIME.** Time is of the essence of this agreement.
19. **ADDITIONAL TERMS AND CONDITIONS:** _Subject to buyer obtaining 80% loan at current interest rate for 30 years. All loan fees paid by buyer. Seller to take back a 2nd Note & Deed of Trust in the amount of $10,000.00 at 10% interest, payable in monthly installments of $212.48 and due in 5 years. Seller to pay up to $250.00 for termite repair work._

The undersigned Buyer **has read both sides of this agreement** and acknowledges receipt of a copy hereof. Buyer acknowledges further that he has not received or relied upon any statements or representations by the undersigned Agent which are not herein expressed.

Valley Real Estate Company DATED _July 1, 20XX_ TIME: _11:30 a.m._
By _Donald Duncan_
Broker's Initials: _DD_ Dated _July 1, 20XX_ , _Bruce B. Buyer_ Buyer
Barbara A. Buyer Buyer

ACCEPTANCE

Seller accepts the foregoing offer and agrees to sell the herein described property for the price and on the terms and conditions herein specified.
COMMISSION. Seller hereby irrevocably assigns and agrees to pay to _Valley Real Estate Company_ the Broker in this transaction, in Cash from proceeds at close of escrow, for services rendered: _6% of Purchase Price_

In the event that Buyer defaults and fails to complete the sale, the Broker shall be entitled to receive one-half of Buyer's deposit, but not more than the commission earned, without prejudice to Broker's rights to recover the balance of the commission from Buyer. The mutual rescission of this agreement by Buyer and Seller shall not relieve said parties of their obligations to Broker hereunder. This agreement shall not limit the rights of Broker provided for in any listing or other agreement which may be in effect between Seller and Broker, except that the amount of the commission shall be as specified herein.

The undersigned Seller hereby acknowledges receipt of a copy hereof. DATED _July 1, 20XX_ TIME: _5:00 p.m._
Valley Real Estate Company
By _Donald Duncan_ _Samuel Seller_ Seller
Seller

Chart 2-2. Residential purchase agreement

Whether you use a pre-printed form such as the one shown in Chart 2-2 or a tailor-made agreement, your agreement should provide the following "contingencies" or safeguards for your protection. (A contingency is something that must take place before your purchase or sale is completed and money and title are transferred.)

- *The deposit received from the buyer* and what will happen to it if the agreement is canceled.

- *Personal property to be included in the sale*, spelled out very specifically. (Take the time to list all the movable items that are to be included with the real property transfer and avoid numerous problems later. Are the curtains considered "window coverings"? Will a naked light bulb be substituted for the hanging Tiffany lamp? Are the towel bars considered attached and hence real property, or are they personal property?)

- *Date for the close of escrow* and what will happen if the closing is delayed.

- *Division of of shared expenses between buyer and seller*, called "prorations," and the date to be used for computing them.

- *Default provisions* or what will happen if either party doesn't live up to the agreement.

- *Termite inspection,* including who pays for the inspection and who pays for remedying any deficiencies disclosed in the inspection, as well as who pays for the recommended preventive measures listed in the report.

- *Other property inspections* (which might include a roofing inspection or a general building inspection).   The buyer is typically given 10-14 days to inspect the property or have a professional inspection made of the house, its systems and structure. There may be inspections for lead and radon levels. Even the neighborhood itself may be subject to inspection.

- *Financing arrangements.* A clause should be written in the purchase agreement that allows ample time for the buyer to apply for and be approved for a loan. Time to make an application is typically 10-14 days and time for loan approval is usually 30 days.

- *Occupancy date* when the buyer may move in. (Will the seller remain in the residence after the close of escrow? If so, what will his rent be?)

- *Stipulation for payment of real estate commissions,* if applicable. (Commissions are paid only upon close of escrow, and the agreement should provide for payment.)

- *Title.* The buyer should be given ample time to review the preliminary title report of the commitment of title. Usually the buyer is given 10 days from receipt of the report to give his approval.

- *Covenants, conditions, and restrictions* (CC&Rs—limitations placed upon the use of land by its owner, the governing operation of a condominium, cooperative or, common interest development). When buying a condominium, a cooperative, or a home in a common interest development, a provision for the approval of the condominium documents, bylaws, budget, or other conditions should be included. Usually the buyer is given 10-14 days from receipt for this approval.

- *Contingency for the sale of the buyer or seller's current home.* Either party may need to add a contingency for the sale of their current home. The time limit on this condition may be set at 30-60 days.

- *Insurance.* You may want to write a contingency into the purchase agreement that allows for cancellation in the event the buyer is not able to obtain homeowner's insurance.

- *Disclosures.* A contingency will be written into the agreement that provides for the buyer to approve the seller's disclosures as to such items as earthquake hazards, flood hazard, lead in the home (if built prior to 1978), or other material facts or defects as required in your state. The time limit for these disclosures is typically 10 days.

- *Attorney review.* You may want to provide for the review of the agreement by your attorney. The time limit is generally set at between five and 10 days of signing the initial agreement.

Although many of these contingencies may be included in the pre-printed purchase agreement form, you may need to add an addendum to provide for any special concerns you may have. The contingency time periods are negotiable and can vary according to the special circumstances of your purchase or sale. When a contingency cannot be satisfied, the purchase agreement may be canceled and your deposit returned. Each contingency should be approved and signed by all parties to the contract, noting their agreement.

Be sure that your purchase agreement provides ample protections for both buyer and seller.

How Will Contingencies Written into the Contract Protect Me?

The contingencies that are written into the purchase contract protect all parties against certain events that may occur between the time the offer to purchase is made and the time the sale is finalized. You want to consider carefully the contingencies written into your contract, as they are the legal way of allowing you to change your mind. They allow you an "out" if you so choose or a negotiating tool if certain things are found that you cannot accept.

Each time a contingency is removed, both the buyer and seller should sign off to show their approval. If there is a disagreement, you should work with the seller to come to terms that you can both agree upon.

A Typical Misunderstanding: Although Pete and Jane know they have credit problems and may have trouble finding a mortgage for their new home, they decided to go ahead with their offer, as they can always keep trying to find financing and at least they have the property tied up so that no one else can buy it.

The Way Things Really Are: Pete and Jane's purchase agreement with the seller provides that they have 10 days to apply for a loan and 30 days to receive a loan approval. If they do not find financing within that time period, the seller may choose to cancel the agreement and find new buyers for his property. Pete and Jane should provide for an extended period of time to find a mortgage and ask the seller to sign his approval.

 Look at the cutoff dates for any contingencies written in your purchase agreement. If these dates pass, you will lose your right to rely on these contingencies as a remedy for approval or disapproval of those items.

What Is a Real Estate Transfer Disclosure Statement?

A *transfer disclosure statement* is a document that reveals a property's known defects. In some states, certainly in California, sellers of residential property consisting of one to four units (houses through fourplexes) must furnish their buyers with a completed real estate disclosure statement for every property sold.

These are typical of the questions that sellers must answer in writing for their buyers:

- Is the house built on filled or unstable ground?
- Do you know of any flooding problems on your property or on any adjacent property?
- Do you know of any structural additions or alterations, or the installation, alteration, repair, or replacement of significant components of the structure upon the property, completed during the term of your ownership or that of a prior owner, completed with or without an appropriate permit?
- Do you know of any inspection reports, surveys, studies, or notices concerning the property?
- Do you know of any violations of government regulations, ordinances, or zoning laws regarding this property?
- Has the roof ever leaked while you have owned the property?

- Are the water supply pipes copper, galvanized, or plastic?
- Are you aware of any excessive rust stains in the tubs, lavatories, or sinks?
- Are there any extension cords stapled to baseboards or underneath carpets or rugs?
- Is the furnace room or furnace closet adequately vented?
- Are you aware of any built-in appliances that are in need of repair or replacement?
- Are you aware of any other conditions that could affect the value or desirability of the property?

The buyers must receive a copy of the disclosure statement at some time before the title is transferred. If possible, it should be in their hands before they sign the purchase agreement. Should they receive it after signing the purchase agreement, they will have between three and five days to cancel the sale.

Real estate agents provide the necessary forms for handling this disclosure requirement as a matter of course. Whenever there's no agent involved, the seller has to do it. Forms for this purpose are available through Professional Publishing (**www.profpub.com**), as well as through your local Board of Realtors' office. You can find valuable information on the RESPA (Real Estate Settlement Procedures Act) form on the Internet at **www.hud.gov/offices/hsg/sfh/res/respa_hm.cfm**.

Does all of this sound as if Ralph Nader has discovered that real estate buyers need more protection than what they've had in the past? You're right. "Caveat emptor" no longer applies to real estate transactions. It's now "caveat venditor." Sellers are the ones who now must beware, not buyers. By law in some states, they're liable for any damages the buyer incurs because of their negligence or failure to comply with the disclosure statement regulations.

Are There Any Other Disclosures That Have to Be Made?

Sometimes real estate agents act as the seller's agent, sometimes they act as the buyer's agent, and sometimes they do a kind of balancing act, acting on behalf of both seller and buyer. The nature of their relationship can influence a transaction significantly in one way or another, so the principals ought to know who's working for whom.

Most state laws now require real estate agents to disclose their relationship and their duties to buyers and sellers whenever a transaction involves a single-family residence or a small income property (one to four units).

The agent must first explain whether he or she is working for the seller, for the buyer, or for both the seller and the buyer, and then all parties must sign a disclosure statement to this effect. The agent who works for both the buyer and the seller is termed a "dual agent" or a "transactional broker." To view a sample agency disclosure statement, you may look on the Internet at **www.profpub.com**.

TIP If there is anything in the agreement that does not make sense to you, ask your escrow officer or consult an attorney. Do not sign until you thoroughly understand and feel that you can accept all the conditions stipulated in the agreement. You don't want to be stuck with something you didn't bargain for, and you surely don't want to take a chance on losing either the property or your deposit money.

TIP If you suspect that the sellers have remodeled or altered their house recently, check with the local building department to make sure that they secured a building permit for the work. If they didn't get a permit and you buy the house, you may get stuck with the consequences. You may have to get a permit yourself and then see that the work passes inspection. If you don't take care of the problem once you own the house, you will have to disclose this when you eventually sell the property.

Chapter Three

The Title Search

You've opened escrow and the closing process has officially started. Now what? The next step in the process is the title search. In this chapter you'll learn who performs this search, why it's necessary, and how issues that are raised during this process can be resolved.

What Happens Right After Escrow Opens?

Right after escrow is opened, the escrow/closing officer orders that a title search be conducted to trace the chain of title back through every available record. This title search will determine whether the person representing himself or herself as the current owner actually has legal ownership and hence the right to sell the property at all. The search will also reveal what, if any, defects exist on the title. Just as a life insurance company will not insure a person without a thorough physical examination, a title insurance company won't issue a policy of title insurance without doing a thorough title search.

The results of this search are compiled into what is called in most Western states a *preliminary report* or "prelim." In some states it's called a *commitment of title*; in others it's called an *encumbrance report*. No matter what it's called, it reflects the conditions under which a title company is willing to issue a policy of title insurance. Still other states handle their title search results somewhat differently. Their title search firms issue an *abstract of title*, "abstract" for short, which reflects the various documents in the chain of title without giving any determination as to the title's condition.

How Is a Title Search Performed?

In order to trace a property's chain of title, a title company examiner searches the records of the county recorder, county assessor, and other government taxing agencies to locate any and all documents that might affect the title to a given property. Most title companies have their own "plant" department, where they keep duplicates of recorded documents, along with copies of certain recorded documents from offices and courts at the federal, state, county, and municipal levels, any of which may affect titles. Thus, the examiner generally doesn't even have to leave the building to search through these documents.

In his search, the title examiner has four primary determinations to make:

- The exact description of the property
- The estate or interest in the property
- The vesting of the estate or interest
- The exceptions (liens, encumbrances, and defects) affecting the particular vested interest

The first step the examiner takes is to locate the property. He or she does this either by the county assessor's parcel number or by the company's own indexing system.

I should note that each title company may have a slightly different system for indexing its documents. Some use a tract- or lot-book system, which is a hand-posted system of recording and indexing documents according to the property description and assessor's parcel number. Some use an outside service that supplies the information to them on microfiche or computer printouts that have specific codes designed for efficiency and ease in tracing the complete history of a particular property.

The county recorder's office itself indexes by name only, using something called a *grantor-grantee index*. This system is not efficient enough for a title company's search, however, because it lists documents alphabetically by name only, without cross-referencing them to property description. Using this index alone, the examiner could easily confuse one piece of property a person owns with other parcels he or she may own in the same county.

After locating the property and the assessor's parcel number, the examiner notes the current property taxes and looks for any delinquent taxes, assessment bonds, or tax liens.

> **A Typical Misunderstanding:** Sears and Macy's filed several judgments against Howard some time ago, but they were in another county. Surely they won't show up during escrow.

> **The Way Things Really Are:** Howard's escrow company will do a "GI" name run on him (check his name in the general index) and will find all the outstanding judgments against him. They'll have to be paid in escrow.

Next the examiner searches the chain of title, often back through the 1800s, to determine whether there has been a "break" in the chain. Every buyer's and seller's name and every document recorded against that particular piece of property must be checked and verified for authenticity and correctness. The examiner actually pulls out and carefully examines each and every copy of the pertinent documents that have been recorded. The examiner then looks up the names of all the grantors and grantees in the general index, an index that lists all the things that apply to a person by name, such as liens, judgments, assignments, and powers of attorney, whether related to a piece of property or not. The examiner must check the name of every owner thoroughly to be sure it is OK. Often a middle initial is used on some documents and omitted on others. He or she must ascertain if the different names all refer to the same person. Are Shelley B. Smith, Shelley Bradford Smith, and Shelley Smith all the same person, or are they three different people? In a situation where title is in the name of Shelley B. Smith and she conveys title as Shelley A. Smith, the error would definitely be considered as critical and it would not be passed by a title company.

The examiner next checks the parcel maps and surveys to report every open easement and right-of-way and reads every pertinent document to be sure the property description is exactly the same as the parcel in question. He or she looks at adjoining properties to see if there is an easement or right-of-way that might have been recorded at some later date in the chain. He or she then reports on every existing deed of trust, judgment, lien, or other encumbrance on the property.

This checking of the title by owner's names, property address, and property description is an efficient and thorough method for locating and verifying information.

Your closing officer can explain in detail how the search was conducted and how documents were located for your property and, if you are interested in seeing for yourself just how a search is made, your escrow officer can even arrange a tour of the title plant she uses, to show you how the documents are indexed and a title is searched. As someone involved in a property transaction, you should feel free to call the title plant for further information or to request copies of recorded documents.

"WILL THE REAL SHELLEY B. SMITH PLEASE STAND UP!"

How Long Does a Title Search Take?

Depending upon the number of documents the examiner must review, a title search will take anywhere from one hour to two weeks to complete.

What Kinds of Things Does the Search Reveal?

The report compiled from the title examiner's findings, the first of many escrow documents you will receive, provides the following information to show the condition of title as of a specific date:

- The vested owner's name as disclosed in public records
- The current real estate property taxes, including whether they are paid or unpaid and the date of the last property assessment
- The outstanding liens, restrictions, easements, or other types of encumbrances
- The property's legal description of record
- The conditions under which the title company will issue title insurance
- A *plat map* (picture or drawing) showing the location and dimensions of the property as found in recorded documents

For the closing officer, the preliminary report is the key that unlocks the door to completing escrow. This information shows her what items, if any, must be cleared up in order for the title to be conveyed from the seller to you as the new buyer under whatever conditions you have agreed to take title. The report makes no guarantees about insuring the title to the property you are buying. It merely informs you of the contents of documents found in the public records exactly as they appear there and guarantees you only that the search made by the title company is complete. You are not protected against title defects that fail to show up in the records or against documents that are part of the records but have been improperly executed. Only a title insurance policy written for the new owner will insure the title that is being sold and will protect the buyer if there are any defects that do not show up in the records.

Copies of the report go to the buyer, the seller, the lender, and the real estate agent for their evaluation. Only after the buyer and the lender accept those items that have been reported against the property can title insurance be issued and escrow closed. Any defects that make the title "unmarketable," that is, any defects that deny the seller the legal right to sell the property, must be removed before someone buys it.

Many times the report will reveal that the seller actually owns the property with someone else. If, for instance, title shows up as Samuel P. Seller as to an undivided 1/2 interest and Skip Smith as to an undivided 1/2 interest, both Samuel and Skip would have to sign the deed. If Skip is out of town or unavailable when he's needed, his absence could complicate matters and delay the closing.

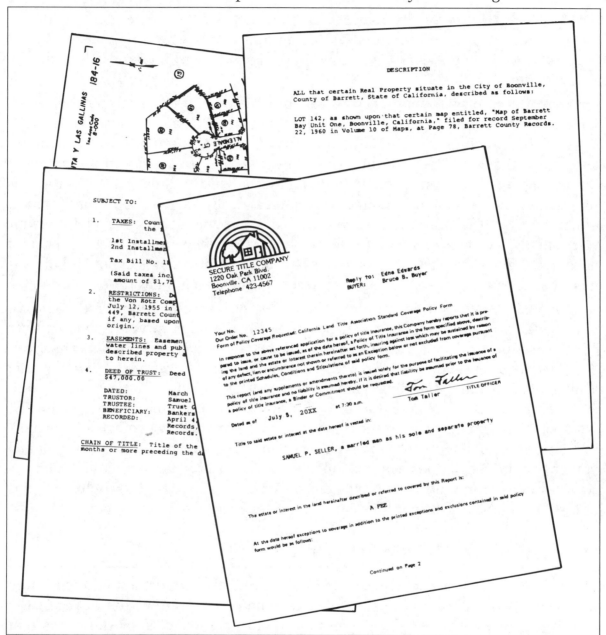

Chart 3-1. Title search documents

A Typical Misunderstanding: Margaret and her Aunt Evy own 41 acres of land on the outskirts of Fresno. A developer has offered Margaret a price that she considers quite attractive. The problem is that Aunt Sally lives on a commune in Readfield, Maine, and is pretty hard to get hold of. Margaret feels pretty sure that her aunt would approve of the transaction, but getting her approval could take a lot longer than the developer is willing to wait. Margaret decides to sign all the papers herself and to send her aunt half of the proceeds.

The Way Things Really Are: Margaret cannot sell the entire parcel without Aunt Sally's written approval. Aunt Sally's name will appear on the preliminary report as an owner, and her signature will be required on the grant deed.

Sometimes title shows up as being held by a trust or it might be in probate pending final disposition of an estate. Either situation would delay the close. When children inherit property from their parents, they frequently assume that they can go ahead and sell the property right away. They don't realize all the time-consuming legal procedures they must follow before they can legally transfer title. For example, there must be a confirmation of the parents' deaths, as well as a confirmation of the validity of whatever trusts are involved. Even when a surviving joint tenant wants to dispose of property that had been held in joint tenancy with someone now deceased, there must be evidence both of the other joint tenant's death and of payment of inheritance taxes. Getting all those papers together takes time.

If a defect, such as a lien or encumbrance, appears on the report and you have not agreed to take title subject to the defect, notify the seller or your escrow officer of your disapproval. For example, if back taxes are due on the property and you don't want to be held liable for them, get them paid in escrow; if a lien exists against the seller and you don't care to assume it, get it paid off in escrow as well; if there's a judgment recorded against the property, get it cleared and obtain the releases showing clearance. If the seller has not removed these defects by the closing date, you can usually stop the purchase and take steps to get back any money you have paid. Ask to look at all the documents listed as encumbrances on the title, so you can examine them before the close of escrow. These would include copies of the covenants, conditions, and restrictions, any easement rights, etc.

Who Pays for the Title Search?

Most often the cost of the title search and the resulting report is included in the title insurance policy premium, which may be paid by either the buyer or the seller or split between them, depending upon local customs or the terms that they have negotiated.

What Should I Do with the Preliminary Report?

Look your preliminary report over very carefully and do the following:
- Verify that the stated escrow closing number is correct.

- Note the date on the report, because it indicates that the title is as indicated only up to that date, not after.

- Note how title is given and find out whether the vested owner can legally convey title, that he or she is not a minor, for example.

- Look over the listed exceptions, the things that the title insurance company will not cover, and ask yourself whether you should take any steps to eliminate them.

- Secure a copy of any CC&Rs (covenants, conditions, and restrictions) mentioned in the report and determine whether you would be able to abide by them.

- Obtain copies of any easements, ask the title insurance company to draw them on the plat map for you, and figure out whether they will interfere with any future proposed uses you have for the property.

A Typical Misunderstanding: Easements and rights-of-way are so common that Greg figures there's no need to locate them exactly on his plat map. They couldn't possibly interfere with his plans to put a pool in his backyard.

The Way Things Really Are: An easement or right-of-way could easily be located right where Greg plans to put his pool. He should check his plat map carefully and identify any easements before calling in the pool company.

If you find anything objectionable or unclear about the preliminary report, ask questions about it now. Clear up the matter while you can still do something about it. If it cannot be settled or answered to your satisfaction, stop the purchase until the matter is resolved. Your escrow officer should be able to explain any item listed in the preliminary report and should be able to answer any questions you may have. Ask, by all means.

Might Someone Order a Preliminary Report on a Property Even if It's Not in Escrow?

Yes, anyone may order a title search and preliminary report alone for a fee of $250-$300 in situations involving neither an escrow nor title insurance.

Should I Inspect the Property Again After Receiving the Report?

Yes, do take the time to inspect the property personally with the report in hand, and ask questions about it when you do. Compare the apparent boundary lines with those shown on the plat map. Don't assume that a fence, a row of trees, or a hedge marks the actual boundaries. The seller may have built a fence on the property without having a survey performed to accurately determine the property lines. A title search will not necessarily reveal an encroachment, such as an incorrect placement of a fence. That fence may very well be five feet inside the neighbor's yard, and you wouldn't want to move into a new home only to start arguing with your neighbors right away about moving their dilapidated fence.

A property survey performed by a professional surveyor is the only way to locate property boundaries with certainty. If you are applying for a mortgage, your lender may require that a new survey be performed. If you have any doubts as to the boundary lines and your lender does not require a survey, you might ask the seller to provide you with one or negotiate to share the cost to have a survey done.

There are other things you might check that affect title to real property, things that normally do not appear in the public records. They include zoning restrictions, renters' unrecorded leases or month-to-month rights, water rights, persons with a right to title by adverse possession, and work being done on the property that could possibly lead to the filing of a mechanic's lien after you buy the property.

A Typical Misunderstanding: Rudy decides to buy a charming Victorian house in Petaluma, California, because it's zoned commercial and would make an ideal professional office. He starts running the ads as soon as he gains possession.

The Way Things Really Are: Although it is zoned commercial, for the past 50 years this Victorian has been used as a personal residence. To change the use from residential to commercial, regardless of the zoning, Rudy will have to conform with all the applicable commercial codes, both city and county. Conformance may involve adding firewalls, additional bathrooms, wheelchair ramps, and fire escapes. It may even require removing the cooking facilities. Before acquiring it, Rudy should find out what the building requires for change of use.

What Are CC&Rs?

Covenants, conditions, and restrictions (CC&Rs for short) are limitations placed upon the use of land by its owner. They are usually included in the deed and specify what uses will be permitted or prohibited on the land. They are created in appropriate deed clauses, in special agreements, or in a general plan affecting an entire subdivision. In some parts of the country they are referred to as "condo docs."

Covenants are promises to do or not to do certain things. A promise not to raise chickens in your backyard or a promise not to put up a clothesline are examples of covenants.

A Typical Misunderstanding: Bill and Jeannine don't feel they need to bother reading the CC&Rs for their planned unit development. Aren't all CC&Rs standard anyway? The other homeowners will surely love the opportunity to buy fresh eggs from local chickens. Bill's pet rabbit, Charlie, is so cute that everyone will adore him.

The Way Things Really Are: Bill and Jeannine should take the time to read their CC&Rs. Expressly forbidden in them could be the raising of chickens and rabbits, and then Bill and Jeannine would be faced with the difficult choice of moving out or getting rid of their menagerie.

Conditions are stipulations or qualifications in a deed that, if not complied with, may give the grantor or his or her heirs the right to demand the property back. This is otherwise known as a *reversionary right*. For example, a seller could specify that he will convey his property to a buyer on the condition that the buyer not sell intoxicating liquors on the property. If this condition is not complied with, the property may revert back to the seller, his heirs, or his successors.

Restrictions encompass a general classification for various types of limitations on the use of real property They fall into two categories: private restrictions and public restrictions.

Private restrictions are those imposed on a property by its owner to ensure a degree of uniformity in the development of a neighborhood, such as limiting the use of land to residential purposes only. Such restrictions may not, of course, be unlawful or contrary to public policy, nor may they be unreasonable.

Public restrictions are best exemplified by zoning ordinances, which are said to be designed to "promote public health, safety, comfort, convenience, and general welfare." These ordinances place limitations on the use of land within certain areas in accordance with a general policy that has been adopted. Many communities have developed master plans for zoning that cover the future pattern for freeways, recreational, airport, or shoreline development.

You should be aware that zoning ordinances are a separate obligation from CC&Rs and that zoning ordinances may not necessarily conform with CC&Rs. As an example, say that a buyer gets a zoning variance to put a duplex on his property but he fails to comply with the CC&Rs, which call for "a single family dwelling only." Despite the zoning change, the owner may not violate the CC&Rs in actual use.

What Is an Easement?

An easement is a right granted by a property owner to another person allowing some land to be set aside for certain purposes, or it may be a property right reserved by a former owner. Easements are commonly granted for pipelines, telephone cables, access roads, power lines, and the like. Thus, if access to your property is possible only by crossing your neighbor's land, you may try to get an easement from her for the right to use that portion of her property.

Basically, there are two types of easements: *appurtenant easements* and *easements in gross*:

- An *appurtenant easement* is an interest in property set aside for things such as roads. Once created, it will normally stay with a property from owner to owner, being transferred with the title whether it is named in the deed or not. Problems could occur if your neighbors are using an access across your property, so you should make a personal inspection to try to determine whether your property is subject to this type of easement. Obviously, if a road runs through your property and continues onto your neighbor's land and you can see that someone is using it, you should suspect that an appurtenant easement exists, even if it is not mentioned in the preliminary report.

■ An *easement in gross*, normally obtained, say, to bring in a telephone line, must be described in the deed in order to pass with the title. As a buyer, one of your main concerns would be to note whether there is an easement in gross located right where you may have plans to build or expand in the future. You surely don't want to add a room to your house only to find out later that it is directly over a utility easement and the utility company has to dig up a broken pipe underneath your living room.

As a buyer, your main concerns about easements are whether they are recorded or not, whether their location and use will disturb your own use of the property, and whether their present uses can be expanded by their terms. How would you be affected if that access road across your land, which now serves a nearby farm, later must carry scores of cars when the farm is sold and the property is developed into a factory? What would you do if the friendly neighbors who now own the common driveway that both of you share should sell to someone who won't help with patching the pavement and filling the chuckholes? Recognize that if there is an easement involved in a property transaction, it may cause you headaches later on.

Here's a sample of one recorded easement that was obviously designed to reduce headaches for those people who live around a golf course:

> An easement and specific right of way for ingress and egress and seizure and the immediate search, recapture, retrieving, and recovery of errant golf balls for a period of 5 minutes immediately following the departure of any golf ball from the confines of the club golf links, as reserved in the declaration by Virginia Country Club of Long Beach, a corporation, recorded in book 16402, page 291, Official Records.

Here's an instance where not having an easement presented a real problem. Several of my clients were trying to buy 650 acres on the top of a mountain overlooking the Pacific Ocean. Not only was the view magnificent, but the prospects for the property were outstanding, because it could be subdivided easily. It was priced reasonably and seemed like a very good deal for the buyers—until the preliminary report came out. What a shock! That report showed that there was no legal access to the property whatsoever. The snag was that the paved roads surrounding the 650 acres were all privately owned by individuals, not by the county, and these individuals were not willing to give access over their roads. There was no other way to enter except maybe by helicopter. Eventually, after months of negotiations, legal pleadings, and entanglements, the individual owners were persuaded (for a price, of course) to give access rights over their privately owned roads and escrow finally closed.

The lesson to be learned from this last example is that reading the preliminary report carefully is very important to ensure that you can use a property as you intend to use it. Never assume just because your property is surrounded by paved roads that you automatically have the use of them. You may not.

What Are Liens and Encumbrances?

Liens and encumbrances are the two most common defects on a property's title. By themselves, they do not make a title unmarketable, because the seller has the legal right to sell his or her property subject to the existing liens and encumbrances, but any buyer should understand them, be aware of them, and be willing to accept them.

Encumbrances include anything that limits or affects the title, such as mineral, timber, or water rights held by the seller or a third party; easement rights permitting others to cross the property; and restrictive covenants in the deed limiting use of the property.

Liens are also encumbrances, but they arise only when a property becomes security for the payment of a debt. A lien is a legal claim against a property or a person to ensure payment of a debt. A lienholder has the right to go to court to sell your property if you don't pay off the debt. This claim against a property makes transferring title or selling a property impossible without first either paying off the debt or assuming it.

Liens may be *voluntary* (a mortgage or deed of trust), *statutory* (property taxes), or *involuntary* (a judgment affecting all the property an owner has or acquires during the legal life of the lien).

Statutory and involuntary liens fall into four main categories:

■ **Property tax liens.** These are placed against a property when the property taxes are not paid on time. They are given precedence over all other claims. If they remain delinquent for five years, the property will be sold off to pay the taxes. Whenever a property is foreclosed upon, taxes are always the first debts paid.

■ **Judgment liens.** These are general liens resulting when a person suing another person wins a judgment from a court for the sums owing and records an abstract of that judgment.

■ **Mechanic's liens.** These are recorded with the county by contractors, subcontractors, materials suppliers, or workers who wish to be paid for their delinquent bills covering labor or materials on new construction, land improvements, or remodeling projects.

- **Federal or state liens.** These result from unpaid federal or state taxes, personal and inheritance taxes being the most common.

The seller normally has to clear all liens from the property before he or she can sell and deliver clear title to the buyer. Any money used to satisfy these liens will be deducted from the seller's sales proceeds. Remember that special assessments (such as city assessments levied to repair a street) and recorded judgments (such as a mechanic's lien or unpaid bills resulting from a court action) will all have to be paid off in order to close escrow. If you're the seller in such a situation, be aware that these "hidden" liens will cost you money at closing time.

A Typical Misunderstanding: Fred has sold his house and it's due to close escrow in three weeks, but the property taxes have to be paid next week. He figures that the taxes should be the new owner's responsibility, so he decides not to pay them.

The Way Things Really Are: In escrow Fred will have to pay all the property taxes and the property-tax penalties he owes. They will show up in the title search as a lien on the house, a lien that has to be paid in order for escrow to close. If he has the money available to pay them when they're due, he should pay them, so he can avoid having to pay a penalty for late payment.

What Is a *Lis Pendens*?

A *lis pendens* is a notice that a lawsuit is pending. Such notice warns anyone with an interest in a property that there's a dispute in progress over title or possession and that any later buyers, lenders, or tenants will be bound by the final resolution. Most title companies refuse to insure the title of a lis pendens property.

When a seller is trying to back out of a sale and a buyer is trying to preserve his right to purchase, the buyer usually records a lis pendens so that nobody else will be able to buy the property until the squabble is settled.

A Typical Misunderstanding: Three weeks into a sales escrow, Patrick discovers that the offer that he has accepted from Jenny and Ed for his property is 10% below what it's worth in today's market. He decides to accept a "backup" offer that is higher than theirs, so he sends a notice of cancellation to the escrow company.

The Way Things Really Are: Jenny and Ed have performed every obligation required of them in order to buy Patrick's property and close escrow on time. Patrick, therefore, has no justifiable excuse to cancel escrow. Jenny and

Ed refuse to agree to the cancellation, so they file a lis pendens on the property in order to warn other prospective buyers that title to and possession of the property is in dispute.

Only specific types of lawsuits are proper subjects for recording a lis pendens. They include the following:

■ Specific performance or recision of real estate agreements

■ Judicial foreclosure of a trust deed

■ Foreclosure of a mechanic's lien

■ Cancellation of a grant deed or other conveyance

■ Slander of title

■ Divorce proceedings

■ Declaration that a building is uninhabitable

■ Actions to re-establish lost land records

Anyone wishing to record a lis pendens must first file a lawsuit concerning one of these proper subjects in state or federal court. After filing the lawsuit, the litigant may record a lis pendens.

Lawsuits that are not proper subjects for recording a lis pendens include the following:

■ Foreclosure as a result of a trustee's sale

■ Actions to recover attorney's fees

■ Actions for breach of a real estate contract that seeks only monetary damages

■ Actions for recovery of a brokerage commission

■ Actions against partners or stockholders who own the property jointly as a partnership or corporation.

Is It Possible to Take Title Subject to Certain Exceptions?

Yes, you may agree to take title subject to exceptions, such as current property taxes, easements, assumed liens, trust deeds, and CC&Rs, but you should be absolutely certain you know what they are. Look at the numbered items on your preliminary report.

They are the exceptions for this particular property. Make a check list of these exceptions, verify them, and go over the following questions:

■ Are there any unpaid special assessments for roads, sewers, or other major improvements?

■ Are there any tax liens on the property?

- Are there any outstanding judgments (collection agency bills, etc.)?

- Is the current owner's name correct? Is ownership held by a trust, partnership, or corporation, which might complicate the consummation of your transaction?

- Are there any mortgages or deeds of trust that are assumable? If there are, what are the amounts and the interest rates?

- Who is the current lender? Will the new buyer be able to obtain financing from him? (This might save the seller from having to pay a prepayment penalty.)

- If there is any new construction involved, was a notice of completion recorded and, if so, when? (If a notice was recorded, then the original contractor has 60 days from the recording date to file a lien; all other persons must record their claims within 30 days. If a notice was not recorded, claimants have 90 days from the actual date of completion during which to file. Any lien resulting from land improvements prior to recording of a trust deed has precedence over the trust deed.)

- What are the current taxes and when was the last assessment year?

After you have read the preliminary report and checked off the exceptions, inform your escrow officer whether the existing loans will be paid off or whether you will be taking title subject to these liens. This information is vital to the smooth processing of your escrow—so vital, in fact, that it will be discussed in more detail later under the subject of assumptions.

What Is an Attorney's Certificate of Title?

As mentioned before, the procedure used in tracing a chain of title is slightly different in some Eastern states, where an attorney rather than a title company is hired to examine all the recorded documents relating to the title. The attorney makes a report of his findings in what is called an *abstract* or *certificate of title*. This report details both what records were examined and what encumbrances currently exist against the title; it is essentially the same as a preliminary report. It is not insurance of marketable title nor does it insure against undisclosed defects, such as forgery, clerical errors, undisclosed heirs, improper interpretation of wills, and so on.

If the attorney makes a negligent mistake in her title search, naturally you may sue her for any losses you suffer due to her negligence, just as you may sue a title company under the same circumstances.

Be sure you check with the local zoning department about zoning restrictions and future planned use of your property. Title companies cannot and do not insure against zoning changes.

How Can I Work with the Title Officer to Resolve Title Issues?

After reviewing your copy of the preliminary title report or abstract of title, there may be certain factors, such as an unknown right-of-way, a utility easement, or an unknown lis pendens or judgment against the seller, which could delay or slow down your closing and jeopardize your sale. If left unresolved, these issues could postpone or cancel your closing.

You will want to work with your title officer or closing agent to resolve these issues in ample time before your closing. If you are uncertain as to a title issue found in the report, ask the title officer to explain it to you. Ask specifically how the issue can be resolved and what steps are necessary to clear up any potential problems. Even if you are represented by an attorney, it is wise to be certain yourself that any title issues are taken care of and a new title report is issued, removing any questionable items. Ask for a revised copy of the title report, showing the clear title.

A common title issue that can occur is one in which the seller is found to own the property with someone else and the other party is out of town. The other party must be located and arrangements made for him or her to sign the closing documents. This problem is solved by obtaining a power of attorney for the absent party.

Delinquent taxes, assessment bonds or tax liens, and judgments all can become a problem to delay the close of escrow. Judgments filed in a county other than the county where the property is located will also show up on the title report. These outstanding judgments will have to be paid at closing.

One type of judgment that is not uncommon is a judgment against a person with a name similar to yours. Most title and escrow companies will accept an affidavit from the affected party that states he or she is not the party named in the judgment. Oftentimes a judgment from a creditor, say a major department store, will show up, but it's against a person with a similar name. Your title officer or closing agent will contact the department store or creditor in question and resolve this issue.

It may be that a judgment shows up that you weren't aware existed, but that is in fact your obligation. These will have to be satisfied or paid off before escrow can close. Often, if money is owed, the creditor will agree to a release just as long as the monies owing are paid at the close of escrow.

Problems can occur in the tax description of your parcel of land. A small discrepancy between the tax description and the survey is normal, but a significant difference can become a problem. If the tax description is too small, for example, portions of the parcel may be part of another tax block and lot and you could lose that land due to failure to pay land and realty taxes. Any tax description that describes only a portion of your parcel needs to be corrected. Notify your title officer so that this issue can be resolved before closing.

Chapter Four

Holding Title: Your Options and Why They Matter

At this point in the closing process, escrow has been opened and the title search has been performed. If you are the buyer, you will soon be taking possession of the title to the property. This chapter will go over the different ways that you can hold title and why they are important.

Why Should I Be Concerned About Holding Title?

One of the most important aspects of the entire closing procedure is how you take title, because not only does it determine how you will be insured, but it also has significant legal and tax consequences. It can even create some unanticipated complications in the future when you decide to transfer the title to someone else.

So much depends upon the precise way you hold title, in fact, that you should not rely on advice from a real estate agent, escrow or closing officer, or friend when you are trying to determine how to hold title. You would be wise to consult your attorney or tax consultant about the best way for you to hold title in your particular circumstances.

> **A Typical Misunderstanding:** Bill and Judy are a married couple in their late 20s who have never given estate planning a second thought. They do their own income taxes and haven't yet needed an attorney for anything. They decide to take title to their first house the same way all their friends have, as joint tenants.

> **The Way Things Really Are:** Joint tenancy may not be the best way for Bill and Judy to take title. They have three small children and want the property to pass to their children in case they both die. Bill and Judy need to secure more information about holding title before they make up their minds.

What Are the Most Common Ways to Hold Title?

There are four common ways to hold title to real property:

- Joint tenancy
- Tenancy in common
- Community property
- Sole and separate property

Joint tenancy. The main distinguishing characteristic of joint tenancy is the *right of survivorship*. If one of the joint tenants ("tenants" here means "owners," not "renters") dies, his or her interest passes automatically to the surviving party or parties instead of being tied up in lengthy probate proceedings. When two or more people own a property as joint tenants, they own an undivided equal interest in the property and have the same rights to the use of the entire property, that is, neither co-tenant can distinguish which portion of the property he or she owns. Once a joint tenancy has been created, no joint tenant can sell his or her interest without terminating the joint tenancy. If either sells his or her interest, the buyer comes in as a tenant in common rather than as a joint tenant.

For example, if Appleby, Baker, and Crabtree hold a piece of property as joint tenants and Crabtree sells his interest to Duffy, Duffy buys in as a tenant in common. If Duffy dies, his share goes to his heirs, rather than to Appleby or Baker. Appleby and Baker remain joint tenants and each has the right of survivorship to the other's interest. Upon their death, their interest would never go to Duffy.

A joint tenant who chooses to sell his or her interest may do so without the consent of the other owners, unless the owners specify otherwise in a contract among themselves. This situation sometimes occurs when a husband or a wife wants to leave his or her interest by will. Remember that a joint tenant cannot leave his or her interest to anyone else but fellow joint tenant(s) in his or her will, not even to his or her children. As for pledging the property as collateral, one joint tenant acting alone may sign a deed of trust making his or her interest in the property security for a loan; this action does not terminate the joint tenancy.

Tenancy in common. When two or more persons buy property together, whether their shares are equal or unequal, they are said to hold the property as tenants in common.

Tenancy in common is so standard as a form of ownership for unrelated buyers that it is generally presumed to be the way they hold title if nothing else appears to the contrary. The shares are also presumed to be equal, unless they are listed otherwise on the deed, and each of the tenants has equal rights of possession. Each co-tenant owns an undivided interest, but unlike a joint tenancy, these interests need not be equal and may arise from different conveyances and at different times.

There is no right of survivorship as in a joint tenancy, so if one of the tenants-in-common should happen to die, his or her interest would not revert automatically to the remaining tenants. Consequently, each tenant in common should note in his or her will the person or persons to whom his or her share will pass. Unrelated property buyers usually buy as tenants in common rather than as joint tenants because they want their property to go to their heirs and not to the surviving joint tenants. Each individual co-tenant can sell or mortgage his or her interest in the property, but acts only for his or her own share and cannot bind anyone else's interest.

Community property (similar to tenancy by entirety but has no right of survivorship). Holding title to real property as community property is a type of ownership available to married couples only. At present, there are nine states that are considered "community property states": Arizona, California, Idaho, Louisiana, Nevada, New Mexico, Texas, Washington, and Wisconsin. (The Marital Property Act defined Wisconsin as a community property state, but individual circumstances will dictate how this act is interpreted. Check with a knowledgeable expert if you need an interpretation.)

These states regard any property purchased during a marriage as community property. Both husband and wife have an equal right to possess the property during their marriage and, in some states, upon the death of either spouse, the survivor automatically receives half of the community property and the other half passes to the lawful heirs. Neither holder of community property may sell the entire property without the consent of the other, yet either holder may sell his or her own share without notifying the other. If either dies and leaves no will, the surviving holder may acquire the property, but unlike joint tenancy, either holder may will his or her half interest to others if he or she so chooses.

Sole and separate property. Holding title as sole and separate property means that no one else has any interest in it. If you are married and want to take title this way, you may, but you should record a quitclaim deed from your spouse to yourself so that no community interest could be claimed at a later date. (This applies only in community property states.) The quitclaim deed transfers any interest or right you may have in a property, but remember that it does not make any guarantees or warranties as to the condition of title.

As you have probably observed, these four ways of taking title offer extremely varied possibilities. In general, if you have children, or plan to, you will most likely want to consider taking title under community property or as tenants in common, since you will likely want your children to inherit your property, something that joint tenancy does not permit.

In California, property of a married person is either separate property or community property. Community property law presumes that all property acquired during marriage is community property or co-owned unless it is proven to be sole and separate property. If it is separate property, it may be held in severalty (sole and separate), in joint tenancy, in tenancy in common, or in partnership. If one spouse is to hold property in severalty, a quitclaim deed is required to release any interest of the other spouse. Whether the property of a husband and wife is separate property or community property may become extremely important whenever there are actions affecting community property, such as divorce or probate proceedings.

A Typical Misunderstanding: Dick and Sam want to buy a property together as partners. Dick is married and living in a community property state, while Sam is single. Dick thinks that his wife won't approve of the partnership or of the property, so he decides to take title to his half as his sole and separate property. His wife, then, won't have any interest in the property.

The Way Things Really Are: In a community property state, Dick may indeed take title to half the partnership property as his sole and separate property, but unless his wife signs a quitclaim deed specifically denying herself an interest in the property, she still does have an interest, whether she was named on the grant deed as an owner or not. Dick wouldn't have any difficulty acquiring the property by himself, but he would have some difficulty divesting of it by himself.

Step-by-Step Procedure for Completing and Recording a Quitclaim Deed

1. Obtain a blank quitclaim deed form. Use the one in the back of this book or get one from an escrow or title company.

2. If you're the least bit fearful of making a mistake, make a photocopy of the form and follow steps three through nine below, using a pencil and making a "rough draft" of all the information you want to include on the recorded copy. Then transfer this information to the actual form you plan to record. Your recorded copy should be neat and legible, with a minimum of additions, corrections, and deletions.

3. Under "RECORDING REQUESTED BY," put your own name, unless, of course, you're filling out the deed for someone else who is making the request. Under "MAIL TAX STATEMENT TO," put "Same as Below," so the persons granted the property will receive the tax bills at the same address where they normally receive their mail.

4. Under "WHEN RECORDED MAIL TO," put the names and a single address of the persons to whom the deed should be mailed.

Chart 4-1. How to complete and record a quitclaim deed (continued on next page)

5. Put the word "None" on the line after "DOCUMENTARY TRANSFER TAX $." Because no money is changing hands, there is no liability for a transfer tax.

6. After "City of," put the name of the city or town where the property is located, and after "Tax Parcel No." put the same assessor's tax parcel number which appears on the property's tax bill, grant deed, or title insurance policy. Double-check this number. It's absolutely crucial. An incorrect number will make the quitclaim deed refer to another property entirely.

7. In the space before the words "FOR A VALUABLE CONSIDERATION," put the names of those who appear on the original grant deed, and be sure the names are exactly alike, middle initials and all. If you can't find the deed, check the title insurance policy. Then put the word "DO" in the space before "HEREBY" if more than one person is granting the quitclaim or "DOES" if there is only one person involved.

8. After the words "QUITCLAIM TO," enter the names of the persons who are receiving the title, along with the way they intend to hold that title.

9. After "County of" and "State of," include the county and state where the property is located, and then enter a legal description of the property. This description should correspond to the one given in the original grant deed or in the title insurance policy.

10. Date and sign the quitclaim deed in the presence of a notary. The notary will then acknowledge the signatures by signing and stamping the deed with his or her official seal.

11. Take the quitclaim deed to the county recorder's office and pay the recording fee. The recorder will stamp the deed with the date and time and index it in the county's official records.

Chart 4-1. Continued

May I Change the Way I Hold Title After Escrow Closes?

Yes, you certainly may change the way you hold title after escrow closes. You may change the way you hold title at any time, generally without tax consequences, too. (Check with your attorney or tax consultant to find out how the change will affect your particular circumstances.) You may effect the change yourself or you may ask your escrow officer to help you do it when you're ready. You simply deed the property from yourself (yourselves) to yourself (yourselves) in the new manner in which you wish to hold title. Some common examples of changing the form of ownership include terminating a joint tenancy, putting property in trust for a child, and giving property to adult children.

RECORDING REQUESTED BY:
 Bruce B. Buyer
MAIL TAX STATEMENT TO:
 Bruce B. Buyer
WHEN RECORDED, MAIL TO:
 Mr. & Mrs. Bruce B. Buyer
 12 Allendale Ct.
 Boonville, CA 91002

302211

RECEIVED OCT 1 3 20XX

RECORDED AT REQUEST OF
SECURE TITLE CO.

AT 2 O'CLOCK P. M.
BARRETT COUNTY RECORDS

FEE $ 5⁰⁰   V. L. GRAVES
COUNTY RECORDER

Recorder's Use Only

302211

ORDER NO.

ESCROW NO.

QUITCLAIM DEED

DOCUMENTARY TRANSFER TAX $___NONE___
COMPUTED ON FULL VALUE OF PROPERTY CONVEYED, OR
COMPUTED ON FULL VALUE LESS LIENS & ENCUMBRANCES
REMAINING THEREON AT TIME OF SALE.
Unincorporated Area_____ City of __Boonville__
Tax Parcel No.__184-162-21_____

BRUCE B. BUYER AND BARBARA A. BUYER, his wife as Joint Tenants

FOR A VALUABLE CONSIDERATION,   DO   HEREBY QUITCLAIM to:

BRUCE B. BUYER AND BARBARA A. BUYER, HIS WIFE AS COMMUNITY PROPERTY

the real property in the County of __Barrett_____, State of__California____, described as:

LOT 142, as shown upon that certain map entitled "Map of Barrett
Bay Unit One, Boonville, California," filed for record September
22, 1960 in Volume 10 of Maps, at Page 78, Barrett County Records.

Witness my hand this __13__ day of __October_____ 20**XX**.

Bruce B. Buyer
    BRUCE B. BUYER

STATE OF California   )
) s.s.
COUNTY OF   Barrett   )

On _____October 13_____ 20**XX**,
before me, the undersigned, a Notary Public in and for said County
and State, personally appeared

    Bruce B. Buyer and
    Barbara A. Buyer

proved to me on the basis of satisfactory evidence to be the person**s**
whose name**s** is (are) subscribed to the within instrument and
acknowledged that __they__ executed the same.

Barbara A. Buyer
    BARBARA A. BUYER

WITNESS my hand and official seal:

Edna Edwards
Notary Public in and for said County and State

NOTARY SEAL

OFFICIAL SEAL
EDNA EDWARDS
Notary Public

MAIL TAX STATEMENT AS DIRECTED ABOVE

Chart 4-2. An example of a quitclaim deed

Agreement	Person	Property Split	Property Sale	Lease Expiration	Inheritors	Creditors	Federal Estate Tax
JOINT TENANCY WITH RIGHT OF SURVIVORSHIP	Two or more people (spouses or others)	Equal shares according to contract or money paid	No consent necessary	Depends on the agreement in the contract	Survivor becomes sole owner (property split evenly if more than one survivor); no will necessary	Levy a judgment	Full estate taxed (assumed that first to die provided all funds for property unless survivor proves other-wise); spouse can claim marital deduction
TENANCY IN COMMON	Two or more people	Equal or unequal shares	No consent necessary	When one person sells shares, others continue tenancy in commmon	Passed to person named in will; divided by state if no will	Subject o creditors' claims	Portion of estate taxed according to property split; spouses can claim marital dedcustion
COMMUNITY PROPERTY	Spouses only	Equal shares	With partner's consent	At divorce or by mutual consent	Survivor becomes sole owner; no will ncecesary	Safe from spouse's creditors	Hal of estate taxed; spouse can claim marital deduction
TENANCY BY ENTIRETY	Married couples only	Each undivided interest	Both must sign documents	Divorce or mutual consent	Survivor becomes an owner in severalty	Creditors of one party cannot en-force their liens against the property	Could result in only partial utilization of federal estate tax
SOLE PROPRIETORSHIP (SOLE AND SEPARATE PROPERTY)	One person	One undivided share	No consent necessary	When property is sold	Passed to person N/A named in will; divided by state if no will	N/A	Full estate taxed

Chart 4-3. Consequences of how title is held

You may even change the way you hold title by simply making up a written agreement and putting it in a safe place. Should you change your mind later, you merely tear up the agreement. That's all there is to it. You don't have to record this agreement if you don't want to, but you probably should record it unless you have some particular reason for not doing so.

On the next page, you'll find an agreement you might use yourself if you should ever want to change the way you hold title from joint tenancy to community property. And you'll find a blank agreement form in the back of this book.

In What Other Ways Can People Hold Title?

As real estate prices climb, some people are joining together with others to pool their resources and buy property together as a group. Although the two most frequently used forms of real estate co-ownership are tenancy in common and joint tenancy, you might want to consider such alternate methods of co-ownership as *partnerships*, *joint ventures*, or *corporations*.

Partnership. An association of two or more persons who as co-owners carry on a business for profit is called a partnership. It is created by an agreement between two or more persons to take care of business jointly and share the profits. It may be a *general* partnership, where each partner is liable for the debts of the partnership, or a *limited* partnership, where each limited partner's liability is limited to the amount of his or her investment and he or she is not otherwise liable for the debts of the partnership. Holding title in partnership with others allows any number of partners to have an equal or an unequal interest in a property. Each partner has equal rights of possession, but only according to the partnership agreement.

AGREEMENT TO CHANGE TITLE FROM JOINT TENANCY TO COMMUNITY PROPERTY

1) PARTIES:

Parties to this agreement are ___Bruce B. Buyer___

and ___Barbara A. Buyer___ .

2) RECITALS:

a) The parties hereto are husband and wife, residing in the County of ___Barrett___ _____, State of ___California___ .

b) They have heretofore held property in their common or separate names, and may hereafter do so.

c) They hold portions of their property in joint tenancy only as a matter of convenience of transfer.

d) This agreement is entered into with the full knowledge on the part of each party of the extent and probable value of all of the property and estate of the community, and of the separate and joint property of each other, ownership of which would be conferred by law on each of them in the event of the termination of their relationship by death or otherwise.

e) It is the express intent of the parties hereto that all their common properties are and shall be their community property.

3. AGREEMENT THAT ALL PROPERTY SHALL BE COMMUNITY:

Each party hereby releases all of his or her separate rights in and to any and all property, real or personal and wherever situated, which either party now owns or has an interest in, and each party agrees that all property or interest therein owned heretofore or presently or hereafter acquired by either from common funds shall be deemed to be community property of the parties hereto, whether held in their separate names, as joint tenants, as tenants in common, or in any other legal form. The parties understand that this agreement will automatically, without other formality, transfer to the other a one-half interest in any separate property now owned and that such transfer could constitute a taxable gift under Federal and State law.

4. AGREEMENT MODIFIABLE IN WRITING ONLY:

This agreement shall not be modified except in writing signed by both parties, or by the mutual written surrender or abandonment of their said community interest in accordance with the laws of said State pertaining to the management of community property, or by the termination of their marriage by death or otherwise.

DATED: ___October 13___ , 20**XX**

___Bruce B. Buyer___
Bruce B. Buyer

___Barbara A. Buyer___
Barbara A. Buyer

Chart 4-4. How to change title from joint tenancy to community property

Joint venture. Like a partnership, a joint venture is an agreement between two or more persons to conduct a business enterprise jointly for profit. Unlike a partnership, which may involve any number of different enterprises, a joint venture involves only a single enterprise.

Corporation. A corporation involves interested parties each putting up a sum of money toward making the down payment for a property in return for shares of stock and becoming a shareholder in the corporation. The unique feature about a corporation is that it has all the legal aspects of a single person. Land owned by a corporation cannot be attached for personal debts or judgments rendered against any of its shareholders. A creditor can attach only the person's shares in the corporation. On the other hand, if the corporation cannot pay its debts, none of the shareholders can individually be forced to pay a creditor, although the corporation's assets, including its real property, can be reached and sold to pay a debt.

To form a corporation, you do not need to have a New York Stock Exchange listing or even an income-producing business. You must, however, file certain papers with the state. The shareholders must draw up articles of incorporation, bylaws, and a shareholders' agreement. Each state has its own requirements regarding the proper legal form for these documents and for filing them with the secretary of the state where the corporation is to be located. You may consult an attorney to draw up articles of incorporation and other necessary paperwork. There are also several books available on forming your own corporation, which might be useful as reference material.

No matter which type of co-ownership or group ownership you consider, you should discuss the full terms of the co-ownership, and perhaps even write them out in detail, before making your final decision. The entire group should understand as completely as possible the intentions and desires of each person involved. Even the best-intentioned people cannot possibly predict what will happen to them when they become co-owners of land with all the responsibilities it entails.

What's a Living Trust? Can I Hold Title in a Living Trust?

A living trust, sometimes called an *inter vivos trust* by attorneys, operates during one's lifetime and is revocable at any time before death. The person who creates the living trust (also known as the *settlor*) acts as his own trustee so long as he lives. He maintains full control of everything just as if there were no living trust. The difference is that in a living trust he doesn't hold title in his own name. The trust holds title and the trustee then buys and sells property on behalf of the trust. When the settlor dies, the successor trustee takes immediate control and turns the property over to the beneficiary or beneficiaries without having to go through a lengthy probate or make the details of the estate public.

Naturally, a husband and wife may form a joint trusteeship if they so choose. When one of the co-owners dies, the survivor takes control.

Lest you think that living trusts are only for strange people in strange situations, you should know that there is a popular do-it-yourself book on living trusts called *Make Your Own Living Trust* by Denis Clifford (Nolo Press, 2002, 5th edition). Should you wish your living trust to hold title to the property you are buying, instruct the escrow officer to make out the papers referring to you as the trustee or trustees. The deed would read "Bruce B. Buyer and Barbara A. Buyer, Trustees under their Declaration of Trust dated xx/xx/xx."

Take the time to inform yourself more fully about living trusts by visiting with a knowledgeable attorney or by reading the Clifford book.

A Typical Misunderstanding: Phil and Sylvia want to transfer their home into their newly created living trust, but they are afraid that this transfer will cause their property to be reappraised, causing their property taxes to be raised. Phil tells Sylvia that placing their property in a living trust may help protect their property from a judgment or attachment by their creditors.

The Way Things Really Are: Phil and Sylvia need not worry about their property taxes being raised from transferring their home into their living trust. A transfer into a revocable living trust does not cause a reappraisal or revaluation of property for tax purposes. Phil and Sylvia need to realize, however, that their living trust will not provide protection against a lawsuit or judgment or attachment by any of their creditors.

 You will be eligible to use the IRS Code 121 $250,000 ($500,000) for a married couple) principal residence tax exemption when holding title in a living trust.

Chapter Five

The Building Inspection and the Termite Inspection

After opening escrow and requesting a title search, the next step is to order inspections on the property. In this chapter I'll review the types of inspection to order, how much they cost, who pays for them, and why these reports often cause problems that must be solved before the closing.

What Type of Inspections Should I Order?

A pest and termite inspection is generally ordered on a property as soon as possible after opening escrow. You will want a copy of the pest inspection report to determine the extent of any infestation and the remedies possible to correct any problems that are found.

In addition to a termite report, you may want to order a complete building inspection by a licensed building contractor or inspection service. For a nominal fee, around $150-$300, a qualified contractor or inspector will give the building an overall structural inspection covering all major systems, such as the foundation, plumbing, electrical, roof, and heating. These inspections are generally well worth their cost, especially for those who are novices about building construction. Plan to accompany the inspector on the inspection tour so you can see for yourself whether a problem is major or minor.

What Is a Termite Inspection and What Protection Does It Give?

A termite inspection used to consist of an inspection for termites that was confined to the ground floor of a building and its underside only. Nowadays a ter-

> **TIP** Whether you conduct the inspection yourself or have someone do it for you, be sure to include in your original purchase agreement the following statement: "Offer contingent upon buyer's full inspection (or inspection by a licensed contractor) and approval of the property within five business days after acceptance by the seller." These inspections may be in addition to the required disclosures provided by the seller and will be considered a contingency of closing. Your acceptance of an inspection report can be made a condition of your agreement to purchase the property. By adding this statement, you are free to negotiate the price and other terms of the house first, and then you may renegotiate the price after the inspection, or you may have an escape if the results of your inspection are not to your satisfaction.

mite inspection is much more comprehensive than that and, strictly speaking, it's no longer even called a termite inspection. It's called a *structural pest control inspection*, but most people still call it a termite inspection anyway because they're accustomed to the term.

Today's termite inspection involves checking for signs of wood damage and potential wood damage throughout a building, no matter what the cause. Inspectors now check for fungus, dry rot, faulty grade levels, earth-wood contacts, water leaks, scattered wood scraps and cellulose debris on the subsoil, and excessive moisture conditions. They also check for evidence of subterranean termites, drywood termites, dampwood termites, and other wood-destroying pests, such as certain varieties of beetles.

A termite inspector's report shows two types of work to be performed:

- Corrective work to remedy current infestation
- Preventive work to inhibit future or threatened infestation

A Typical Misunderstanding: The house looks terrific, all freshly painted. The yard is beautifully landscaped and cared for. Lisa won't need a termite or building inspection. She can see for herself that the place is in great shape.

The Way Things Really Are: Looks can be very deceiving. Lisa may be dealing with a seller who painted over a water-damaged ceiling without repairing the leaky roof or who hung pictures over holes in the walls. Only a thorough inspection by someone who knows buildings well will give her the assurance she needs that the building is sound.

In addition, the report will quote a price for having the inspector's company actually do the recommended work. With the report, termite companies generally include a work authorization form. They require an authorization, signed by the seller, before they will begin the work.

Pest control companies that do termite inspections are licensed and regulated

STANDARD STRUCTURAL PEST CONTROL INSPECTION REPORT
(WOOD-DESTROYING PESTS OR ORGANISMS)
This is an Inspection report only—not a Notice of Completion.

ADDRESS OF PROPERTY INSPECTED	BLDG. NO.	STREET	CITY	DATE OF INSPECTION
	12	Allendale Ct.	Boonville	July 5, 20XX

GETTEM TERMITE CONTROL COMPANY
612 Seventh St., Boonville, CA 91002   Telephone 423-7654

Affix stamp here on Board copy only. A LICENSED PEST CONTROL OPERATOR IS AN EXPERT IN HIS FIELD. ANY QUESTIONS RELATIVE TO THIS REPORT SHOULD BE REFERRED TO HIM.

FIRM LICENSE NO. 1981	REPORT NO. 737	STAMP NUMBER 94936

Inspection Ordered by (Name and Address) Bruce B. Buyer, c/o Security Title
Report Sent to (Name and Address) Same as Above
Owner's Name and Address Samuel P. Seller, c/o property address
Name and Address of a Party in Interest
INSPECTED BY: Al Hart   LICENSE NO. 465   Original Report ☒ Supplemental Report ☐ Number of Pages

YES	CODE	SEE DIAGRAM BELOW	YES	CODE	SEE DIAGRAM BELOW	YES	CODE	SEE DIAGRAM BELOW	YES	CODE	SEE DIAGRAM BELOW
X	S—Subterranean Termites			B—Beetles—Other Wood Pests			Z—Dampwood Termites			EM—Excessive Moisture Condition	
X	K—Dry-Wood Termites			FG—Faulty Grade Levels			SL—Shower Leaks			IA—Inaccessible Areas	
X	F—Fungus or Dry Rot			EC—Earth-wood Contacts		X	CD—Cellulose Debris			FI—Further Inspection Recom.	

1. SUBSTRUCTURE AREA (soil conditions, accessibility, etc.) 100%   See 1
2. Was Stall Shower water tested? 1 O.K.   Did floor coverings Indicate leaks? No
3. FOUNDATIONS (Type, Relation to Grade, etc.)   Concrete O.K.
4. PORCHES . . . STEPS . . . PATIOS   Concrete O.K.
5. VENTILATION (Amount, Relation to Grade, etc.)   Adequate
6. ABUTMENTS . . . Stucco walls, columns, arches, etc. None
7. ATTIC SPACES (accessibility, insulation, etc.)   Accessible   See 7
8. GARAGES (Type, accessibility, etc.)
9. OTHER   See 9

DIAGRAM AND EXPLANATION OF FINDINGS (This report is limited to structure or structures shown on diagram.)

General Description Two story stucco frame residence, furnished and occupied, composition roof and unimproved underarea.

There are areas of a building which we are not able to inspect. Although we make a visual examination, we do not deface or probe into window or door frames or decorative trim. The interiors of hollow walls are not inspected unless noted below and were not inspected at this time as they are inaccessible. We did not move built-ins, appliances, furniture, raise floor coverings or move storage unless otherwise specified within this report. These areas will be inspected if they are made accessible by the owner at his expense. Showers over finished ceilings are not water tested unless water stains are evident on the ceiling below in which case recommendations will be made for further testing. Detached wood fence or garden trellises are not part of this report. If the owner desires further information on the condition of the roof, we recommend a licensed roofing contractor be contacted. This inspection is only on the structures indicated on the diagram below.

1. SUBSTRUCTURE:
FINDING: 1. Cellulose debris and evidence of subterranean termites noted in the subarea as indicated on the diagram.

RECOMMENDATION: 1. Remove cellulose debris from the subarea and take away from the premises. Treat the entire subarea soil with registered chemicals for the control of subterranean termites.

2. ATTIC SPACES:
FINDING: 7. Evidence of drywood termites noted on rafters in the attic area as indicated on the diagram.

RECOMMENDATION: 7. Drill and chemically treat local drywood termite infested timbers in visible and accessible areas as indicated on the diagram.

3. OTHER:
FINDING: 9. Fungus infection noted in sub-floor as indicated on the diagram. Condition appears to be due to previous leak that has been repaired.

RECOMMENDATION: 9. Remove surface fungus and treat area (s) with a fungicide.

Estimated Cost:$ 250.00

Signature Al Hart

Chart 5-1. Standard structural report for pests

by a state structural pest control board and all of their inspection reports must be filed with this board. The board makes available to the public copies of any report filed on a building during the preceding two years.

Having inspected and cleared a building, the pest control company guarantees only that the building is structurally sound as of the inspection date and according to the specific limits given in the clearance. Those areas listed on the report as inaccessible or requiring further inspection, for example, would not be covered. The company does not guarantee that the building will continue to be structurally sound in the future, either. Conceivably, on the day after the inspection, termites could invade the place and a toilet could begin to leak at its base, and these conditions could cause real structural problems next year. The damage they cause would not be covered by the inspector's company.

Who Requires the Termite Inspection?

The termite inspection is generally required by the buyer and the lender. That's why the buyer, not the seller, usually pays for the inspection. The buyer wants to be sure that the building is sound enough to outlast his ownership and the lender wants to be sure that the building is sound enough to outlast the mortgage. Neither the inspection nor clearance of the inspection is required by law.

Who Orders the Termite Inspection?

Just as any of those involved in a real estate transaction may open escrow, any of them may order a termite inspection. Generally the real estate agent, if instructed to do so, will order the inspection from a reputable pest control company. If there is no agent involved, either the buyer or the seller may do it simply by calling a termite company and giving them the property address, the escrow company's name, and the escrow number.

How Do I Find an Inspector?

You can locate a pest inspector by looking in the yellow pages of your local telephone directory under "Pest Inspections." When speaking with the company, ask for references, the fee for the initial inspection, and the scope of their report. You may ask your real estate agent for suggestions of reputable inspection companies in your area. Ask how soon the inspector can perform the inspection and how quickly the report will be prepared. You can check on the Internet at **www.pestworld.org** or **www.pestcontroldirectory.com**; both sites will list inspection companies for your area.

Compare fees among inspectors. An inspection may cost from $75 to $500, depending on the scope of detail to be covered and the size of your home. Compare the type of written report that will be issued following the inspection. Ask the home inspector if his company carries an errors and omissions (E&O) policy to cover any mistakes the inspector may make. You may be relying on this report to negotiate further costs with the seller and you want to be sure that everything is included. You may want to be certain that the inspector is bonded and certified.

Look under "Building Inspection Service" for a list of those overall building inspection companies that will examine all the structural, electrical, plumbing, roofing, and other systems in your property. You can look on the Internet at **www.ashi.com**, the Web site for the American Society of Home Inspectors. ASHI is a nationwide, non-profit professional association and is selective in accepting applicants for membership. Members must have performed at least 750 home inspections or 250 inspections in addition to licenses and experience. Applicants must also pass a written exam, receive approval on at least three sample inspection reports, and perform a satisfactory home inspection before a review committee. Another association, the National Association of Home Inspectors (NAHI), works to regulate home inspectors. At their Web site, **www.nahi.org**, you will find a list of all their members in your state. The association offers free brochures for homebuyers. For free copies you can contact the NAHI office at (800) 448-3942 or e-mail info@nahi.org. Perhaps an easier source on the Internet to locate a building inspector may be to go to your search engine, type in the words "real estate, home inspectors, your city."

Whenever you choose a building contractor or an inspection service, be certain that the person you choose is licensed with the state as either a contractor or an inspector and that he will prepare a written report of the findings. Ask if the report will be a checklist or if it will be a complete overall view. Having this written report could be very useful later in case a lawsuit arises because of undisclosed structural damage.

Why Do Termite Reports Cause Problems at Closing?

Termite reports cause numerous problems in your closing, as many as any other single cause, for several reasons.

One is that the company that inspects a building also submits an estimate for doing the work. In other words, the termite company is given the responsibility of determining the extent of the work to be done and the charges for doing it and, after the work is completed, the company also clears the report. If the inspector finds that some work needs to be done, he usually gets the job to do that work. If he doesn't find anything wrong with the structure, he doesn't get any work. Needless to say, he is rather thorough in his inspection. That's good to some extent, but it can be troublesome, too.

Another reason why termite reports cause problems is that the inspector determines how the corrective and preventive work is to be done. Frequently there are several ways to remedy a problem, but the inspector is inclined to indicate just one of those ways on his report, and often it's the most expensive one, the one that will yield him the most work. I know of a case where an inspector called for $4,000 worth of work, which later was done satisfactorily in another way for $5. In another case, an inspector called for $500 worth of work, which later was completed for $2.

The termite inspector can wield awesome power in real estate transactions because his clearance is frequently an essential element required for escrow to close. Because large sums of money are involved in most real estate transactions, many people overlook the savings that are possible. Like Las Vegas gamblers who have forgotten the value of a dollar, they pay out large sums for termite repairs that might be done for much less. Even a relatively new house will often cause termite report problems in escrow. A new house might have wood scraps on the subsoil left there by the builder or it might have wooden forms for the concrete foundation still imbedded in the soil. These problems have to be remedied for clearance, and sellers become angry that they have to pay the cost of the remedy. Can you blame them?

How Can a Seller Avoid Outlandish Termite Repair Bills?

Actually there are several ways you might protect yourself from having to pay outlandish termite repair bills.

Obtain a termite report before you offer your property for sale. With this information, you will know before negotiating a sales price exactly what your maximum liability for structural damage will be, and you will also have the option of having all the work performed before possibly scaring the buyer with the extent of the work required for clearance. If you opt to obtain a termite report on your building before putting it up for sale, you will, of course, have to pay for the inspection fee yourself. The buyer could later accept this report or reject it and order another at his own expense.

Select an inspector who has a reputation for being fair and who will clear work that you or others have done. Because real estate agents deal with these companies all the time, they will have had enough experience to be able to make good recommendations. Tell an agent what your primary concerns are and ask for recommendations.

Set up the inspection appointment for a time when you are able to accompany the inspector. If possible, try to arrange an appointment with the firm's owner to do the inspection, even if it means waiting longer for him. Owners tend to be more disposed to explaining the work, suggesting inexpensive alternatives, and letting you do certain work yourself. Cooperate cheerfully, but ask for an explanation of the damage findings on the spot. If you can, get the inspector to itemize his estimate of repairs so you can determine how much each part of the total job costs.

Do not hesitate to get two or more termite reports if you feel the first estimate for work is excessive (sellers sometimes feel this way) or if you feel it doesn't show all the work that you think the property requires (buyers sometimes feel this way).

Once you get a written report, scrutinize it carefully. Try to understand all that it says. If the findings, recommendations, and estimates all seem reasonable, go ahead and hire the company to complete the work. If they seem unreasonable, discuss them with the inspector and see whether he will accept any alternatives. If not, do the easiest work yourself in a way you deem best and ask a contractor or independent carpenter to bid on the balance. (You won't have to pay for their bids.) Look in your daily newspaper's service directory and you will likely find independents who advertise that they specialize in doing termite work at 20%-33% off the termite companies' estimates and also guarantee that their work will pass inspection. Be careful whenever you deal with independents, however. Check their references and pay them in full only after the work has been completed and inspected.

Some termite companies will not issue a clearance unless they were hired to do the termite work, so you may have to pay another company to inspect the work that you and/or an independent contractor complete. For this reason, don't quibble with a termite company over anything less than a hundred dollars, because securing an inspection by another company will surely cost you that, and each termite company's estimate for the work it does itself also includes clearance of the report at no additional charge.

Because an institutional lender will generally require a current termite report before approving any new loan, it is often helpful to the lender and it will speed up your loan request if you submit a copy of the current termite report along with your loan application.

Who Pays for Termite Clearance?

The buyer and seller should determine through negotiations who will be responsible to pay for the corrective and preventive work recommended by the inspector. In general, the seller agrees to pay for the repair work, or at least a portion of it, while the buyer pays for the termite report and any preventive work. Often the buyer will add a statement to the purchase agreement stating that he is willing to buy the property provided that the termite work does not exceed a certain sum. If the report lists a substantial amount of work to be completed, you might even want to take a second look at what you are buying or at the price you are paying for the property.

Who is to pay for the termite report and what termite work needs to be done should all be fully explained to your escrow officer, because these bills are usually paid through escrow by the escrow holder at closing.

What Happens When the Termite Report Can't Be Cleared Before the Close of Escrow?

Whenever the work necessary to clear a termite report cannot be completed prior to the close of escrow, the balance of funds due the termite company must then be held in escrow for release upon the buyer's and the seller's written assurance that the work was done to their satisfaction. Include the conditions for release in your escrow instructions because, whereas the seller will most always agree that the work is satisfactory, the buyer won't necessarily agree, and the buyer must also approve the corrections made.

Be certain you verify your lender's policy regarding termite clearance, since some institutional lenders do not permit escrow to close before all of the termite work has been completed.

How Can I Negotiate a Lower Price or Get Out of the Deal if I Object to the Inspection Reports?

Under the purchase agreement, you will be given the opportunity to either accept the termite and other inspection reports or cancel the transaction. If you do so within the time limits set in the contract, your deposit money is refunded and no penalties are charged. Often a buyer may find items in the inspection reports that are not acceptable but these can be used to negotiate a lower price from the seller or other compensation. You may think that the small items found in the inspection report are minimal amounts, but take the time to add up all the suggested remedies. They may come to hundreds, even thousands, of dollars. Be sure to put your objections in writing and deliver a copy to the seller, the real estate agent, and the closing officer or attorney.

A Typical Misunderstanding: John and Sylvia found items of concern in their building inspection report, but felt it was too late to negotiate a lower purchase price with the seller. After all, the purchase contract had already been signed.

The Way Things Really Are: John and Sylvia should carefully read the expiration time and dates for their approval of any inspection reports. In practice, negotiations with the seller can continue up until the day of closing, based on provisions set in the purchase agreement. When a serious item is found in the inspection report, negotiations on settling the matter can begin at that time.

A Typical Misunderstanding: Jim and Danielle were advised by friends to have their new home inspected by a licensed building inspection company. Although the home was newly built, Jim and Danielle still wanted the added protection of an independent inspection company to check for any defects before they signed the final closing papers.

The Way Things Really Are: Many builders will add a clause in their purchase contract that will not allow the buyer to have a building inspection company look at the property before they close escrow. Look carefully at your contract with your builder. Try to negotiate the option that allows a qualified inspection before you close.

 A building and pest inspection should not be replaced by the disclosure statements furnished by the seller. The disclosure furnished by the seller discloses only those items that the seller knows about or suspects.

Can a Buyer Get Insurance Covering Other Potential Building Problems?

Yes, in most states a buyer can now get a home warranty insurance policy that insures against plumbing, electrical, heating, and major appliance problems for one year after escrow closes and is renewable annually thereafter.

This kind of policy has become quite popular because it offers welcome peace of mind at a reasonable price. It is especially attractive to buyers who have just emptied all of their savings accounts and piggy banks to make the large down payment required to buy a house, only to live in fear that they might encounter some unforeseen and expensive repair bills that might cause them to either lose the house or eat lots of beans. A basic policy costs approximately $250.

Before buying a policy, discuss it with a sales agent and read it carefully, since a basic policy contains certain exclusions that may be significant. Typically, a basic policy excludes the roof, air conditioner, refrigerator, laundry machines, outside sprinkler system, and swimming pool, but they may be included for an additional charge. Also, ask whether there is a charge for every repair visit and, if so, how much the charge is.

Two companies offering this coverage are American Home Shield (P.O. Box 849, Carroll, IA 51401-9901, (800) 247-2429, **www.americanhomeshield.com**) and First American Home Buyers Protection (P.O. Box 10180, Van Nuys, CA 91410-0180, (800) 444-9030, **homewarranty.firstam.com**). First American offers contracts in Spanish.

Sellers forced to relocate before their house is sold are also fond of home warranties because coverage begins soon after they apply for it and they don't even have to pay the premium until the house sells, regardless of how many repairs the house requires once the warranty is in force.

A Typical Misunderstanding: Margi and Fletcher didn't bother to apply for a home warranty plan when they moved from their lovely house in Maine because it was in perfect condition and they thought it would sell in no time.

The Way Things Really Are: Margi and Fletcher's charming and historical house languished on the market for two years without attracting a buyer. In that time, pipes cracked, appliances rusted, and plumbing fixtures began to leak. They had to pay for all the repairs themselves. Had they applied for an all-inclusive home warranty policy, the policy would have covered all the problems and they wouldn't have had to pay a cent in premiums until the house sold.

TIP Responsibility for paying the premium on a home warranty insurance policy, like many other escrow charges, is negotiable. No matter who pays it, though, be certain that the premium has been paid the day escrow closes, for often the buyer will have to use the policy the very next day, when he or she moves in and learns that the heater or air conditioner doesn't work.

Chapter Six

Loans and Financing Basics

T he biggest obstacle that most homebuyers face is coming up with enough money for a down payment and closing costs. The variety of loan programs today means that financing a property is much less difficult than it used to be, but the wide variety of financing options can be confusing. In this chapter I'll go over the basics of financing, including how to secure a loan, how much to borrow, and why your credit history plays such an important role. At the end of the chapter I've included a typical timetable for the entire loan process.

Why Is Financing So Important?

Unless you have just inherited a fortune, acquired some clandestine capital, or saved religiously for years, you will probably have to borrow most of the money you need to pay for the property you want to buy. You'll have to get some financing—perhaps even a lot of financing. If there is sufficient financing available, you'll be able to buy the property. If there isn't, you simply won't be able to buy it, no matter how much you want it.

Why Should I Shop Around for Financing?

Because the various costs involved in borrowing money will likely be the biggest expense in acquiring your property, the financing you get is extremely important—important enough for you to negotiate good terms with the seller if the seller is lending you the money to buy the property and important enough for you to shop around as much as possible for conventional financing if it's needed.

When you shop around for conventional financing, you will find that types of loans, loan fees, and interest rates vary from lender to lender. Variances in the rates may appear at first to be small, 2% at most, but these seemingly small variances have very direct and important consequences. Consider that, depending on the size of the loan, even a ½% difference in the interest rate may add an extra $30 or $40 to your monthly mortgage payments. Consequently, if you shop around for the money you need, you'll be glad that you did every month you own the property.

The following chart shows how varying interest rates affect the amount of the monthly payment on an $80,000 loan.

6.5%	7%	7.5%	8.0%	8.5%	9.0%	9.5%	10.0%
$505.65	$532.24	$559.37	$587.01	$615.13	$643.70	$672.68	$702.06

Chart 6-1. Monthly payment (fully amoritized)—$80,000 for 30 years at various interest rates

Besides considering the rate, consider also the length of your loan. 15-year loans are becoming more and more common because they save borrowers thousands in interest costs and are paid off twice as fast as 30-year loans. Contrary to what most people think, the payments on a 15-year loan are not twice what they would be on a 30-year loan. They're only slightly higher, because most of each payment during the first years of a loan goes toward interest; very little goes toward paying off the principal.

Here's an example. Let's say you get an $80,000 loan at a 10% interest rate, fully amortized, where the payments are structured to pay off the loan completely over a designated period of time, in this case over 30 years. After making monthly payments of $702.06 for 15 years, you would still owe the lender slightly more than $65,000. Had you been making payments of only $157.63 more every month for those same 15 years, you wouldn't owe the lender anything. Your loan would be fully paid off.

A Typical Misunderstanding: Dennis learns that the seller of a certain property will give him good terms. He doesn't know how he'll make the payments, but he'll figure that out later. He's always felt that getting a loan is the biggest problem in acquiring real estate.

The Way Things Really Are: The very first thing Dennis should consider is how he's going to meet those payments he's obligating himself to make every month. People lose their properties when they overextend themselves, and that could happen to Dennis.

How Much Will a Lender Lend Me?

Let's assume that your loan is customary, that is, somewhat less than the purchase price. Lenders will lend you a percentage of that price, varying anywhere

TIP

Be wary of a 15-year mortgage if you think you might have difficulty making the larger monthly payment at some time. A 15-year loan cannot be extended to a 30-year loan, whereas a 30-year loan can be paid off in 15 years.

Some 15-year loans are not fully amortized. Be wary of them. They require a large balloon payment after you've made payments for 15 years. Be sure you understand whether your loan is fully amortized or not.

Another alternative to the 30-year loan is the biweekly loan, which is amortized over 30 years. With a biweekly loan, you make payments every two weeks instead of monthly. You pay half the normal monthly payments every two weeks, or a total of 26 half-payments a year, which equals 13 full payments per year. The extra month's payment each year reduces the principal balance faster and a 30-year loan is paid off in 19-22 years.

One way to circumvent having to make a balloon payment on a loan that isn't fully amortized is to make higher payments, just as if the loan were fully amortized. You can turn a 30-year loan into a 15-year loan by doing the same thing. In fact, some real estate advisors recommend that borrowers who want a 15-year loan ought to get a 30-year loan instead, so they have the option of making smaller payments based upon a 30-year amortization schedule when times get tough. In most cases, you may make higher payments based on an appropriate amortized schedule even though your loan calls for lower payments. If you choose to pay your loan off in this way, make sure you indicate clearly to the lender that you want the excess funds applied to the loan principal. Mark each check with the words "Apply Excess Funds to Principal Only."

from 60% to 95%; generally it's 80%. Commercial property almost never exceeds 70% of the purchase price, while residential property, on the other hand, may secure a 90% loan.

There are even loan programs that offer 100% financing, requiring no down payment. These alternative loan programs are valuable for borrowers with limited available cash to use in their purchase, but the loan program may carry higher fees and interest rates.

Also, much depends on whether you will live there or rent it out. Lenders invariably lend a higher percentage on owner-occupied property. For example, suppose you find a house you like for $100,000. A lender might offer you a loan of, say, 90% of $100,000, or $90,000, if you were planning to occupy it yourself. You would have to come up with a down payment of $10,000 plus the loan fees and other closing costs. If you were buying the same house strictly as an investment and you were planning to rent it out, the lender would lend only 70% or 75% of the purchase price, and you would have to come up with a larger down payment.

A Typical Misunderstanding: James and Marcy thought they'd hit pay dirt when they heard that they could obtain a loan for 100% of the purchase price of their new home. With no down payment required, they could finally afford to buy a home.

The Way Things Really Are: Although loan programs providing 100% financing with no down payment are available for qualified buyers and may be the best alternative for some borrowers with limited cash, James and Marcy would do well to consider the additional fees and higher interest rates that typically are associated with a 100% financing loan program. James and Marcy should compare the monthly payment obligations under a 100% loan program with those of a traditional 80% loan program.

Although loans based upon a percentage of the appraised value are not so common as those based on the purchase price, you should know that the FHA (Federal Housing Administration) and DVA (Department of Veterans Affairs) base their loans solely on their appraisal figures. For example, if they appraise your $100,000 house at $80,000, they may want to offer only 80% of this $80,000, their appraisal figure, which amounts to a loan offer of only $64,000.

Except for DVA and FHA loans, a loan based on an appraisal figure rather than a purchase price figure generally indicates that the sales price is higher than what the banks consider the true value to be.

How Should I Prepare to Get a Loan?

The first thing to do, even before you begin shopping around for a loan, is to determine what is the greatest monthly payment you can make. The property you are buying is security for the loan, but you must be able to meet the monthly payments or the lender will have the right to foreclose. To determine your ability to pay back a home loan, lenders generally use a ratio based upon your gross monthly income being so many times the amount of the monthly mortgage payments. The commonly accepted rule of thumb for this type of evaluation is that your gross monthly income must be three or four times the monthly payments. For example, if your monthly payment is $900, then your monthly income from wages, dividends, interest, and bonuses should be between $2,700 and $3,600. Naturally, this rule of thumb will vary depending on inflation and on the lender's individual policy.

Of course, if you should be buying income property, something you intend to rent out, the income you can expect from the rents may be added to the rest of your monthly income in making a determination.

In addition to figuring out what you can afford to pay every month according to your income, you ought to think about setting aside some funds just in case you should suffer a financial setback sometime during the life of the loan. Many financial advisors recommend that borrowers set aside a three-month reserve of mortgage payments in a separate "peace of mind" savings account for use in case of "rainy days."

Next, you should know how lenders determine a loan, that is, how they figure the maximum amount they will lend on a property. Generally, they do it in one of two ways—as a percentage of the purchase price or as a percentage of the appraised value.

The property you intend to buy will always be appraised by the lending institution. They appraise it before they make a loan because they must protect their investors' money. They want to be sure that, if you should stop making the payments on your loan, they can get their money back by reselling your property.

Just remember that each lender's appraisal figure is somewhat arbitrary. There is no such thing as an exact property value. It is the lender's appraisal, however, on which they will base their loan commitment. One bank may consider that your intended property is located in an up-and-coming area and thus offer you a larger loan, which is, of course, to your advantage. Another lender may consider that the same property is declining in value or has no growth potential and thus offer you a much lower loan. Each lender has different self-imposed rules and regulations, but all of them base their appraisals on the probable market value of the property during the life of the loan.

Generally speaking, most loans are based on the purchase price, though occasionally a loan will be based on the appraisal figure alone. Some lenders follow a policy of giving a loan commitment on whichever is the lower figure, the appraised value or the purchase price.

How Should I Go About Shopping for a Loan?

If we assume that there's no real estate agent involved, here's what you should do to secure a loan:

- Pick up an interest rate "stat sheet," which some title and escrow companies prepare for their customers. These stat sheets list the prevailing interest rates and the loan fees for institutional lenders in the area.

- Call or visit several banks and/or savings and loan offices. Consider first those where you normally bank. Sometimes they give their own customers special concessions such as a reduced interest rate when the monthly payments are automatically deducted from a checking account. Then consider any lenders that relatives, friends, or acquaintances have recommended.

- Call several loan brokers. See what they have to offer. They sometimes have connections with out-of-town lenders that would otherwise be unknown to you. Be aware that there are some unscrupulous loan brokers that make promises and ask for up-front money from applicants; once they get it, they do nothing. Should a loan broker ask for up-front money, do some checking into the broker's reputation. Under no circumstances should you ever give a

SECURE TITLE COMPANY
1220 Oak Park Blvd.
Boonville, CA 91002
411 423-4567

Interest rates for: July 25, 20XX

Lenders	Terms					Remarks
American Mortgage	**80% loan** 9 1/4% + 1 1/2	**Pts+** 135	**To** 203,150			FHA & VA
	80% w/2nd	**Pts+**	**To**			8 1/2% + 4 points
	90% loan 9 1/4% + 2 1/2	**Pts+** 135	**To** 203,150			
Boonville Bank	**80% loan** 8 3/4% + 2	**Pts+** 150	**To** 100,000			Call for quotes on non-owner-occupied single-family & 2-4 units
	80% w/2nd 9% + 2	**Pts+** 150	**To** 203,150			
	90% loan	**Pts+** 135	**To**			
Helpful Financial	**80% loan** 9% + 1 1/2	**Pts+** 250	**To** 98,750			Second, home improvement loans, also commercial
	80% w/2nd 9 1/4% + 2	**Pts+** 250	**To** 203,150			
	90% loan	**Pts+** 135	**To**			

Chart 6-2. Sample rate sheet for loans

loan broker more than $100 in up-front money. He should be paid for his services after he secures you a loan, not before.

■ Browse the Internet for the best available rates, terms, and qualifying conditions. One good Web site, **www.e-loan.com/s/show/purchase**, will search all available sources for the loan type and amount you are looking for. Under the "Home Purchase" tab, click on the "Search Mortgage Rates" link and you will find anywhere from 10 to 20 different loan options for your specific loan amount. Click on "Loan Details" and a description of the loan product will be shown, together with a "Rate and Payment Forecast." The margin for adjustable rate loans will be shown, in addition to the annual and lifetime cap for the loan. If you click on "View Closing Costs," a breakdown of the closing costs associated with the loan will be shown, as well as the "third party fees," such as the appraisal fee and credit report fee. The title company or attorney closing fees will also be estimated.

This information will help you determine how much you will need to come up with by the day of closing for the down payment. Keep in mind that your closing costs may add an additional 3%-6% of the mortgage amount to the cost of your home.

Other things to consider when comparison shopping for a loan:

■ Ask about interest rates and loan fees. (Be sure to ask about all of the fees already mentioned.) Ask if you can "lock in" the interest rate for a specified period of time.

- Compare the percentage each lender is offering, that is, whether your loan would be 70%, 80%, or 90%. Also, note whether the loan would be based on the appraisal or on the purchase price.

- Ask how quickly the lender can appraise the property. This is important because generally you have a set time (negotiable between you and the seller, but it can be as short as 15 days) in which to obtain financing or a loan commitment once you sign the purchase agreement with the seller; if you cannot get a fairly quick appraisal, you might not be able to buy the property at all. If, for example, the lender is busy and says that no one can get out to appraise the property for two or three weeks, you will want to go elsewhere to find your loan.

- Ask what types of loans are available (conventional, FHA, or VA).

- Prepare a "Loan Shopper" (you'll find a blank copy of this form in the back of the book) side-by-side comparison of the terms being offered to you by the various lenders, and think carefully about which loan would be the best for your circumstances.

	Lender One	Lender Two	Lender Three
Initial interest rate on note	9½	9¾	10½
Fixed, variable, graduated, other	variable	variable	fixed
Amortization due date	30 yrs.	20 yrs.	15 yrs.
Points and other fees (total)	1½	2	2½
Pre-payment penalty	no	no	yes
Assumability (specific requirements)	yes, one only	yes	no
Interest rate cap	4 pts.	5 pts.	—
Index used	U.S. Treasury Securities	11th District Cost of Funds	—
Interest rate adjustments	every 3 months	every 6 months	
Co-borrowers allowed	yes	yes	yes
Maximum negative amortization	none	none	—

Chart 6-3. Loan shopper form

Your chances of obtaining a loan depend to a great extent on whether money is "tight" or "easy" when you are making your purchase. Lenders change their loan policies constantly, depending upon conditions in the national and local money markets and the local real estate market as well.

Whatever you do, don't give up. If one lender denies you a loan, try another and another and another until you find a willing lender. Every lender has its own needs and policies, and you will discover that you can get a loan if you keep trying. When the money market is tight, being turned down for a loan repeatedly can be very discouraging, but persistence pays off. Keep at it. Even if people tell you money isn't available, keep trying. After all, lenders are in business to make money, and they can make money only by lending out their customers' deposits.

You might be surprised to learn that there are certain lenders who make loans on non-conforming properties for non-conforming borrowers. No, I'm not referring to loan sharks. I'm referring to legitimate lenders willing to take more risk in exchange for higher fees and interest rates. They will make loans on properties that have liens against them and they will lend to applicants with bankruptcies in their past. Seek these lenders out if you keep getting negative responses to your loan inquiries.

A Typical Misunderstanding: The Bank of Central California turns down Jack's application for a loan to acquire a new house. He figures that they rejected him because of a questionable credit rating and that there's no sense wasting any more time applying to other lenders.

The Way Things Really Are: Each lender has its own credit requirements and its own supply of available money. Jack may have had the credit he needed to qualify, but that particular bank may not have had any money to lend on a long-term first mortgage right then. Jack may very well be able to get the money he needs from another lender.

If there is a real estate agent involved in your transaction, he or she will shop for the loan, asking all the right questions, and then bring you the information and the loan applications, and he or she will submit your completed loan application to the lender in question. This is a major advantage of having an agent. The agent provides a loan broker's services at no extra charge. Not only does he or she do the legwork, but the agent will probably have a better knowledge of the lending market and will probably know which lenders are more receptive to someone with your qualifications and needs.

Who Will I Be Dealing with Regarding My Loan?

During your loan shopping process, you may be dealing with a mortgage broker, a loan officer, or your real estate agent. You might want to consult with a mortgage broker, especially if you have special needs in finding a loan. Mortgage brokers often have resources that an individual may not know about. A broker may also have suggestions and ideas on how best to help you qualify for a loan. A good mortgage broker may help you write backup letters required by a lender and will help you prepare your loan application in the most favorable terms possible. While the mortgage broker cannot prepare documents for you, he or she can give you advice on the best way to prepare your documentation.

If you want to obtain your financing yourself, you will deal with a loan officer at the bank or lending institution of your choice. The loan officer will give you a list of items that will be required to complete your loan application. The officer will be your contact throughout your loan approval process. When dealing directly with the bank's loan officer, you will want to carefully review your documents before submitting them to the bank. Once entered into your loan file, the information may be hard to change.

For example, you may have submitted a bank statement or other documentation showing negative credit items, which the bank may not have required and you may have overlooked. Once the lender becomes aware of these negative items, it will make them part of your credit profile. Be careful to submit only the required items, and check these documents over for any derogatory comments that may affect your credit score.

However, when answering lenders' questions, be as truthful as possible. The computerization of bank and credit accounts is becoming so thorough that dishonest answers are likely to be uncovered when the lending institution does its independent investigation. If you have had some problems repaying debts in the past, you should explain this to the loan officer handling your case rather than misstate the facts and have the lender discover the truth from some other source.

Once your loan has been approved and your escrow/closing officer is notified of the lender you will be using, your next communication will likely be with your closing or escrow officer. She will know the status of your loan documents and when they will be ready for closing. She will notify you of the amount the lender will require you to pay at closing and any other miscellaneous fees.

What Information Do Institutional Lenders Generally Require?

Institutional lenders will almost always ask the following questions:

- How much cash and what liquid assets do you have? The lender will request a copy of your bank balance, your savings account balance, and an accounting of your stocks and bonds.

- What type of work do you do for a living and what is your current income?

- How many current debts do you have? All current debts in your family will be considered, as well as possible future debts, such as schooling and common necessities.

- What is your credit history? This involves an investigation of your entire past with regard to loans and buying on credit.

- Do you have adequate credit references? Borrowing from banks ranks higher than borrowing from finance companies.

- What is your past banking experience? Your banks will be contacted for information regarding the size of your accounts, the length of time you have banked with them, and the average amount of money you have on hand in the accounts.

- How old are you, your spouse, and your children? Age is considered because your earning potential usually declines when you get beyond a certain age.

- How much do you wish to borrow and what repayment schedule do you desire?

Lenders ask for all of this information, and sometimes a whole lot more, because they want to make sure that they can resell their loans to other banks. They might sell their loans on the secondary mortgage market to other lenders, such as Fannie Mae, insurance companies, and pension funds, both here and abroad. Consequently, lenders verify almost every asset on your loan application and check out every negative credit rating, no matter how insignificant. The more documentation you give a lender in the beginning, the faster your loan will be processed.

You may speed up the loan processing by providing the lender with copies of your federal tax returns for the previous two years, copies of your last three months' bank statements, and a copy of the current fire insurance on the property (in refinancing situations). You may speed up the loan processing even more by getting prequalified as a borrower before you actually need your loan, so that when you do need it, the lender will be able to move quickly.

What Can I Do if I Have Bad Credit?

You may still qualify for a loan, despite credit problems you may have had in the past. There are companies that specialize in "credit repair," which promise to "clean up" or wipe your credit report clean. You can do it yourself with a little time and persistence. There are certain steps that you can take to clean up your credit report. In most cases, you can qualify for a loan with late payment histories on your credit report, but the lender will want explanations of each late payment made and the reason why the payment was late.

The first step you need to take is to request a copy of your credit report from one of several credit reporting agencies. These are private agencies and they make their money selling your credit to lenders or marketing companies. These are the three main credit reporting agencies:

Experian
P.O. Box 2106
Dallas, TX 75002-9506
www.experian.com
(888) 397-3742

Equifax Information Services, LLC
P.O. Box 740241
Atlanta, GA 30374
www.equifax.com
(800) 685-1111

TransUnion, LLC
Consumer Disclosure Center
P.O. Box 1000
Chester, PA 19022
www.transunion.com
(800) 916-8800

If you have been denied credit in the past 30 days, you can request a free copy of your credit report. Many credit agencies will give you a free copy of your report once a year. Once you have received a copy of your credit report, read through it and note any errors or items that you may want to dispute. Under the Fair Credit Reporting Act of 1970, you are entitled to certain rights in regards to your credit report. You have the right to ask the agency to check the information for you. The credit reporting agencies are required to answer your requests for verification of information and must do so within certain specific time limits.

What Is a FICO Score?

Many lenders rely on a credit score report from the credit reporting bureaus called a *FICO score*. This type of scoring is a way that lenders determine the likelihood, based on certain criteria, that you will pay your bills on time. In essence, your credit history is condensed into a single number. This number is calculated by using scoring models and mathematical tables that assign points for pieces of information that are believed to best predict your future credit performance.

A company called Fair, Isaac and Company (www.fairisaac.com, 415 472-2211) studied millions of people and how those people used credit. They found factors in their results that have proven to predict future credit performance. The credit score considers such criteria as your late payments, the length of time you have had established credit, the amount of credit you use in relation to the amount of credit available to you, the length of time at your current residence, your employment history and any negative credit information reports, such as a bankruptcy, charge-off, or collection. Under the FICO system, credit files are rated on a numerical scale from 300 to 900. The higher your score, the better your chances of obtaining a loan. The average FICO score is around 699, with a score of 800 being excellent. A low FICO score could mean the difference between qualifying for a loan and being denied credit. One of the most important tools you can use to improve your chance of getting a favorable loan, one with the best interest rate and terms, is to improve your FICO score. To obtain your credit score, visit **www.myfico.com**.

There may be several ways to increase your chances of improving your credit or FICO score. You can begin by making every effort to pay your bills on time. Late payments and collections can have a dramatic impact on your score. Try not to apply for credit too frequently. Oftentimes, having a large number of inquiries on your credit report can lower your chances for a high credit score. Reducing your credit card balances can improve your credit score. If you have reached your maximum on any of your credit cards, consider paying down some of these card balances or distributing the balances more evenly among your cards. If you have derogatory credit items on your credit report, try to remove or explain anything that may be removed or explained.

You may request that certain derogatory items be removed from your credit report if they appear after seven to 10 years. Unless challenged, most all bankruptcies, liens, and judgments will remain on your credit history for 10 years. Late payments, charge-offs, repossessions, and convictions will remain on your report for seven years. It is a little-known fact that the only credit information required to stay on your credit report for seven to 10 years is delinquent child support. Although the credit bureaus are allowed to put the negative information on your credit report for up to seven or 10 years, they don't have to. You have the right to challenge and dispute negative information and have it removed if the information is misleading and not an accurate reflection of your current creditworthiness. In general, you can request to have derogatory information deleted that is over 120 days old.

For those items on your credit report that are correct, but that you feel require an explanation, such as paying late due to losing your job or incurring unexpected medical bills, you may send a brief statement (up to 100 words) explaining the situation that caused you to pay late. This statement will be placed in your credit file and disclosed each time your credit file is accessed.

If the credit bureau is still reporting items in your credit report that you feel are incorrect, you should ask them to reinvestigate the disputed items and also request the names, addresses, and phone numbers of the companies with which the credit bureau is verifying the disputed items.

Professional credit repair services remove the negative items from your credit report, whether they are true or not, in just this fashion. They keep sending the credit bureau letters denying everything, including late payments and other derogatory items, knowing that about half of the items will be removed simply because the company cannot verify the disputed item. The credit repair service continually requests a reinvestigation until the credit bureau or the subscriber fails to comply in the time allowed.

When asking for information on your credit report, be as specific as possible and back up your request with any pertinent documents that will verify your claim.

Credit reporting agencies make mistakes and any mistake will remain on your credit report until you or someone else brings it to their attention. I have seen many instances where someone's credit report included erroneous information from the credit report of another person with a similar last name or a similar Social Security number. The error can be a small matter of a few dollars or a serious error involving a lien or a foreclosure.

Be sure to check your credit report carefully and accurately. Your credit report is the first thing a lender will look at when considering your request for a loan.

A Typical Misunderstanding: Jonathan thought his credit was so bad that he couldn't qualify for any type of loan. He noticed ads for credit repair services that promised to "clean up his credit" and make him creditworthy again. He decided to pay the fee and have a credit repair company clean all his debts off his credit report.

The Way Things Really Are: Jonathan needs to realize that there is no magical formula to take away bad credit. Jonathan's explanations and attempts to correct the problem himself will confirm to the lender that he is using good judgment and is trying to correct his credit history and that he is trying very hard to become creditworthy.

How Can I Be Sure Nothing Will Go Wrong with My Loan Application?

One of the best ways to be sure nothing will go wrong with your loan application is to submit all the documentation the lender requires as soon as possible after requested. Stay on top of your loan application, checking on it daily, if need be, to be sure the loan approval processing is proceeding on schedule. Ask your loan officer if any documents—inspection reports, title reports, insurance verifications—are missing that she may be having difficulty in obtaining. Offer to help get copies of these documents from the title company or from your real estate agent and hand them in to her. Verify that the appraisal of the property is done on time and is promptly submitted to your lender. You can check that any verifications from banks or from your employer are processed on time.

There are several steps that your lender will take with your loan application:

an underwriter will review it, then a senior underwriter, then a processor, and then a closer, and finally a supervisor underwriter will check it again. Most loans must follow government-mandated guidelines on what must be documented and which documents must be in your loan file, so lenders are careful that everything in your file follows those rules to the letter.

Can I Still Qualify for a Loan if I Am Self-Employed?

A lender will consider you self-employed if you own a 25% or greater interest in a business. You can still qualify for a loan, and there are several things you can do to make your loan approval process easier and faster. Lenders look at job stability and potential for growth in your business. Although you don't have a W-2 statement from an employer, you can still show the lender that you are a conscientious borrower and a good credit risk. If you are self-employed, you will be asked to supply the lender with the following items:

- Tax returns for the last two years
- Signed federal business income tax return, if you have a corporation or partnership
- Current profit and loss statement for your business (you can prepare this yourself and it can be handwritten)
- An explanation of your business, including your customers and your projections for the future
- An explanation of your expertise in your field and your years of experience
- Current bank statements for the last three months
- Copies of any business licenses

Many self-employed borrowers maintain only one bank account for their personal and business enterprise. This is acceptable to the lender, as long as you can separate the business expenses and income from the personal expenses and income. You should try to maintain a savings account, as lenders view a history of saving as a big plus in your credit evaluation. Your savings account may be small, say $500-$1,000, but the fact that you do save something will greatly help your creditworthiness.

If you are self-employed, do whatever is necessary to maintain a good credit record. No matter how large or small your company income is, a poor credit record will harm you more than anything else. There are lenders who specialize in self-employed borrowers and you should look to them first for your loan. These lenders tend to be more open-minded in looking at your tax returns and business history. If they see an upward trend, that your income is rising each year, they will look favorably on your loan application. You should explain any large expenses, and it would be very helpful to have a letter from your accountant confirming the financial status of your company. There are no absolutes in qualifying for a loan and there is no reason you will be automatically disqualified for a loan just because you are self-employed.

Is There a Loan for a First-Time Homebuyer?

Many lenders participate in the Community Home Buyer's Program, sponsored by Fannie Mae, which is specifically tailored for the first-time homebuyer. This type of loan provides financing for low- to moderate-income buyers who might not qualify for a loan on traditional criteria. Under this loan program, you do not need to have a credit history and it allows you to show a willingness to pay by presenting paid utility bills, payments to a landlord, and other sources of credit or services.

An important feature of the Community Home Buyer's Program is the 3/2 option. This means that you can buy a home with only 3% down of your own funds, instead of the usual 5%, and the remaining 2% can be a gift from relatives or borrowed from friends. Other loan requirements, such as your income-to-debt ratios, are relaxed under this program and you are not required to have a specific percentage of the purchase price in a reserve or checking account as required for a conventional loan.

The disadvantage of this program is that there are limits on the amount of the loan you may apply for. To qualify for a loan, you must earn no more than the area median income (with exceptions for specified high-cost areas). You may want to check with your local bank to see if it offers this loan program and what the loan limits are for your area. You can learn more from the Fannie Mae Web site, **www.homepath.com** (or part of **www.fanniemae.com** as of November 2002).

> **A Typical Misunderstanding:** Thomas and Kristen have been renting a modest two-bedroom apartment for five years, trying all the while to save part of their salaries to use as a down payment on a home. No matter how hard they try, they can't seem to save enough to buy anything they'd want to call their own. Prices rise faster than their savings, and they begin to despair of ever being able to buy.

> **The Way Things Really Are:** Thomas and Kristen can afford to buy their home now by buying with a 95% mortgage and private mortgage insurance. Although they might be on a tight budget for a while, they are still better off buying with a 5% down payment rather than waiting until they have accumulated a 20% down payment, because their income should increase over time and so should the value of their home.

How Do I Get Prequalified for a Loan?

To get prequalified, select a lender that is both competitive and cooperative and explain that you are looking for a property to buy but haven't found one yet. Say that you would like to get a commitment letter based upon your personal financial information so you will be able to move quickly when you locate a suitable property. The commitment letter should state that the lender will lend you a specified amount on certain general terms, based upon your personal information and contingent upon their final appraisal of the property.

This commitment letter is not a loan guarantee commitment in which the lender would guarantee all the terms of the loan. It is more general than that. It is strictly a preliminary commitment showing that you're a qualified buyer who can act quickly. Sellers want to know whether a potential buyer can qualify for a loan. They don't want to tie up their property for months before they know whether the buyer can complete the transaction.

Most lenders charge nothing for a commitment letter, though they may hesitate to give you the commitment in writing. Tell them that you must have it in writing to show your prospective seller that you can qualify for a loan. Remember: lenders want your business as much as you want theirs.

You may obtain a prequalification letter from a lender over the Internet. Start your search by going to your favorite lender's Web site and entering in a request to prequalify for a loan. You will need to enter some general information, such as the type of loan you would like to qualify for, the property type, whether single family or commercial property, the property usage (such as owner-occupied or rental property), the purchase price, if you can document your income, your gross monthly income (before taxes), your available cash, and your total monthly debt (including cars, student loans, and credit card balances). There are many excellent Web sites that offer a prequalification letter. You can type in "prequalify for a loan" in any one of the major search engines and a list of lenders and mortgage Internet brokers will appear.

As an example, go to **www.countrywide.com** and click on "Home Purchase." You will be offered several options to consider. You might visit "Calculators" and choose to look at "How much can I afford?" You can also visit "Loan Advisor" to learn which types of loans might best suit you. To speak with a loan representative, you can call (800) 556-9568.

How Can I Use the Internet to Qualify and Obtain a Loan Faster?

It is becoming possible in some cases to get a loan approval and even an actual loan commitment in just a few minutes at your real estate agent's office or over the Internet from your home computer. New computer software is being developed that can quickly and objectively run through your loan application and credit report and tell you if you will be a good credit risk for a lender's loan programs. The program will also tell the lender if you are likely to make your loan payments on time. Some large lending institutions are striving for a system in which the loan officer will be able to enter your basic information, income, debt, and assets and your credit report into an underwriting system that will come up with a basic decision within minutes.

The Internet has provided lenders with the means to approve and fund a loan more quickly and more efficiently than ever before. You may want to begin by checking your real estate agent's Web site. Agents are offering valuable information on their Web sites, such as current mortgage interest rates, credit report resources, and home inspection services. You can look at various Web sites to compare loan interest rates and programs. Here are a few typical mortgage sites: **www.homemortgageguide.com**, **www.mortgagemart.com**, **www.rate.net**, **www.bankrate.com**, and **www.mortgageloan.com**. If you have a favorite lender, such as Wells Fargo, GMAC, Washington Mutual, Bank of America, or Chase, you might want to visit their Web sites to determine their current mortgage interest rates and programs.

Helpful Hints to Consider When Taking out Loans

- Weigh the advantages and disadvantages of each different type of loan available to you: conventional (ask about the current types available), FHA, and VA.

- Be ever aware of the time limit you have in which to close escrow. You must know how soon you can get the loan.

- Ask your banker or real estate agent for help if you don't understand something.

- Make sure that any special agreements with the lender are in writing. Take nothing for granted.

- Read the loan forms thoroughly.

- Understand that interest rates may vary from the time a lender quotes you a figure to the time your loan is actually processed.

- Consider locking in your loan rate if you feel rates will be going up in the near future.

- Get a loan commitment in writing from the loan officer and be sure you know when the commitment will expire. Most commitments are good for 30 days. Do not, whatever you do, rely on verbal agreements.

- Request an extension well ahead of the expiration date, if you think you will need one. Most lenders will honor this request, although they may very well change the interest rate.

- Know the annual percentage rate. Know whether it is variable or fixed.

- Know if the loan will carry a prepayment penalty for early payoff.

- Know exactly how much the lender will lend you.

- Know whether you need a co-signer or security other than the property you intend to buy.

- Know whether the lender will permit any secondary financing.

TIP The most important thing you can do to improve your chances for getting the loan of your choice is to know your credit score before applying for your loan. The second most important thing you can do is to know your qualifying ratio of total monthly expenses to total monthly income. You can look at ways to improve your credit rating and reduce your monthly income-to-expense ratio before you submit your loan application.

A Typical Misunderstanding: John and Louise locked in their rate with their mortgage broker, so they didn't worry how long it took to complete their loan application. After all, their rate was locked in, so they were protected.

The Way Things Really Are: Rates may be locked for certain specified periods of time, typically 10, 15, or 30 days, after which that rate expires. John and Louise could be forced to accept the prevailing interest rate at the time of the closing of their loan.

How Can I Be Sure That I Will Get the Locked-in Interest Rate on My Loan?

Before you lock in an interest rate with your lender or mortgage broker, ask how long they anticipate your loan will take to process. If lenders are quite busy, your loan approval and processing may take several weeks and a locked-in rate may not be in your best interest. In a busy time, you may want to add 15 days or more to the closing date to take into account delays that may occur. It's typically best to lock in your rate 15 days before your loan is scheduled to close. Your interest rate will depend on how many days in advance you lock in your rate. The longer the rate is locked in, the higher the interest rate the bank may need to quote.

How Might I Calculate How Much Cash I'll Need to Close My Purchase?

Complete the cash-to-close worksheet much like the sample that follows (there's a blank copy of this worksheet in the back of the book) and you'll have calculated how much cash you'll need to close your escrow. Generally, your closing costs will come out to between 3% and 5% of your loan amount.

ANALYSIS OF CASH TO CLOSE

Full purchase price of new house	$ 100,000	A
Loan amount requested	$ 80,000	B
Down payment needed (without closing costs)	$ 20,000	C=A-B
Closing cost estimate (3-5% of loan amount)	$ 2,400	D

TOTAL CASH NEEDED TO CLOSE $ 22,400   E=C+D

SOURCES OF CASH NEEDED TO CLOSE

Amount from sale of present house	$ 10,000	F
Amount of cash deposit	$ 1,000	G
Amount from savings & checking accounts	$ 1,400	H
Amount from gifts	$	I
Amount from stocks or other securities	$	J
Amount from other sources (secondary financing, etc.)	$ 10,000	K

2ⁿᵈ Note + D.T. to Seller

_____

_____

TOTAL CASH AVAILABLE FOR CLOSING $ 22,400   L=F+G+
                                                H+I+J+K

NOTE: "L" must be equal to or greater than "E."

Chart 6-4. Cash-to-close worksheet

What Loan Fees Do Lenders Charge?

The various fees charged by institutional lenders for making a loan vary considerably from lender to lender.

First, there's the loan or application fee that the lender charges to process your loan. Usually this is a set fee, say a flat $150, $1,000, or even $2,000. Whatever the amount, just keep in mind that this fee covers only the cost of processing your loan papers, nothing else.

Second, there is a charge called points, a charge to originate a loan based on the amount of the loan itself. Borrowers pay points only once, before they receive any loan proceeds. One point is one percentage point (1%) of the loan amount, two points is 2%, three points is 3%, and so on. If your loan was $80,000, each point would equal $800. Four points on such a loan would be $3,200. Each point you pay will raise the effective yield on a 30-year loan by 1/8%. If you pay 2 points, for example, your 8½% interest rate will be raised to 8¾%. Points may vary from one all the way up to six, depending on the money market, that is, the availability of money to loan. Determining who will pay the points is a matter for negotiation between buyer and seller. FHA loans stipulate that the buyer may not pay more than one point.

Third, there's a credit report fee, something charged to check out your credit and your employment. This fee is usually minimal, considering the other sums charged. It will range from $50 to $175.

Fourth, there's a tax service fee to cover what the lender has to pay an outside agency to keep informed as to the status of your property taxes. Your lender wants to be notified if you fail to pay your property taxes and the property comes into jeopardy of being sold for back taxes. But because no lender has time to check twice a year to see whether all of its borrowers have paid their property taxes, it hires an outside tax service agency to provide this information—and naturally it charges its borrowers for the service. Usually the charge will run between $50 and $75 over the life of the loan.

Fifth, there may be miscellaneous loan fees for processing and appraising. These may be called document preparation fee, loan discount fee, underwriting fee, administration fee, appraisal review fee, and warehousing fee.

Lumped together, the loan fee, points, credit report fee, tax service fee, and any miscellaneous fees all may add up easily to hundreds and even thousands of dollars. More important, though, you have to pay all of these fees in advance, before you can ever receive the loan proceeds. Either they are paid into escrow and turned over to the bank once you get your loan or, more generally, they are deducted from the loan proceeds. As a consequence, the loan fees are actually added to your down payment and must be paid up front. They generally amount to 3%-5% of the loan. Some of these fees may be nonrecurring: you pay them only once. Other fees may be recurring, paid over time, such as monthly or annually.

So, you see, it is exceedingly important that you shop around for both a favorable interest rate and the best possible loan fees.

A Typical Misunderstanding: Even though the loan fees turn out to be double what he thought they would be, Oliver figures that he had better go through with his loan anyway. Loans are hard to get.

The Way Things Really Are: Lenders all charge different loan fees. Oliver should shop around when he has the chance, and he should get an estimate of his loan fees in writing before deciding to go ahead with the loan.

Nonrecurring Closing Costs Associated with Your Loan	Items Required to Be Paid in Advance
loan origination fee	prepaid interest
loan discount fee	homeowner's insurance
appraisal fee	VA funding fee
credit report fee	up-front mortgage insurance premium
lender's inspection fee	
mortgage broker fee	mortgage insurance
tax service fee	reserves deposited with lender
flood certification fee	homeowner's insurance impounds
flood monitoring fee	property tax impounds
document preparation fee	mortgage insurance impounds
underwriting fee	nonrecurring closing costs
administration fee	closing/escrow settlement fee
appraisal review fee	title insurance
warehousing fee	mortgage insurance
	recording fees
	pest inspection

Chart 6-5. Closing costs and when they're paid

What Is an Escrow Impound Account?

Your lender may require that you place a specified amount in an escrow account, which will be held by the lender for payment of your property taxes and homeowner's insurance. This amount may be up to two months' worth of the taxes and insurance payments. Lenders like to set up impound accounts because it provides them with assurance that the property taxes and insurance will be paid on time.

Most impound accounts allow your lender to collect 1/12 of the annual expenses each month. This amount will be included as part of your monthly mortgage payment. Generally you will be required to place two months of homeowner's insurance and two months of property taxes to set up your impound account. You may be offered the option of waiving this requirement, but lenders often charge up to a quarter point on your interest rate for choosing not to contribute to an escrow account.

Your lender will perform an analysis each year to determine if you have sufficient funds in your escrow account or if you are due a refund. Any excess amount over $50 must be returned to you. If you do not receive an annual statement of your escrow account, contact your lender or the HUD Office of Consumer and Regulatory Affairs. You are entitled to file a complaint if the lender does not comply with the escrow account regulations. You would send the complaint to the Director of Interstate Land Sales/RESPA Division, Office of Consumer and Regulatory Affairs, Department of Housing and Urban Develop-ment, Room 91-46, 451 7th Street, SW, Washington, DC 20410.

There are currently about 14 states (California, Connecticut, Iowa, Maine, Maryland, Massachusetts, Minnesota, New Hampshire, New York, Oregon, Rhode Island, Utah, Wisconsin, and Vermont) that have passed laws requiring the lender to pay interest to you on your escrow funds. In some states lenders will allow you to set up a separate account into which you place a certain amount of money and then pay the insurance and property taxes yourself. These *pledge accounts* must be set up before you close on the house.

If you would like to find out if your lender is required to pay interest on your impound account, check with the Mortgage Bankers Association of America (MBA). You can find them on the Internet at **www.mbaa.org**. The MBA has a current list of the states that have passed laws requiring lenders to pay some form of interest on the escrow impound account.

Is There a Way to Save on Financing and Loan Fees?

When shopping for your loan, you may be most concerned about finding the best possible interest rate. But in order to save on financing and loan fees, you will want to look at other considerations in addition to a low interest rate.

Take a careful look at the closing fees associated with your loan, the loan type or length of the loan, and other provisions written into the mortgage, such as a prepayment penalty clause. Your loan should be tailored to fit your individual needs and fit comfortably into your financial plans for the future. As you are speaking to lenders and comparing rates and terms, ask to see an estimate of the closing costs that will be associated with your loan. Many of these closing loan fees may be negotiable and some may be eliminated altogether. There are several steps you can take before applying for your loan that can save you money and reduce your loan fees.

Among all the negotiations that will be involved in your property purchase, negotiating a favorable loan will be one of the most important. Your first step is to understand which fees are negotiable and which fees can possibly be deleted. There will be lender-related fees, which are generally negotiable, and there will be government-related costs, such as recording and property tax fees, which will not be negotiable. With careful negotiating, you could save hundreds of dollars on your loan fees at closing and over the life of the loan.

Negotiable Loan Closing Costs	Nonnegotiable Loan Closing Costs
loan origination fee	transfer taxes
application fee	state/county tax stamps
processing fee\document preparation fee	recording fees
notary fee	property tax fees
underwriting fee	government-related fees
wire transfer fee	utility fee
funding fee	
points	
survey fee	
credit report fee	

Chart 6-6. Negotiable and nonnegotiable closing costs

TIP Title and escrow companies will not establish your impound account. Your lender will set up and maintain this account.

In addition to negotiating with the lender to pay reduced loan fees, the second most important step you can do to ensure that you get the best loan and the best rate and terms is to know your credit score before you apply for your loan. Refer to "What Is a FICO Score?" to learn about this type of credit scoring and how you can improve your score. Remember: the higher your FICO score, the better your chances are of obtaining the best interest rate and the best loan terms.

A valuable money-saving tool is to consider paying your mortgage off in a shorter time. You can save thousands of dollars in interest if you pay your mortgage twice a month. Ask to have your lender prepare an amortization schedule of your current loan based on an additional monthly contribution of your principal payment. For example, you may be able to include an extra $100 monthly to be paid directly on your principal loan balance.

Be cautious of lenders that charge large up-front fees or points, have high interest rates, assess prepayment penalties, or require balloon payments. Guard against these loan practices by carefully reading your loan documents and checking the interest rate, fees, and terms of the deal.

Ask if your closing agent has the ability to download your closing package using what is called a *digital delivery* system. Many lenders offer this type of system to transmit your closing documents to the title company. The online form of transmittal can save you paying a courier fee, which can cost $45-$55. There may be a small fee for the digital system, but it will be less than for using a courier service.

Closing on your loan at the end of the month will save you having to pay a month's worth of interest. Interest is always collected in arrears. For example, if you close on September 28, you will be charged with only three days' interest at closing. On the other hand, if you close your loan on October 1, you will be required to pay a full 30 days of interest at closing for the month of October.

TIP

Tip #1: Try to negotiate with the seller to pay all or part of your closing costs.

Tip #2: Get a no-point loan. Although you may pay a higher interest rate, this option may help you if you are short of cash and can qualify for a higher interest rate. Finding a no-point loan will cut your closing costs.

Tip #3: Get a no-fee loan. The loan fees may be wrapped into a higher interest rate, but this will save you on the amount of cash you will need to pay up front at closing.

Consider several closing agents and compare their closing costs. Ask for a breakdown of their fees and be sure to ask which fees are negotiable. It may be difficult to compare closing costs, as one closing agent may quote $150 for a "closing fee" and $200.00 for a "title search," while another closing agent may quote $150 for a "settlement fee" and $200 for an "abstract fee." Often closing agents will not disclose until the closing various additional fees, such as notary fees, title examination fees, and document preparation fees. Try to get the title company or closing agent to be specific and include all the fees you will be required to pay at closing.

Ask if you qualify for a *reissue rate* on your title insurance policy. When an existing policy is presented to the title company, a credit will most times be given toward the purchase of the new title insurance policy, equal to 20% to 60% of the face amount of the new policy. Typically, a policy less than one year old qualifies for a 60% discount and a policy two to three years old qualifies for a 20% discount. Try to negotiate such fees as the settlement/closing fee, title search/abstract fee, title insurance fee, survey fee, courier/overnight fee, notary fee, and document preparation fee.

How Do I Know Whether the Lender Is Computing Everything Correctly?

After the loan application has been made in writing, the lending institution will furnish you with a federal *Truth in Lending* statement or, as it's frequently called, the *Regulation Z* form. This form states the estimated costs you will incur in connection with your loan. It must, by federal law, give you, the borrower, the following information within three days of your loan application:

- The schedule of payments.

- The annual percentage rate (APR, also known as the annual interest rate), the total amount of interest to be paid over the life of a loan. All of these items are listed under "prepaid finance charge" on the Regulation Z form. (The APR frequently confuses people, especially because it is almost always higher than the rate stated in the note accompanying the mortgage or deed of trust, because of points, fees, and other credit costs added to the interest rate over the life of the loan.)

- The finance charges (points, interest, and loan fees).

- The total amount of the loan.

- The method used for computing late charges.

- The prepayment penalty.

The Truth in Lending form was designed to protect you, the buyer. Just as the government requires that the contents of packaged foods be itemized, so does it require that all the fees involved in a loan be disclosed. This disclosure protects the consumer from hidden loan costs. You are to sign this disclosure statement as proof that you saw it and approved its contents. The signed document is the lending agency's proof that it complied with the Federal Truth in Lending Law. Study the statement carefully before signing to be sure it contains all of the terms you have agreed to.

Along with the Truth in Lending form, the lender is required under the Real Estate Settlement Procedures Act (RESPA) to give you a copy of the HUD booklet entitled *Buying Your Home: Settlement Costs and Information* also within three days after your loan application. The federal regulation was enacted by Congress in 1974 and is aimed to protect borrowers from unscrupulous lenders and settlement practices. RESPA prohibits most real estate settlement service providers from giving or receiving kickbacks when a federally related loan is involved. Only those services that are actually performed may be charged to the borrower. In the past, it had been a common practice for closing providers, such as real estate agents, title insurers, lenders, and mortgage brokers, to agree to offer kickbacks in exchange for referring customers to one another. The cost of these unearned fees was passed along to the borrower in the form of higher settlement fees.

Address any questions you might have concerning a lender's compliance with the law to the following agencies:

National Banks:
Customer Assistance Group, Comptroller of the Currency
1301 McKinney Street, Suite 3710
Houston, TX 77010
(800) 613-6743
e-mail: customer.assistance@occ.treas.gov
Web: **www.occ.treas.gov/customer.htm**

State-chartered Banks:
Federal Reserve Board
Division of Consumer and Community Affairs
20th and Constitution Avenue, NW
Washington, DC 20551
Web: **www.federalreserve.gov/communityaffairs/national/default.htm**

Federal Savings Banks (savings and loans)—
Office of Thrift Supervision, Consumer Affairs
1700 G Street, NW
Washington, DC 20552
(800) 842-6929
e-mail: consumer.complaint@ots.treas.gov
Web: **www.ots.treas.gov**

Take note that if your property is to be a personal residence and your loan is a refinance, you have the right to cancel the entire loan without penalty if you do so within three working days following the signing of the loan contract. This is called the right of rescission and is another federal consumer protection requirement.

Are There Any Other Disclosures That the Lender Is Required to Give Me?

Depending on the type of loan you are seeking, your lender will be required to furnish you with various standard loan disclosure forms. You will be given an *Equal Credit Opportunity Act (ECOA) Statement*, which states that the lender will not discriminate. You will receive a *Good Faith Estimate of Closing Costs*, outlining the probable costs you will incur in conjunction with your loan. If you are choosing an adjustable rate mortgage (ARM) loan, you will be given a *Loan Disclosure Form*, explaining how an ARM loan works, and a *Consumer Handbook on Adjustable Rate Mortgages*. You will receive the HUD handbook on *Buying Your Home: Settlement Costs and Information*, which explains the closing costs outlined in the Good Faith Estimate. You may be given *Lock-in and Processing*

Disclosures. A *Mortgage Transfer Disclosure Statement* is typically provided, which tells you the percentage of loans your lender sells to an outside serving agency. The *Certification of Authorization* form authorizes your lender to check your credit, employment, and assets. FHA and VA loans require additional disclosures, which your lender will give you upon your loan application.

A Typical Misunderstanding: Dave and Sylvia calculated their closing costs based on the Good Faith Estimate that their lender gave them when they applied for their mortgage. They were not prepared for the final figures that appeared on their closing documents, as they were somewhat different from the figures on the estimate.

The Way Things Really Are: Under Department of Housing and Urban Development (HUD) regulations, the Good Faith Estimate must represent only a reasonable relationship to the charges that the borrower will likely be required to pay at closing and need not be the exact figures. Dave and Sylvia would be wise to ask their lender three or four days before their closing for the final figures needed to close escrow.

The annual percentage rate (APR) indicated on the Truth in Lending statement is the true interest rate your loan is going to cost you. The APR rate is calculated by including the interest rate on your loan together with the points, fees, and any other costs the lender will be charging for your loan. Your 7% loan may actually carry a 7.75% APR rate. Use the APR rate to compare one loan with another and see which loan will cost you more.

Is There a Typical Timetable for a Loan?

Just as there is no typical timetable for your escrow and closing, there is no typical time frame in which a loan may be closed. Some loans may take as long as 45 days or more to close, while other loans may be closed within 48 hours. The time will depend on your lender and the special criteria that must be met in order for your loan to be completed.

In the table on the next page, I have outlined for you the steps that a typical loan goes through. Using this chart you can follow your loan through each stage and know what is expected to happen next and approximately how long that next step will take.

Day	Activity
1–5	Fill out and file loan application with your lender
1–3	Within three days of application, receive Truth in Lending statement
3–10	Lender orders property appraisal
	Credit report, mails out verifications of employment and deposit
5-25	**Processing**
5–26	Loan processor reviews credit report, verifies your debt and payment history, verifies COE.
15–25	**Lender underwriting**
15-26	Loan underwriter reviews loan package and decides to approve or deny loan
	Additional information from borrower is requested
17–27	**Mortgage insurance underwriting**
	If less than 20% down, application is made for private mortgage insurance
17–27	**Pre-Closing**
	Once loan is approved, title insurance is ordered and closing is scheduled
25–45	**Closing**
	Obtain your loan proceeds and present cashier's check to cover the balance of the down payment and closing costs

Chart 6-7. Timetable for a typical loan

Chapter Seven

Loans and Financing: Advanced Topics

In Chapter Six I went through the basics of financing the purchase of your new home. In this chapter I'll describe several different types of loans, to help you decide which one may be right for you, as well as provisions you may want to include or exclude from your loan.

What Types of Loans Are Available from Institutional Lenders?

The three most common types of real estate loans available from institutional lenders are the following: 1) the conventional loan (which may have a fixed rate, a variable rate, shared appreciation, graduated payments, or some combination of these variations), 2) the VA loan, and 3) the FHA loan.

Conventional Loan

The conventional loan, which is the one most often used, has several advantages over the other two. Although it may not always be assumable, it is much less hampered by federal restrictions and red tape than are the other two and there is no set maximum amount that may be borrowed. Virtually anyone who has basic good credit can qualify for a conventional loan. In addition, this type of loan takes the least time to obtain.

VA Loan

The newly originated VA loan, as opposed to one being assumed, is available to eligible Armed Services veterans only. This type of loan is backed by the Department of Veterans Affairs (DVA) and involves a certain amount of governmental red tape. Hence, it takes longer to obtain. Technically, this loan does not require a down payment if the appraisal is the same as or higher than the purchase price, but since the government's appraisal is almost invariably lower than the purchase price, a down payment is almost always necessary. The veteran has to come up with the difference, a sum that may not be borrowed commercially. The veteran may borrow from a friend or relative but not from an institutional lender.

A basic funding fee of 2% must generally be paid for most all VA loans. This fee may be reduced to 1½% if the veteran makes a 5% down payment and to 1¼% with a 10% down payment. The funding fee may be paid in cash or it may be included in the loan. The lender making the VA loan may charge reasonable closing costs and these may be paid by the purchaser or by the seller or shared between the two. The closing costs on a VA loan will include a VA appraisal, a credit report, a loan origination fee, discount points, a title search and title insurance, recording fees, state and local transfer taxes, and a survey. Brokerage fees or a "buyer's broker" fee may not be charged to the veteran buyer.

The maximum DVA guarantee is $36,000 or up to $60,000 for certain loans over $144,000. There is no maximum VA loan amount, but lenders often set a limit of $203,000. Moreover, not all banks, lending institutions, insurance companies, or mortgage companies offer VA-secured loans. You must either shop around or write the DVA for a list of those that offer VA loans in your area. The address for the Department of Veterans Affairs is 810 Vermont Ave., NW, Washington, DC 20420, (800) 827-1000. You can find a VA lender in your hometown area by going to **www.vba-roanoke.com/rlc/VA-e-lenders** on the Internet.

You will need to present a certificate of eligibility to the lender to prove that you are eligible for the VA loan. To request your certificate, you will need to complete VA Form 26-1880 and submit this form to a VA Eligibility Center. The center will issue you your certificate of eligibility. You might want to request VA Pamphlet 26-4 (VA-Guaranteed Home Loans for Veterans) or VA Pamphlet 26-6 (To the Home-Buying Veteran) from your VA loan office. Additionally, you can find VA loan information on the Internet at **www.homeloans.va.gov**.

VA loans have four major advantages over conventional loans: 1) they usually carry lower interest rates and do not require a down payment, 2) they are assumable by either veterans or non-veterans, 3) there is no prepayment penalty, and 4) there is no mortgage insurance premium required.

The major disadvantage of the VA loan is its long processing time and its abundant paperwork, both of which simply mean that more things can go wrong.

FHA Loan

FHA loans are sponsored by the Federal Housing Administration, a federal agency whose main purpose is to encourage home ownership. This loan is similar to a VA loan, except that an FHA loan is open to anyone with good credit, not just to veterans, and it has a maximum limit. This limit varies according to the average cost of a house in a particular area and it is revised upward periodically to compensate for inflation. Because FHA loans are supposed to benefit buyers with moderate incomes, the loan limits are at the lower end of the housing scale. You can check on the Internet at **www.fhatoday.com/mtg_limits.htm**, for the current limit in your area, or you can reach HUD at 800-697-6967.

An FHA loan is like a VA loan in many respects—it is assumable, it carries no prepayment penalty, it requires lots of paperwork to satisfy government bureaucrats, and its down payment may not be borrowed commercially, unless the buyer is at least 62 years old or is assuming an existing FHA loan. The FHA allows either the buyer or the seller to pay for the points on the loan and permits 100% of the closing costs to be financed. The entire down payment may be in the form of a gift.

The FHA provides mortgage insurance as a condition of the loan and charges the borrower ½% of the loan balance as a premium. Because of this mortgage insurance, the FHA will lend as much as 97% of the purchase price. This type of loan is referred to as a section 203 (b) mortgage and is the most popular FHA loan. Since the requirements for a down payment are lower than on conventional loans, the interest rate may be slightly higher. Some of the closing costs may also be included in the mortgage amount. With a section 203 (b) mortgage, you are allowed to make extra payments toward the principal when you make your monthly payment, repaying the loan faster, or you can choose to pay off the balance at any time, as there is no prepayment penalty on this type of loan.

FHA mortgage insurance works the same way as the private mortgage insurance (PMI) already mentioned, except that it cannot be canceled when the loan balance declines to 80% of the property's market value. Nonetheless, the person who pays off an FHA mortgage, whether prematurely or at the end of the term, may apply for a refund of some premium monies. The actual duration of the mortgage will determine the amount of the refund. For detailed information, look on the Internet at **www.pueblo.gsa.gov/cic_text/housing/100-questions/new-home.html** and **www.pueblo.gsa.gov/cic_text/housing/home-insure/mortgage.htm**.

Incidentally, if you are the one who makes the final payment on an FHA mortgage and the FHA fails to contact you about a refund of mortgage insurance premiums within two months following the payoff, you may contact them at Distributive Shares Branch, Room 2239, 451 Seventh St., SW, Washington, DC 20410, 800-697-6967. Give them your FHA case number and ask for a refund application. You can search the database at **www.hud.gov/offices/hsg/comp/refunds/index.cfm** and type in your name or case number.

To get an FHA mortgage, you approach one of the institutional lenders that are FHA-approved and you make an application. You can also apply on line at **www.fhatoday.com**. You may be surprised by the large number of FHA-approved lenders and by the variety of their FHA loan offerings. They offer adjustable rate mortgages, growth equity mortgages, and graduated payment mortgages, as well as standard fixed-rate mortgages. You select the one most suited to your needs. You can find information on the Internet at **www.hud.gov/fha**.

If you wish more detailed information on loans, consult one of the numerous books on the subject. *The Mortgage Kit* by Thomas C. Steinmetz (Chicago: Dearborn Trade, 2002, 5th edition) is one good example. This book and others like it are available in the real estate or personal finance sections of bookstores and libraries.

Keep in mind that we are concerned here with so-called primary or first loans only. Secondary loans are covered later.

How Does a Variable or Adjustable Rate Loan Work?

Whereas a fixed rate loan has one interest rate for the life of the loan, a variable or adjustable rate mortgage (ARM) loan (here we will call them all "adjustable rate" loans) has an interest rate that changes periodically according to whatever interest rate index it is tied to. These are the indices most commonly used:

- Six-Month Certificate of Deposit (CD) Spot Index—This index is the weekly average of the interest rates paid by institutions on negotiable six-month certificates of deposit. Because it reflects every blip and swing of the market, it can change quickly.

- One-Year Treasury Spot Index—This index is the weekly average interest paid by the U.S. government on funds borrowed for one year. It changes more slowly than the CD index.

- Treasury 12-Month Average Index—This index is the yearly average of the monthly interest paid by the U.S. government on actively traded securities. It changes more slowly than either of the preceding indices.

- 11th District Cost-of-Funds Index—This index is the monthly weighted average cost of what banks on the West Coast pay for their various deposits and for the advances they get through the Federal Home Loan Bank Board of San Francisco. It moves at a tortoise's pace compared with the other indices.

More and more newspapers list these indices every week in their real estate or business sections, so you can get some idea how they act over an extended period of time and how they compare with one another at any particular time.

Some lenders might use the One-Year Treasury Spot Index and add four percentage points to get their rate, while others might use the 11th District Cost-of-Funds Index and add three points. These points are the lenders' *markup*, also called the *margin* or *spread*. Whatever they're called, they're what lenders need to cover their overhead and make a profit.

Adjustable rate loans come up for review periodically, sometimes every month, sometimes every six months, sometimes every year, sometimes every five years. When they come up for review, the lender adjusts the interest rate according to the index that controls it and according to whatever caps the loan has.

An interest rate cap may limit the amount the loan rate can change at each review, say 2%, or it may limit the amount the loan rate can change over the life of the loan, say 6%. A payment cap limits the amount that the payment itself can change from one review to the next.

Besides being adjustable in interest rates and sometimes in payments, adjustable rate loans may be either *negative* or *non-negative*. A negative loan allows for negative amortization; a non-negative loan does not. (*Amortization* is the paying down of the loan balance with each payment: a portion of the payment pays the interest owed and a portion pays down the loan balance.)

A loan that allows for negative amortization lets the borrower make constant payments whether those payments cover the full interest owed or not. If they don't cover the full interest owed, then the shortfall is added to the principal balance and the balance grows month after month. A borrower whose interest rate has increased several times but who continues to make a constant payment every month may wind up owing more than he originally borrowed.

A non-negative adjustable rate loan requires the borrower to make payments that cover the current interest owed at the very least, so the principal won't increase. In order to ensure that the principal does not increase whenever the interest rate rises, a non-negative loan provides for payment changes.

Some adjustable rate loans allow you to convert to a fixed-rate loan beginning with the second year and extending to the fifth year. These so-called *convertible* loans relieve you from worry about future interest rate increases, but they may carry a higher loan fee at the outset and another fee at the time of the conversion.

While adjustable rate loans have their uncertainties, they generally offer some flexibility for dealing with those uncertainties. Should your interest rate index bump your payment up, you may pay the higher payment or exercise other options open to you, such as extending the term of the loan by as much as a third of the original term or paying off part or all of the principal without incurring any pre-payment penalty.

Be sure you check the figures over carefully before you elect to extend your loan, though, for extending the life of a loan beyond 15 or 20 years doesn't really decrease the payment very much. Look at the figures.

10	15	20	25	30	35	40
$1,057.21	$859.69	$772.02	$726.97	$702.06	$687.74	$679.32

There are all kinds of variations in these loans. Make sure you understand any variations in the loan you're being offered. You don't want any nasty surprises when you're locked in and can't do anything about them.

Your adjustable rate lender will send you written notification of any rate adjustment at least one month before the new rate is to go into effect. This notification will tell you the old and new index rates and your current and new interest rates. Because lenders make mistakes when adjusting loans, check your adjustable rate loan's interest rate adjustment. Look in your loan documents for the index used and the margin, and make sure that the lender's calculations are correct.

Normally, the index rate available 30 days prior to your adjustment date determines the adjustment. For example, if your loan is supposed to be adjusted on the first of August and it's based on the 11th District Cost-of-Funds Index, the lender will use the index published at the end of June or beginning of July. That rate reflects the rate that prevailed during May. To that index add the lender's margin and you'll have the applicable rate. If the index is 6.75% and the margin is three points, your new rate will be 9.75%.

Should you discover that the lender has erred, call the loan-servicing department and ask for an explanation.

What Other Financing Arrangements Are Available Through Institutional Lenders?

With housing prices getting out of reach to all but the more affluent, institutional lenders are trying various new kinds of financing arrangements so that more and more people can qualify to buy. The whole idea behind them is to reduce the down payments and/or the monthly payments that would be required for old-style loans.

Adjustable rate fixed mortgage loans, *shared-appreciation mortgage loans*, and *graduated-payment mortgage loans* are just three of the more popular new financing arrangements being tried today, but they serve to illustrate how lenders are changing their ways of doing business to accommodate changes in the marketplace.

Adjustable rate fixed mortgage loans would seem to be a contradiction in terms. Actually they're a hybrid. They start out as fixed rate loans, generally for a five- or 10-year period. Then they become adjustable for the remainder of the term. These loans benefit the borrower, because they have lower initial rates than normal fixed rate mortgage loans and hence allow the borrower to qualify for a higher loan amount. Most of these loans have maximum lifetime interest rate caps and no prepayment penalties and they allow no negative amortization.

Lenders using *shared appreciation mortgage (SAM) loans* reduce the interest rate normally being charged in exchange for an equity interest. The borrower pays the lender this equity interest at some time within a certain number of years when the house is either sold or refinanced. SAMs reduce the monthly payments considerably and enable buyers to qualify for buying a house that would be out of their reach otherwise. Real estate agents and mortgage brokers both arrange such loans.

Graduated payment mortgage (GPM) loans have lower initial monthly payments than standard fixed rate level payment loans, but gradually their payments rise to a level that will amortize the principal balance over the remaining life of the loan. The objective of GPMs is to reduce the initial payments while the borrower's income is low, in the expectation that the borrower's income will increase later. GPMs enable a buyer to buy a house at today's prices and pay for it comfortably with smaller payments in the beginning and larger payments later, when he or she can afford them. If you are attracted to a GPM loan, be sure to get a listing of the fixed schedule of payments, so you'll know long in advance exactly when the payments are going to change.

A Typical Misunderstanding: Christine and David, madly in love, are newlyweds who are anxious to buy their first home. They grab the first adjustable rate mortgage loan offered to them, thinking that it must be similar to the adjustable rate mortgage loan that their friends Virgie and Bud were most pleased with.

The Way Things Really Are: Adjustable rate mortgage loans differ significantly. Some can be more favorable to the lender than to the borrower. After six months of honeymooning in their dream home, Christine and David notice that their payment has increased by almost a hundred dollars and they get scared. When they look more closely at their mortgage terms, they find that it has no cap at all, that the interest rate could change every month after the first six months, and that the initial interest rate was nothing more than an inducement. It wasn't set according to the index that was going to determine the interest rate throughout the rest of the life of the loan. Christine and David learn their lesson the hard way. Now they rent. They wish that somebody had warned them to ask about the "little things" before they ever got their loan.

Before choosing the loan you will be living with for the next 15, 20, or even 30 years, ask your lender these five very important questions:

1. What is the initial interest rate based upon?
2. What is the interest rate after the first six months based upon?
3. How much and how frequently can the interest rate change in a year?
4. What is the cap on the interest rate over the life of the loan?
5. How will an interest rate change affect my monthly payments?

Try to determine what the worst-case scenario might be for the loan you're contemplating. You don't want to be surprised later and lose your property.

What Is a Construction Loan?

A construction loan is a temporary loan to you by the lender to pay the building contractor, either in installments or in one lump sum at the end of construction. Under an installment construction loan, the lender will usually lend you between 70% and 100% of the permanent loan amount you will need after the house is completed. Your equity in the land will be counted as cash in your favor and will go toward both the permanent mortgage and the construction loan. The interest rate on a construction loan can be based on the prime rate plus extra interest or it can be at a fixed rate. The lender may charge points. Generally you will be charged interest only on the money you draw from the loan amount. Most construction loans are written for six months to one year. The builder will request that draws or payments be made during certain phases of construction. These draws will cover the costs of labor and materials during that phase of the building project.

Typically, a draw schedule is created so that the first draw is due when the foundation is completed, the next draw after the roof is in place, the next draw after the mechanical systems such as heating and plumbing are roughed in, another installment when the dry wall is complete and ready for paint, and a final draw or payment upon completion and issuance of the certificate of occupancy. Your lender will require that the builder submit evidence of the work he has completed, which may include lien waivers, to protect you and the lender against any liens that could be placed on the property by one of the builder's subcontractors. The lender may inspect the house before each draw is issued.

Once your house is completed, the lender will close on your permanent loan, pay off the construction loan balance, and pay any remaining balance due to the builder.

An alternative to a simple construction loan is a combination construction/permanent loan. Under this type of loan, you apply for a permanent loan and the construction loan is included in the package. With this type of loan, you pay points only once and you pay only one set of closing costs. At your closing, you will sign documents for your construction loan and, once the house is completed, the construction loan will evolve into a permanent loan with regular monthly payments. Often, you are able to lock in your interest rate at the time of your loan application.

What Is a Jumbo Loan?

A *jumbo* loan is the same as a *non-conforming* loan. It's any loan made by an institutional lender that exceeds the guidelines of the Federal National Mortgage Association (Fannie Mae) or the Federal Home Loan Mortgage Corporation (Freddie Mac) for a *conforming* loan. The limit for a jumbo loan is calculated by the Federal Housing Finance Board and is based on the average price of houses nationally. This limit is adjusted every October. (As of January 2004, it was $333,700.) Lenders can't sell jumbo loans to secondary mortgage purchasers such as Fannie Mae or Freddie Mac, so they have to keep these loans in their own portfolios. Consequently, they will charge slightly higher interest rates on jumbo loans, usually ¼% to ½% higher. This can add up fast. On a $300,000 loan, the difference in interest between a jumbo and conforming loan would amount to about $815 in additional payments a year—or more than $24,000 over the life of a 30-year mortgage. If you live in Hawaii, Alaska, the Virgin Islands, or Guam, the conforming loan limit is $412,500 as of October 2001. This higher limit was authorized by Congress because home prices traditionally have been much higher in those places. Certain lenders, however, known as *portfolio* lenders, keep the loans they originate and do not charge more for jumbo loans.

Should you be shopping for a jumbo loan, note this distinction between portfolio lenders and non-portfolio lenders and turn it to your advantage.

 To find out the current maximum for conforming loans in your area, you can check with Fannie Mae at **www.fanniemae.com** or call your local lender.

What Is a Note?

A *note* used in real estate transactions is actually a promise to pay, a kind of IOU that is both legal and binding. All real estate notes must be in writing and they must state both the amount of the debt and the date when it falls due. You, as the borrower or signer of a note that is secured by a deed of trust, are called the *trustor* or, if the note is secured by a mortgage deed, the *mortgagor*. In the note, you promise to pay a certain sum of money or a consideration to the beneficiary, the lender, and you make a conditional promise in writing to the lender that you will pay the loan according to a specified plan. Most notes are negotiable, which means that the holder of a note may sell or transfer it to another person and the borrower would then make all future payments to the new holder of the note. You can tell whether a note is negotiable by its wording. If it states that you are to "pay to the order of" some person or entity, it is negotiable.

Real estate notes come in two varieties, *straight* and *installment*, which differ in only one respect—what their payments cover. Payments on straight notes cover interest only; the original amount of the loan itself is due in one lump sum upon a given expiration date. Payments on installment notes cover both interest and principal; they may or may not be fully amortized, that is, installment notes may or may not be paid off in full at the due date.

Sometimes people set up installment notes according to a 30-year amortized schedule, but they stipulate that the balance is all due and payable in 10 years. Such a note would have lower monthly payments than one that is fully amortized in 10 years, but it would require a large balloon payment on the due date. Because the terms of all notes are negotiated between the parties involved, don't be afraid to set up terms that you can live with, monthly payments that are within your budget, and a due date that fits in with your long-range financial plans. Review your financial ability carefully. Don't rush into a second mortgage without confidence that you can meet the payments.

If you are a seller considering a second, consult an accountant or a tax advisor before negotiating the terms of the note with the buyer. You might want, for instance, to receive only so much in each year, depending on your tax situation. Review carefully the tax consequences for the length of the loan—three years, five years, or whatever other period suits you—and consider adding a prepayment penalty so you'll have enough money to pay your extra tax liability in case the buyer decides to pay off the note before it's due. No matter what the other terms are in any note you are carrying, be certain that one of them includes a late fee to penalize your borrower for paying late. Some can be notoriously slow at paying, otherwise. Also, check the buyer's credit thoroughly if you're going to be lending him some money. Don't assume that the buyer has a good credit rating. You don't want to be surprised by his bad payment habits sometime later and have to go through a painful foreclosure.

On the next several pages you'll find samples of straight and installment notes and a form for the assignment of a deed of trust, together with instructions for using the assignment form. Blank copies of these forms appear in the back of the book.

They might come in handy sometime if you get involved in owner financing.

If you ever do become an *owner-financier*, the following computer spreadsheet template will come in handy, allowing you to create loan tables with ease. Here's a partial table created by one of the numerous spreadsheet programs available. Besides creating the table, the template calculates the monthly payment.

Borrower:	Dario Miglia
Lender:	Charles Meade
Property:	1012 Laurel Ave., Tarrytown

Principal:	10,000.00
Interest:	9.500%
Term (Years):	7
Starting Date:	11/25/99
Balloon Pmt:	0.00

Calc'd Payment:	163.44

Date	Pmt No.	Prin. Bal. Before Pmt.	Interest	Principal	Prin. Bal. After Pmt.	Cumulative Interest
11/25/01	1	10,000.00	79.17	84.27	9,915.73	79.17
12/25/01	2	9,915.73	78.50	84.94	9,830.79	157.67
1/25/02	3	9,830.79	77.83	85.61	9,745.18	235.50
2/25/02	4	9,745.18	77.15	86.29	9,658.89	312.65
3/25/02	5	9,658.89	76.47	86.97	9,571.92	389.12

Chart 7-1. Loan payment calculator and loan table

Instructions for Transferring a Promissory Note Secured by a Deed of Trust

With all the trafficking in owner financing nowadays, you may at some time be involved in acquiring or disposing of a promissory note or you may be the owner of a property that secures a note being transferred from one holder to another. To make certain that everyone involved is treated fairly and squarely, each party should follow certain steps (Chart 7-4, p. 105).

Why Is a Mortgage Deed or a Deed of Trust Used?

A note itself is a fairly straightforward promise to pay. But to secure collateral for a note, the lender or your closing officer draws up either a mortgage deed or a deed of trust, depending upon which is used in your state. Both of them describe the property against which the loan is written and enable the lender to foreclose on the property held as collateral under certain conditions.

STRAIGHT NOTE

$ __10,000.00__ _____ Boonville _____ (city),

_____California_____ (state), ___August 10___ , 20 __XX__,

__On or before 1 (one) year_____ after date, for value received,

I promise to pay to ___Samuel P. Seller, a married man_____

_____, or order, at

_____Place designated by payee_____

the sum of ___Ten Thousand and no/100ths------------------------------ DOLLARS,

with interest from ___August 10, 20XX_____, until paid at the

rate of __10%__ per cent per annum, payable ___At Maturity._____

_____

Principal and interest payable in lawful money of the United States of America. Should default be made in payment of interest when due, the whole sum of principal and interest shall become immediately due at the option of the holder of this note. If action be instituted on this note, I promise to pay such sum as the Court may fix as Attorney's fees. This note is secured by a Mortgage Deed of a Deed of Trust of even date herewith.

The Deed of Trust securing this note contains the following provision:

In the event Trustor, without the prior written consent of the Beneficiary, sells, agrees to sell, transfers or conveys its interest in the real property or any part thereof or any interest therein, Beneficiary may at its option declare all sums secured hereby immediately due and payable.

Bruce B. Buyer
_____
BRUCE B. BUYER

Barbara A. Buyer
_____
BARABARA A. BUYER

_____   _____

When paid, this Note, if secured by a Deed of Trust, must be surrendered to Trustee for cancellation before reconveyance will be made.
DO NOT DESTROY

Chart 7-2. Example of straight note

INSTALLMENT NOTE
(Combined Principal and Interest in Equal Installments)

$ __10,000.00__ _____ __Boonville__ _____ (city),

_____ __California__ _____ (state), ___August 10___ , 20 __XX__,

FOR VALUE RECEIVED, I promise to pay in lawful money of the United States of America to

____Samuel P. Seller, a married man_____

or order, at ___Place designated by payee_____

the principal sum of __Ten Thousand and no/100ths----------------------- DOLLARS,

with interest in like lawful money from_____August 10_____, 20 __XX____

at __10___ per cent per annum on the amounts of principal sum remaining unpaid from time to time. Principal and interest payable in installments of__Two Hundred Twelve & 48/100 ($212.48) DOLLARS, or more

each, on the ___10th___ day of each and every __month_____

beginning __September 10, 20XX__ and continuing for a period of Five (5)

__years from date hereof, at which time the entire principal balance__

__and interest due thereon shall become due and payable.__

Each payment shall be credited first to the interest then due, and the remainder to the principal sum; and interest shall thereupon cease upon the amount so paid on said principal sum. AND I agree that in case of default in the payment of any installments when due, then the whole of said principal sum then remaining unpaid, together with the interest that shall have accrued thereon, shall forthwith become due and payable at the election of the holder of this note, without notice. AND I agree, if action be instituted on this note, to pay such sum as the Court may fix as Attorney's fees. This note is secured by a Mortgage Deed or a Deed of Trust of even date herewith.

In the event that any payment is not paid within ten days of due date, there shall be paid a late charge of $60.00 on said delinquent payment.

The Deed of Trust securing this note contains the following provision:

In the event Trustor, without the prior written consent of the Beneficiary, sells, agrees to sell, transfers or conveys its interest in the real property or any part thereof or any interest therein, Beneficiary may at its option declare all sums secured hereby immediately due and payable.

Bruce B. Buyer _____   _Barbara A. Buyer_ _____

BRUCE B. BUYER   BARBARA A. BUYER

_____   _____

When paid, this Note, if secured by a Deed of Trust, must be surrendered to Trustee for cancellation before reconveyance will be made.

DO NOT DESTROY

Chart 7-3. Example of installment note

The seller of the note should:

1. Type the following on the back of the promissory note and fill in the blanks:

FOR VALUE RECEIVED, I (WE) HEREBY TRANSFER AND ASSIGN TO

_____

ALL MY (OUR) RIGHT, TITLE, AND INTEREST TO THIS NOTE, SO FAR AS THE SAME PERTAINS TO SAID NOTE, WITHOUT RECOURSE.

DATED: _____

SIGNED: _____

_____

2. Complete the Assignment of Deed of Trust form.

3. Record the Assignment form and have the recorder mail it directly to the buyer.

4. Exchange the assigned note for the money agreed upon.

The buyer of the note should—

1. Order a preliminary title report to verify the liens against the property.

2. Request that the note seller follow the steps above.

3. Exchange the money agreed upon for the assigned note.

The owner of the property affected by the note assignment should—

1. Request that the new holder of the note show evidence of the assignment.

2. If at all possible, contact the old holder of the note to verify the assignment.

Chart 7-4. Instructions for transferring a promissory note secured by a deed of trust

The basic difference between them is the use of a third party (trustee) in a deed of trust, something lacking in a mortgage deed, which is a two-party agreement with the lender holding the mortgage deed until the loan is fully paid. The mortgage deed, most common in the Midwest and East, allows the borrower one year to make up back payments and always requires a court hearing for foreclosure. As we shall see, foreclosure on a deed of trust is simpler.

A deed of trust deeds the property over to a third party for him to hold until the loan is fully paid. Lest you feel uneasy about a third party holding the deed to your property, rest assured that the only power transferred to the trustee is the power to sell the property in the event of a default. That's all.

The trustee is usually a commercial institution such as a title company, a bank, or an escrow company. The trust is established in the following manner: the seller delivers title to you, the buyer, by giving you a deed to the land. If the seller is your creditor, you give him a down payment on the land and sign a deed of trust; if you borrow the money from a third party, you pay the seller the entire purchase price,

RECORDING REQUESTED BY:

Samuel P. Seller

WHEN RECORDED, MAIL TO:

Mr. Colin Smith
148 Michele Circle
Norman, California 91005

RECEIVED DEC 1 1 20XX

RECORDED AT REQUEST OF
SECURE TITLE CO.

AT **2** O'CLOCK *P.* M.
BARRETT COUNTY RECORDS

FEE $ *5⁰⁰* V. L. GRAVES
COUNTY RECORDER

Recorder's Use Only

ASSIGNMENT OF DEED OF TRUST

FOR A VALUABLE CONSIDERATION, the undersigned hereby grants, assigns, and transfers to:

COLIN SMITH, a single man

all beneficial interest under that certain Deed of Trust dated ___August 10___, 20XX

executed by __Bruce B. Buyer and Barbara A. Buyer, his wife__, as Trustor,

to __Secure Title Company__, as Trustee,

and recorded as Instrument Number __302208__ on __August 10__, 20XX

in Book __2450__ at Page __36__

of Official Records, in the office of the County Recorder of __Barrett__
together with the Promissory Note secured by said Deed of Trust and also all rights accrued or to accrue under said Deed of Trust.

Witness my hand this __11__ day of __December__, 20XX.

Samuel P. Seller

SAMUEL P. SELLER

STATE OF California)
) s.s.
COUNTY OF Barrett)

On ___ December 11 ___, 20 XX,
before me, the undersigned, a Notary Public in and for said County and State, personally appeared

SAMUEL P. SELLER

proved to me on the basis of satisfactory evidence to be the person__
whose name__ is (are) subscribed to the within instrument and
acknowledged that ___he___ executed the same.

WITNESS my hand and official seal:

Edna Edwards

Notary Public in and for said County and State

NOTARY SEAL

OFFICIAL SEAL
EDNA EDWARDS
Notary Public

NOTE: This Assignment should be kept with the Note and Deed of Trust hereby assigned.

Chart 7-5. Example of an assignment of deed of trust

using your own and the lender's funds, and sign a deed of trust for the lender. You then place the deed to the property with the trustee.

Your deed of trust is recorded at the county recorder's office, making it a matter of public record, and then it is returned to the lender, who keeps it and the original note until you, the borrower, have completely paid the amount of that loan on the property. Those states using a deed of trust to secure the loan are Alaska, Arizona, California, Mississippi, Missouri, Nevada, North Carolina, Virginia and Washington, D.C. There are 15 states which use both deeds of trust and mortgages to secure the note. Those states are: Colorado, Idaho, Illinois, Iowa, Maryland, Montana, Nebraska, Oklahoma, Oregon, Tennessee, Texas, Utah, Wyoming, Washington, and West Virginia.

States in which the borrower retains legal title to the property are called "lien theory" states. The lender has only a lien on the property as security for the debt and must initiate a foreclosure action if payments are not made. There are 27 lien theory states and they are: Alabama, Arkansas, Connecticut, Delaware, Florida, Hawaii, Indiana, Kansas, Kentucky, Louisiana, Maine, Massachusetts, Michigan, Minnesota, New Hampshire, New Jersey, New Mexico, New York, North Dakota, Ohio, Oregon, Pennsylvania, Rhode Island, South Carolina, South Dakota, Vermont and Wisconsin. There are 15 states in which both a Deed of Trust or a mortgage may be used. Those states are called "intermediate theory" states and they are: Colorado, Idaho, Illinois, Iowa, Maryland, Montana, Nebraska, Oklahoma, Oregon, Tennessee, Texas, Utah, Washington, West Virginia, and Wyoming. State statute ultimately determines how a lender must initiate foreclosure proceedings, whether you are located in a title, lien, or intermediate theory state. Since state laws do change, even some from year to year, you might ask your closing officer how foreclosure would be handled in your state.

How Does a Foreclosure Work?

When you, the borrower, fail to meet your payments on a note, the lender has every right to sell the property given as collateral for the original loan and use that money to reimburse himself for what you still owe. The deed of trust or mortgage deed he holds spells out this right of foreclosure. Although the term "foreclosure" carries an ominous connotation of unfairness about it, it's hardly unfair at all because the borrower actually has quite a bit of time, almost four months in California, in which to make up his back payments. Foreclosures don't happen overnight.

Let's look at the basic outline of a foreclosure under a deed of trust in California. Because consumer-oriented changes in foreclosure law are occurring regularly, you should consult your attorney or escrow company for the specific procedure practiced in your particular area. (You'll find some information about how other states handle foreclosures in Appendix B.)

- The lender gives the trustee (title company or trust company) written notice that you have defaulted, along with the note and deed of trust and a statement of the account.

- The trustee prepares a declaration of default and records this form in the recorder's office of the county where the property is situated.

- Within 10 days from recording the notice of default, the trustee notifies by certified mail the borrower and any subsequent buyers and lenders to whom mandatory notice must be sent that the lender wishes to sell the property to recover his debt and that a declaration of default has been recorded.

- The trustor or junior lien holder has three months in which to pay all sums due and cure the default. A notice of sale is recorded at the county recorder's office and then published in a local newspaper giving the time and place of the foreclosure sale. This may be done only after three calendar months have elapsed from the date of recording the declaration of default. This notice of sale must be published in a newspaper in the city where the property is located at least once a week for three consecutive weeks. At least 20 days before the sale, a copy of the notice of sale will be mailed to all parties who were sent copies of the notice of default.

- The foreclosure sale must be set at least 20 days after the day this advertisement first appears in the local newspaper.

- At least 20 days before the sale, a copy of the notice of sale must be posted on the property and in one public place.

- After the proper time has elapsed and the borrower still hasn't cured his default nor has any junior creditor done so, the property is then sold to the highest bidder. The sale itself often takes place in the lobby of the title company or on the courthouse steps.

- The minimum bid set by the trustee is the balance owing the lender on the note, plus all costs that have accumulated to process the foreclosure. Bids must be in cash or its equivalent.

- The trustee is reimbursed first for his costs, fees, and expenses, and then the holder of the note is paid the monies owed to him. If there is any surplus of funds, subordinate lien holders may make claims for the sums they are owed.

- A trustee's deed is given to the highest responsible bidder. The title passes to the new buyer without any right or period of redemption. The sale is final. Some states allow a period after the sale during which the borrower can still redeem the property.

Note that the holder of a deed of trust does not have to use an attorney to begin foreclosure proceedings. A foreclosure may be initiated merely by giving the

trustee written notice and then letting the trustee handle the matter.

Every step of a foreclosure must be strictly complied with. Failure to publish notices properly, for example, could invalidate the sale. Should you be involved in a foreclosure, be sure to consult your title company or an attorney for the most up-to-date procedures.

A lot depends on whether the default occurs in a state using the mortgage deed system or the deed of trust system. If you have a mortgage deed, rather than a deed of trust, you as the mortgagee have two choices:

- Petition an equity court to sell the property to recover the money loaned.

- Sue the mortgagor in a court of law and obtain a judgment that may be used to force the sale of the property.

As you can see from the outline here, foreclosure gives the borrower ample time in which to come up with the money, anywhere from four months to two years, depending upon state laws. Most lenders do not like to foreclose on property, though, because it costs them time and money. They generally will make every effort to contact the borrower and determine the cause of nonpayment. In addition, the trustee makes every effort to notify all of those who might possibly have an interest in the property to see whether they might want to take over the property.

Sometimes the lender has the right to sue the borrower to get a deficiency judgment if an insufficient amount of money is obtained from a foreclosure sale to make up the amount of money due him. However, most states and courts will not permit a deficiency judgment when the loan is made for the purchase of one's own home.

As a result of 1986 legislation, the interest rate on any foreclosure property loan reverts to 10% during the foreclosure period. Lenders may request a title insurance endorsement to cover this situation.

For further information on foreclosure procedures and on acquiring foreclosure properties, consult *How to Earn Big Profits from California Foreclosure and Distress Properties* by Robert Bruss (251 Park Road, Suite 200, Burlingame, CA 94010) and *Save Your Home: How to Protect Your Home and Property from Foreclosure* by Steven L. Porter (Colorado Springs, CO: Piccadilly Books, 1990, 2nd edition).

What Is a Due-on-Sale Clause?

This clause simply means that the entire note will be due at once if the owner sells or transfers his interest in the property. Since the lender, whether a bank or a private party, has established the loan with you as the buyer and has qualified you as a good credit risk, he will not readily accept a sale or transfer of your property to someone else without demanding complete payment of the loan at once. If a lender wants this protection, he inserts a *due-on-sale* clause into the note. The due-on-sale clause is also known as an *acceleration* or *alienation* clause because the due date is rushed forward and any new buyer is kept from assuming the loan obligation. Most notes do contain this clause. The common exceptions are VA and FHA loans. These loans, therefore, are considered to be assumable, a real advantage that will be explained later under the subject of assumptions.

> **A Typical Misunderstanding:** Mike has a loan on his house with a federally chartered savings and loan. It's an old loan at 7% with a due-on-sale clause that would make the entire loan balance, half the current value of the house, payable in full when he sells. He decides to offer the house for sale with wraparound financing at 12%. His buyer will make one payment every month directly to him and Mike will continue making the old payments to the savings and loan, pocketing the difference. Because the savings and loan won't know there has been a sale, it won't call the loan due.

> **The Way Things Really Are:** The savings and loan may not find out about the sale if Mike keeps making his payments regularly, but then again it may be tipped off inadvertently by something like the new fire insurance policy that shows new owners and, if it is, it could call the loan due.

A sample due-on-sale clause written into a note might read as follows: "In the event Trustor, without the prior written consent of the Beneficiary, sells, agrees to sell, transfers, or conveys its interest in the real property or any part thereof or any interest therein, the Beneficiary may, at its option, declare all sums secured immediately due and payable."

How Can I Tell Whether a Loan Is Assumable?

You can tell whether a loan is assumable or not by considering these factors:

1. Whether there is a due-on-sale clause in the original note (some notes have no due-on-sale clauses at all; look carefully)

2. What the wording of the due-on-sale clause is (some notes have clauses as airtight as a vacuum bottle, prohibiting sales and transfers of every variety, and some have clauses as holey as balloon bread that enable creative buyers to structure transfers to circumvent the strict wording of the clauses)

3. Where the property is located (if the property is not in one of the 17 states listed on page 118, then the due-on-sale clause is enforceable; if it is in one of these 17, then, depending upon certain other factors, the clause may or may not be enforceable)

4. Who the lender is (if the note holder is a federal savings and loan, the due-on-sale clause is enforceable; if it's a state-chartered savings and loan in one of the 17 states, it may be enforceable)

5. When the loan originated (if the loan originated after October 15, 1982, its due-on-sale clause is enforceable, no matter what; if it originated during a window period in one of the 17 states and with certain lenders, it may not be enforceable).

All of these factors and dates may sound confusing. They are. But they are extremely important to anyone assuming a loan. If you're involved in an assumption, consult current source material and/or an attorney and satisfy yourself that you're on safe ground before you go ahead with the transaction.

How Do Assumptions Work?

An assumption occurs when you, the buyer, take over the seller's existing loan. Because a house in the United States sells on the average of every three to five years, the homeowner still normally owes a sizable sum of money on his first loan when he is ready to sell, but the interest rate on that loan is likely to be lower than what a new buyer's would be. Now, if the money market is tight and lenders aren't readily lending, if you simply cannot obtain a loan even though your credit is good, or if you have enough cash available and you don't want to take out a high-interest loan, you may work out an agreement with the seller whereby you assume his loan and take over his liability.

Lenders have the right both to charge an assumption fee and to raise the interest rate if there is a due-on-sale clause in the original loan. If there is none, they cannot charge any additional fees nor can they raise the interest rate. An assumption of a loan without a due-on-sale clause is most often beneficial to you as a buyer, for you may avoid both the current interest rates and the many costly closing and loan fees.

If you can arrange an assumption, you will need to sign an Assumption Agreement with the lender. Later your escrow officer will record a Substitution of Liability form at the county recorder's office. With that, you will have formally assumed the seller's loan.

Remember that your escrow officer is available to help you sort out the details about assumptions and about your lender's particular policy regarding assumptions, too. Once you have determined that an assumption is available, she will write the lender and ask for a Statement of Condition (also known as a Beneficiary's Statement) of the loan, to include the remaining balance, the interest rate, monthly payments, and any delinquencies. You, the buyer, generally pay a small fee ($65-$150) to obtain this Statement of Condition.

Note that with a new loan there is usually a 30-day grace period before the first payment is due, but there may be no grace period at all when there's an assumption. Be sure to ask your escrow officer when the first payment will be due after you assume a loan.

What Is "Subject-to" Financing?

Taking title "subject to" an existing loan means quite basically that you agree to take over the payments while the loan remains in the seller's name. There are no documents or agreements with the lender. You receive the grant deed and make the payments.

This method of financing greatly benefits you as the buyer because you assume the loan at the old interest rate and without having to pay any new loan fees. (Occasionally there may be a loan transfer fee of $60-$100.) It does mean, however, that you will normally have to make a larger cash down payment to pay the difference between the sales price and the loan balance, although you may, of course, take out a second loan.

Subject-to financing may be used only with a loan that has no due-on-sale clause in the original agreement, that is, unless the parties involved wish to take the risk upon themselves that the loan won't be called due. If there is a due-on-sale clause in the original agreement, the loan probably won't be called due so long as the lender has no knowledge that there has been a transfer of ownership, but there is always the possibility that the lender will discover the "sale" and call the loan due. In this kind of financing, the buyer is dealing strictly with the seller, not with the lender.

How Does an Assumption Differ from a "Subject-to"?

Here's a quick comparison of the differences between the two:

Assumption

- Old borrower (seller) is released from any liability for the loan.
- A Substitution of Liability is recorded, thereby releasing the original borrower from any responsibility for the debt.
- New borrower makes the monthly payments.
- The lender may change the interest rate.
- The lender may charge an assumption fee.
- If there is a due-on-sale clause in the original note, the consent of the lender is required. If there is no such clause, consent is not required.

Subject-to

- The old borrower (seller) retains ultimate liability for the loan.
- No document is recorded and no recorded agreement is made between the lender and the new buyer.
- The new borrower makes the monthly payments.
- Neither the interest rate nor the other terms of the note are changed.
- There are no costly loan fees.
- There should be no due-on-sale clause in the original note.

What Is Private Mortgage Insurance and How Can It Help Me Buy a House?

Private mortgage insurance (PMI) insures lenders against losses when they have to foreclose and can only sell their foreclosure properties for less than the loan balances. Let's say that a lender lends a young couple $142,500 to buy a $150,000 house. They live there for a year, fall upon hard times, and stop making payments. The lender forecloses, takes the house back, and resells it for the best price anybody will pay at the time, $135,000. Somebody has to take the loss on this loan. Without PMI, the lender has to take the loss; with it, the insurer takes the loss.

Most lenders now require PMI whenever they lend more than 80% of the appraised value of a property. Some lenders will even lend as much as 95% of appraised value so long as the borrower secures PMI.

PMI can help you buy a house by enabling you to make a smaller down payment than you would otherwise make. Because many lenders forbid the borrowing of any of the down payment, you wouldn't have to tap all of your savings accounts and all of your rich aunts to come up with a sizeable down payment. You could come up with it yourself comfortably. By making a down payment that is only a small percentage of the price, you'd also be able to buy a bigger house than your savings would otherwise allow, even though you could well afford to make large monthly payments.

Of course, PMI costs the borrower something. There's a start-up fee roughly equal to the annual premium and an annual premium amounting to between 0.6% and 3% of the total loan. On a $100,000 loan with a PMI premium of 0.6%, for example, you would pay $600 at the close of escrow and $50 per month thereafter. You pay the premiums directly to the lender along with your loan payments.

More than a dozen companies offer PMI. Your lender will have two or three preferred insurers and will generally use the one most likely to approve your loan.

Most lenders will allow you to terminate PMI when your loan balance is 80% of the value of your house or less, a requirement that may be met by a reduction in the loan balance and/or by appreciation in the value of the house. Across the U.S. as a whole, mortgage insurance is required for 10 years, while in California, the average is four to five years.

Should you believe that your loan balance is low enough to warrant the cancellation of your PMI, contact your lender and find out what you need to do for the lender to drop the PMI requirement on your loan. With the requirement dropped, you'll save having to pay the PMI premiums every month.

A Typical Misunderstanding: Ted and Cynthia knew that the equity in their home had reached 20% of the value of their house, but they assumed that their lender would send them notification of their right to cancel their PMI insurance premium obligation. They decided to wait until their lender wrote them a letter before they stopped making the PMI monthly premium.

The Way Things Really Are: Lenders in many states are not required to tell you when your loan has reached the point where PMI insurance is no longer required. Ted and Cynthia could be paying PMI premiums for 10 years or longer without knowing that all they needed to do was contact their lender and notify them that their equity had reached or exceeded 20% of the value of their home.

When Does the Lender Submit Escrow Instructions?

After you have chosen your type of loan, filled out your loan application, and received a commitment in writing, your lender will then submit instructions to your escrow officer. These instructions specify the conditions that must be met in order for the loan to be completed. Do your best to meet these conditions within the time limits set by the lender. Remember: lenders give a loan commitment for a specific period of time, usually no more than 30 days.

All lenders, whether institutional or private, will require that at least four conditions be met prior to the close of escrow:

- The loan documents must be executed by the buyer.
- The title insurance in the amount of the loan must be issued to insure the lender's interest.
- The title policy must show only those exceptions approved by the lender.
- Fire insurance must be issued for at least the amount of the loan, with the lender named as loss payee.

Institutional lenders do not, as a rule, deposit their check along with these instructions. They will disburse their loan proceeds (the actual loan amount, less their fees and any prepaid interest) only at the close of escrow and upon notification that their deed of trust has been recorded. Interest will, of course, begin to accrue from the date when this loan proceeds check is disbursed to your escrow officer.

With the First Loan Approved, Where Might I Obtain Additional Needed Financing? Should I Consider Seller Financing?

Let's suppose now that you have succeeded in getting your first loan but that it's not quite enough for you to consummate the purchase. Money is tight, but you need to borrow more. You need to negotiate a second loan. Since you have already received the maximum first loan obtainable from an institutional lender, you most often cannot borrow more from them right away. They simply will not write a second loan on the same property because they are restricted by regulation from lending more than their allowable maximum. They cannot afford to take the chance either, for if you default, the holder of the first loan is always paid first from the proceeds of a foreclosure sale, while the holder of the second may lose out.

Even though the first loan holder cannot provide you with any more money, you may apply for *secondary financing* through "non-institutional lenders." These lenders include private parties (the seller, a friend of yours, a relative, etc.), mortgage companies, pension funds, trust funds, and so on. These non-institutional lenders are not regulated as heavily and usually do not have as rigid a credit investigation as the institutional lenders.

Regardless of the company or person, however, non-institutional lenders must stay within the usury laws, which set a limit on the interest that anyone may charge. Usury laws vary from state to state, so be sure to verify the current allowable interest rates for your area, but make note that many types of lenders are exempt from usury laws as they now exist. Verify this with your escrow officer.

Because some institutional lenders will not permit secondary financing in conjunction with their first loan, be sure to ask the lender of your first loan whether they will permit secondary financing at all. Indeed, you would be wise to ask this question when you originally inquire about your first loan. If you didn't ask about secondary financing before, you can always call and ask your lender about it when the matter becomes an issue. Even if they do consent, they will insist that their loan be superior to all other loans or credit liens. If you have more than one loan on your property, one is always junior to the other; under a foreclosure action, the senior lender collects first and then the junior lender. If you fail to make your payments either to the institutional lender or to the seller who is carrying a second, the loan will be foreclosed and the institutional lender will get to collect its money first. Any money left over goes next to the seller holding the second loan up to the amount of his loan. If any money is left after that, it goes to you.

A Typical Misunderstanding: Interest rates on new loans are so high that Robert assumes he would be wasting his time even to look for a house right now. He knows that without a bank loan he could never afford to buy any property. He can't possibly scrape up enough cash.

The Way Things Really Are: Robert should be out looking for his house. When bank loans are not readily available, a seller will usually have to help finance the sale of a property if he wants to sell it at all. Then, too, many properties have existing financing that the buyers can assume. There are very few buyers who have all the cash necessary to purchase a property, no matter what the market conditions happen to be.

Let's look at one example of secondary financing to learn more about how it works. The first and most common place to look for a secondary loan is the seller. After all, he wants to sell his property and, if he believes in you and thinks you're a good credit risk, he may be agreeable to becoming the secondary lender for a short-term loan. Most secondary loans are for a short term, usually from one to five years. The seller doesn't actually lend you cash, but he extends you credit; he "carries back" the note you promise to pay and he doesn't receive that sum in cash that you would otherwise be paying him. Naturally, he will charge an interest fee for lending the money, just as any other lender would. This "carrying back of paper by the seller" occurs fairly frequently in real estate transactions. Those sellers who would otherwise bank this money are often pleased to extend credit to the buyer in this way, since the interest rates on these notes are generally higher than they could get if they put that money in a savings account.

Should a seller be willing to lend on a second promissory note secured by the property you're buying from him, you and he will have to negotiate the terms of this note—interest rate, monthly payments, due date, and other conditions. Once you have settled on the terms, your escrow officer will draw up the note and deed of trust or mortgage deed in accordance with your agreement. Never rely on a friendly handshake to bind the agreement. Insist that a promissory note secured by a deed of trust or mortgage deed be drawn up to act as the legally binding contract between borrower and lender. Then have the deed of trust or mortgage deed recorded. Every lender, institutional or private, should receive a deed of trust or mortgage deed and should keep it together with the note until the buyer has paid off the loan in full.

The seller of a residential property (one to four units only) in California who intends to finance part of the purchase price must provide the buyer a Seller Financing Disclosure Statement. This statement spells out all the terms and conditions of the note.

Be sure to check for mistakes before you sign any note, too, because you will be responsible for precisely the terms written on the note. Mistakes are sometimes made even in the serious business of drawing up loan papers, and these mistakes may be overlooked in the haste of signing a variety of documents. One instance I can remember involved the seemingly innocent substitution of a period for a comma. That little typing error turned this particular conventional note into a demand note, due anytime on demand of the lender! Read every word of any note you sign. Be certain everything is done exactly right and that the terms are correct according to your understanding and your prior agreement.

What Is a Wraparound Loan?

Essentially a *wraparound* is a loan that incorporates an old, existing loan with a new loan made by the seller of a property. The buyer makes one payment to the seller and the seller continues paying any old loans on their original terms. The wraparound gains popularity whenever there are high interest rates and whenever institutional financing becomes difficult to obtain. During those times, people still have to buy and sell property so they turn to wraparounds as a means of financing.

Here's how a wraparound works. Suppose that you have good credit and a good job, but you don't have enough cash for a down payment for a property purchase right now. You come across a house that you like very much and that the seller wants very much to sell. Let's say that he doesn't want all cash for his equity because he doesn't want to pay excess taxes that year. You explain your circumstances to him. He checks your credit and it's good, so you and he work out a wraparound loan.

The existing first loan remains in the seller's name, as it does in a subject-to situation, and he agrees to give you a second loan, that is, to carry whatever you could not make as down payment. He does this for a rate of interest at the current level on both his old loan and the new loan he is offering you. Say, for example, that the selling price is $100,000. The existing first loan is now at $60,000, but you, the buyer, can come up with only $10,000 for a down payment. This leaves $30,000 more to be financed. The seller gives you, the buyer, a loan for $90,000, incorporating the $60,000 of the original loan and the difference between that and your cash down payment, or $30,000, and the seller gives you this loan using one interest rate for the entire amount. Hence, the term "wraparound" was coined, a packaged loan, also sometimes called an "all-inclusive note and deed of trust" because the new loan includes the original loan(s).

Why Haven't Lenders Challenged the Use of Wraparounds?

That's a good question. After all, wraparounds eliminate lenders' opportunities to charge higher interest rates as well as new loan fees on renegotiated loans. The answer is that lenders have challenged this practice.

On August 25, 1978, the California State Supreme Court ruled that a state-chartered bank or savings and loan could not call its loan due or keep a new buyer from assuming a loan, unless it (the lender) could prove that the new borrower's (buyer's) credit was worse than the original borrower's (seller's) credit or that the property had decreased in value (Wellenkamp v. Bank of America).

This case, believe it or not, was over a mere $16 per month additional interest, but the consequences were dire for state-chartered lenders. The decision virtually stopped them from enforcing their due-on-sale clauses.

What Laws Have Passed Since the Wellenkamp Decision That Affect Due-on-Sale Clauses?

Because Wellenkamp was a state decision, it did not apply to federally chartered banks or savings and loans and thrift institutions or to states other than California. However, 16 other states followed in one way or another (Arizona, Arkansas, Colorado, Florida, Georgia, Illinois, Iowa, Michigan, Minnesota, Mississippi, New Mexico, New York, Ohio, Oklahoma, South Carolina, and Washington) and lenders in the other 33 were holding their collective breath. Finally, on June 28, 1982, the de la Cuesta decision (Fidelity Federal Savings & Loan Association. v. De la Cuesta) took the heat off federally chartered savings and loans by excluding them specifically from the terms of Wellenkamp. Then, on October 15, 1982, the President signed into law the Garn-St. Germain bill, which made fully enforceable all due-on-sale clauses originated after that date for both institutional and private lenders.

Since there are some situations that were never meant to trigger a due-on-sale clause anyway, the Garn Act spells out certain exceptions to its provisions. The following situations would not give a lender the right to exercise a due-on-sale clause:

1) transfer to a joint tenant upon the death of another joint tenant, 2) creation of a junior loan, 3) creation of a lease that is three years or shorter in duration and does not contain an option to purchase, 4) transfer to an heir, 5) transfer in a divorce settlement where a spouse becomes the owner, 6) transfer where the spouse or children become the owner, and 7) a transfer into an inter vivos trust in which the borrower is the beneficiary.

Although the main provisions of the Garn Bill affect only those loans created after October 15, 1982, Congress did make special provisions for loans either originated, acquired subject to existing financing, or assumed during the "window period" between the Wellenkamp decision and the Garn Act. These loans continued to be assumable, as they were under Wellenkamp, until October 14, 1985.

To add to all this confusion, I must note here that the governing body for each particular category of lender may deal with matters itself as well. The Office of the Comptroller of the Currency, which regulates national banks such as Wells Fargo, ruled that its banks may enforce their due-on-sale clauses on all loans beginning April 15, 1984. And the National Credit Union Administration, which regulates federal credit unions, ruled that its credit unions may enforce their due-on-sale clauses beginning December 8, 1982.

Remember that these rulings and legislation concerning due-on-sale matters may be changed at any time by further rulings and legislation, so be sure you verify the current status of assumptions and wraparounds with your attorney, your tax adviser, or a well-informed real estate agent before you get involved in any financing that involves a due-on-sale clause.

> **A Typical Misunderstanding:** Josh decided to buy his new home by way of an installment land sales contract. This would surely not trigger the lender to enforce the due-on-sale clause. Josh didn't want the lender to check his poor credit history.

> **The Way Things Really Are:** Lenders have the right to enforce the due-on-sale clause when any transfer of real property takes place. This transfer may be an assumption, an installment land sales contract, a wraparound loan, a contract for deed, or a transfer subject to the mortgage or similar lien.

How Does a Loan Approval Proceed?

Upon receiving your loan application, the lender will order a credit report to verify your financial stability and your ability to make the loan payments. Only after the lender has approved your credit will the property be appraised. From this appraisal, the lender will tell you how much he is willing to lend on the property. As mentioned earlier, this may vary anywhere from 60% to 90% of either the purchase or the appraisal price. Loans given on commercial property, businesses, and so forth usually range between 60% and 70% of the purchase price. Again, as mentioned, the appraisal will take anywhere from two days to two weeks to complete. It is often helpful to give the lender a copy of your preliminary report along with your credit or loan application so they can process your application more quickly. Your escrow officer will mail copies of this report for you if you tell her where you would like them to be sent.

When your application is accepted, the lender will issue you a letter of commitment detailing the terms of the loan. This commitment is usually good for 30 days.

> **A Typical Misunderstanding:** Danielle and Nick were confident they would get their loan. Their loan broker never gave any indications that there might be problems getting approval.

> **The Way Things Really Are:** Danielle and Nick's loan broker is not the person responsible for deciding whether their loan would be approved. The first place a loan goes for processing is the underwriting department. The underwriter will decide if the loan fits the qualifying criteria for that lender and whether they have all the relevant documents they need from the applicant. The loan file may be handed to three or more other loan underwriters before it is sent to the final "loan processing" department of the bank. Lenders must keep a meticulous paper trail of the loan transaction, ensuring that every statement is documented in the event the lender is audited.

Why Should a Request for Notice of Default Be Recorded?

Now let's suppose that you, the borrower, do not have sufficient funds over and above the first loan to meet the purchase price, so you have taken out a second loan from the seller, who has agreed that he'll lend you the difference, so long as he gets some security in exchange. For his protection, he requires that a second mortgage deed or deed of trust be drawn up and recorded. And you agree. The seller, who has given you the second loan, then receives this second mortgage deed or deed of trust, which he holds, as does the institutional lender who holds the first loan until you have paid him off completely.

Should something occur later so that you cannot make your payments, perhaps you cannot even pay the monthly installments to the bank, much less to the holder of the second loan, the bank will foreclose and sell your property to recoup its original investment. If this were to happen, it would leave the seller, who might be out of the country and unaware of your problems, with a total loss. He'd be unable to get his money back for the loan, because the first loan gets first claim in any default proceedings.

To protect himself, the holder of the second loan wants to be certain he is notified in case of any default on the first so he can take over the payments, if necessary, and not lose most or all of the collateral for the loan. In order to be notified promptly of such a possibility, he has the escrow officer prepare a Request for Notice of Default on the first. This form requests the trustee or mortgagee to inform the holder of the second when there is a default in payments or any other breach of the first note that might cause the lender to begin foreclosure proceedings. The trustee or mortgagee notifies the holder of the second within 10 days after the notice of default is recorded. If no Request for Notice of Default has been recorded, the trustee need notify the note holder only within 30 days following the recording of a Notice of Default. The law allows the holder of the second to cure any default on the first in order to protect his interests. He can then proceed to foreclose to get his money back if he chooses to do so.

The holder of the second loan must either ask the escrow officer or trustee to prepare and record a Request for Notice of Default or he must do it himself. It is not done automatically. If one is not prepared during escrow, the holder of the second can prepare and record one after escrow closes simply by giving the escrow officer the pertinent information and the fee for recording.

Are There Any Other Ways to Finance a Property Purchase?

Believe it or not, there are over a hundred ways to structure the financing of a real estate transaction, depending upon the cash position of the buyer and seller and what each needs. Many of these methods are commonly called *creative financing*. Creative financing involves working in conjunction with the existing financing to create a financing package to enable the buyer to purchase the property with better interest rates or terms than conventional lenders are offering.

The creative financing approach is based on the ability of a buyer and a seller to structure an arrangement that is acceptable to both. The structuring is often done by real estate agents who are knowledgeable about financing.

These are the four most commonly used creative financing methods: assumptions, subject-to's, wraparounds, and land contracts.

Are Land Contracts "Creative Financing"?

Yes, they are. They are a fourth alternative to traditional financing and they offer one effective way of getting around due-on-sale clauses. They rely on the principle of *buying on contract*. A Contract of Sale, Installment Sales Contract, Agreement to Convey, or Contract for Deed (these four terms all mean pretty much the same thing) is a type of contract used in connection with the sale of real property where

the seller retains legal title to the property until some future date, usually when the full purchase price has been paid.

The installment land contract is most often used as a security device just like the deed of trust. The seller lends the buyers a certain sum of money for buying real property, but unlike a conventional sale, little or no money is transferred by the buyer to the seller at the time of sale and the seller does not convey title to the property until the full obligation has been paid. The buyers are able to take possession of the property, to move in and use it as if they were the vested owner, but no deed is recorded and the seller holds the deed until the full obligation has been satisfied. The buyers usually put up a relatively small down payment and acquires an equity interest after making periodic payments. When they finally fulfill the contract, they acquire the fee title.

The two main advantages to the buyers using a land contract are that it provides a means to circumvent the due-on-sale clause found in the existing loan, and it offers the possibility that any money paid to the seller will be returned in case of default. When a deed of trust is foreclosed, the borrower is not entitled to the money he or she has paid the beneficiary unless there are surplus funds generated by the foreclosure sale. In other words, the borrower forfeits all his or her payments. In the event of a default under a land contract, however, the borrower is entitled to recover the money already paid toward the principal.

Naturally there are disadvantages to buying property under a land contract, too. These are the primary ones:

- Although the seller is limited by law as to the amount he or she can borrow after the execution of a land contract, the seller could still create new liens against the property or there may be a judgment filed against the seller that

RECORDING REQUESTED BY

Secure Title Company

AND WHEN RECORDED MAIL TO

Mr. Samuel P. Seller
4 Evelyn Court
Sydney, Ill. 50010

302207
RECEIVED AUG 1 0 20XX

RECORDED AT REQUEST OF
SECURE TITLE CO.

AT 8 O'CLOCK A. M.
BARRETT COUNTY RECORDS
FEE $ 4 —   V. L GRAVES
COUNTY RECORDER

302207

————— SPACE ABOVE THIS LINE FOR RECORDER'S USE —————

SHORT FORM DEED OF TRUST AND ASSIGNMENT OF RENTS   A.P.N.

This Deed of Trust, made this 10th day of August , between

Bruce B. Buyer and Barbara A. Buyer, his wife as Joint Tenants
, herein called TRUSTOR,

whose address is 12 Allendale Ct., Boonville, Ca 91002 ,
(number and street) (city) (state) (zip)

Secure Title Company, a California corporation, herein called TRUSTEE, and

Samuel P. Seller, a married man as his sole and separate property , herein called BENEFICIARY,

Witnesseth: That Trustor IRREVOCABLY GRANTS, TRANSFERS AND ASSIGNS to TRUSTEE IN TRUST, WITH POWER OF SALE,
that property in Barrett County, California, described as:

Lot 142, as shown upon that certain map entitled, "Map of Barrett Bay
Unit One, Boonville, California," filed for record September 22, 1960
in Volume 10 of Maps, at Page 78, Barrett County Records.

In the event the real property herein above described is sold or transferred by Trustor herein, the promissory note secured by the within deed
of trust shall become immediately due and payable at the option of the
payee.

TOGETHER WITH the rents, issues and profits thereof, SUBJECT, HOWEVER, to the right, power and authority given to and conferred
upon Beneficiary by paragraph (10) of the provisions incorporated herein by reference to collect and apply such rents, issues and profits.

For the Purpose of Securing: 1. Performance of each agreement of Trustor incorporated by reference or contained herein. 2. Payment
of the indebtedness evidenced by one promissory note of even date herewith, and any extension or renewal thereof, in the principal sum
of $ 10,000.00 executed by Trustor in favor of Beneficiary or order. 3. Payment of such further sums as the then record owner of
said property hereafter may borrow from Beneficiary, when evidenced by another note (or notes) reciting it is so secured.

To Protect the Security of This Deed of Trust, Trustor Agrees: By the execution and delivery of this Deed of Trust and the
note secured hereby, that provisions (1) to (14), inclusive, of the fictitious deed of trust recorded in Santa Barbara County and Sonoma
County October 18, 1961, and in all other counties October 23, 1961, in the book and at the page of Official Records in the office of the
county recorder of the county where said property is located, noted below opposite the name of such county, viz.:

COUNTY	BOOK	PAGE	COUNTY	BOOK	PAGE	COUNTY	BOOK	PAGE	COUNTY	BOOK	PAGE
Alameda	435	684	Kings	792	833	Placer	895	301	Sierra	29	335
Alpine	1	250	Lake	362	39	Plumas	151	5	Siskiyou	468	181
Amador	104	348	Lassen	171	471	Riverside	3005	523	Solano	1105	182
Butte	1145	1	Los Angeles	T3065	899	Sacramento	4331	62	Sonoma	1851	689
Calaveras	145	152	Madera	810	170	San Benito	271	383	Stanislaus	1715	456
Colusa	296	617	Marin	1508	339	San Bernardino	5567	61	Sutter	572	297
Contra Costa	3978	47	Mariposa	77	292	San Francisco	A332	905	Tehama	401	289
Del Norte	78	414	Mendocino	579	530	San Joaquin	2470	311	Trinity	93	366
El Dorado	568	456	Merced	1547	538	San Luis Obispo	1151	12	Tulare	2294	275
Fresno	4636	572	Modoc	184	851	San Mateo	4078	420	Tuolumne	135	47
Glenn	422	184	Mono	52	429	Santa Barbara	1878	860	Ventura	2062	386
Humboldt	657	527	Monterey	2194	538	Santa Clara	5336	341	Yolo	653	245
Imperial	1091	501	Napa	639	86	Santa Cruz	1431	494	Yuba	304	484
Inyo	147	598	Nevada	305	320	Shasta	684	528			
Kern	3427	60	Orange	5889	611	San Diego	Series 2 Book 1961, Page 183887				

(which provisions, identical in all counties, are printed on the reverse hereof) hereby are adopted and incorporated herein and made a part
hereof as fully as though set forth herein at length; that he will observe and perform said provisions; and that the references to property,
obligations, and parties in said provisions shall be construed to refer to the property, obligations, and parties set forth in this Deed of Trust.
     The undersigned Trustor requests that a copy of any Notice of Default and of any Notice of Sale hereunder be mailed to him at his address
hereinbefore set forth.

STATE OF CALIFORNIA,
COUNTY OF Barrett } SS.
On August 10, 20XX before me, the under-
signed, a Notary Public in and for said State, personally appeared
Bruce B. Buyer and
Barbara A. Buyer
————————————— , known to me
to be the person s whose name are subscribed to the within
instrument and acknowledged that they executed the same.
WITNESS my hand and official seal.

Signature *Edna Edwards*
     EDNA EDWARDS

Title Order No. ——————

Escrow or Loan No. 1: 12345

Signature of Trustor
Bruce B. Buyer
BRUCE B. BUYER
Barbara A. Buyer
BARBARA A. BUYER

OFFICIAL SEAL
EDNA EDWARDS
Notary Public

(This area for official notarial seal)

SFT-1   2/76

Chart 7-6. Example of short form of deed of trust and assignment of rents

would further encumber the property. In order to place the contract before all other encumbrances against the property, the buyer should record his or her contract with the county recorder.

- Circumstances may arise in the future, such as the seller becoming bankrupt or incompetent or dying, which would prevent the buyer from obtaining legal title without court proceedings. The buyer would also lose the land if the seller fails to make his or her payments and the loan is foreclosed. If the buyer goes to court at that time, this individual may get his or her payments back, but it is very unlikely he or she will get the property since the seller no longer has it. The situation is similar if the seller goes bankrupt or dies and passes title to his or her heirs.

- Some due-on-sale clauses prohibit contract sales specifically. Should a lender discover that one has occurred, he or she may call the loan due.

- The seller may not have held legal title at the time the land contract was executed. The buyer should obtain title insurance to protect him or herself from this and other matters.

The advantage of the land contract to the seller is the ease with which he or she can eliminate the buyer's interest in case of default. If the contract is not recorded and the buyer defaults, the seller may prepare a notice of termination and regain possession in less time than he or she could if he or she were foreclosing on a deed of trust. Since he or she already has title to the land, the seller does not have to go through a regular court foreclosure.

If the land contract is recorded at the county recorder's office, however, clearing the title of record may become involved and expensive, especially if difficulties arise because the buyer has created liens, subcontracts, or other encumbrances of interest in favor of third parties, or if the buyer simply disappears. If a land contract is recorded, the seller cannot sell the property to anyone else without first obtaining a release from the buyer.

The rules for issuing title insurance on land contracts vary from state to state. The contract buyer's interest can be insured and, if requested, the contract seller's interest can be insured as well, but title insurance companies will insure recorded contracts only.

Any land contract should be drawn up carefully by someone knowledgeable about it. Such a contract should specify, among other things, the exact amount of the obligation, the method of payment, the interest rate, and the monthly payment schedule.

Are There Any Guidelines for a Land Contract?

There are indeed. As further safeguards, you as a buyer employing a land contract should follow these guidelines:

- Draw up a contract that states that the seller is to put the title to the land in trust with an escrow holder or third-party trustee until you complete your payments or default on them.

- Require that the land contract be recorded immediately with the county recorder.

- Have the seller sign a deed to you and deliver it to the trustee together with instructions to give it to you upon completion of your payments. This will prevent him or her from selling or encumbering the title to the land before you receive it.

- Try to get the best financing arrangement possible. Because of the somewhat risky nature of land contracts, sellers often will agree to an extremely small down payment and low monthly payments.

- Specifically forbid the seller from encumbering the title in any way. He or she should not be allowed to bequeath the title to a beneficiary in his will. If the seller dies while you are still making payments, the land should remain under the care of his executor until you have either made all of your payments or defaulted.

- Never allow the seller to put a prepayment penalty clause into the contract penalizing you for paying off the balance at an earlier date than scheduled. For example, if your payments are to be $600 a month, you should be permitted to pay $600 a month "or more."

- Be required to keep the property in good repair and to pay for fire and hazard insurance on the property under terms to be approved by the seller. Be sure you and the seller are both beneficiaries under the policy.

- Have the seller state, in detail, the conditions under which he or she can force you off the land. Make sure you understand them.

- Get the seller to include a clause in which he or she promises to convey all or part of the title to you after you have completed a certain amount of the total payment. For example, after you have made half of the payments, the seller will give you full title to the land and you can give him or her back a mortgage or trust deed for the remaining amount due.

- Give a trustee or third party the responsibility of keeping track of the payments made and the current balances. Over the life of a loan, 10, 15, 20, or 30 years, people move, change jobs, and disappear. I remember one instance in which the trustee (a title company) had changed hands, the original employees were gone, and the land contract was coming due. The seller said one amount was left owing; the buyer said quite another. The title company's file on the transaction was supposed to have contained the documentation for the original deposits, monthly payments, etc., but they were nowhere to be found and there was nothing in the file to prove anything specific. The buyer eventually paid the seller what he felt was due and the seller turned around and sued the title company for the balance (in this case $5,000) that he felt was owing. The problem was that no one could remember whether a $5,000 deposit had been made initially.

While not the most desirable of the creative financing techniques, the land contract offers an alternative when other means of financing won't work for some reason or other. At times this becomes the only way to buy a piece of property.

Amid all the wheeling, dealing, and financial razzle-dazzle of creative financing, both buyer and seller should be cautious. Beware of misinformation, risks, and liabilities. Be certain your real estate agent is well informed, and review any advice you are given with an attorney.

When I Pay off a Loan, What Fees Must I Pay?

When you want to pay off a loan, you will be responsible for paying quite a few fees. Here they are:

- reconveyance fee—The lender or escrow company charges a fee for drawing up a deed of reconveyance, an instrument used to prove that the old deed of trust is indeed paid in full. Ordinarily, the lender will forward a release of claim on the property and the escrow officer will see that it's recorded at the county recorder's office. This, of course, happens only at the close of escrow, when the loan has been paid off. The payoff and the deed of reconveyance clear the title and release the original borrower from the original loan. The fee for this service runs around $75 and is paid by the borrower (seller).

- recording fee—Through escrow, the seller pays about $5 to the county to record the deed of reconveyance.

- forwarding fee—To close out their loans, some lenders collect a forwarding or processing fee, varying from $40 to $100.

- prepayment penalty—Most people sell a property before paying it off according to the original loan. The holder of that loan is then faced with receiving a large cash sum and no further interest on the loan. If interest rates are currently higher than what was specified in the original note, this is a blessing to the lender, but if they are lower or about the same, it's a curse. Whatever the situation, the lender will have to recommit those funds, that is, lend them to someone else, something that cannot be accomplished immediately. Because the lender will likely lose some interest on the sum paid off, the lender may charge a prepayment penalty to recover part of the interest lost on the money.

Is There Anything I Can Do to Avoid Paying the Reconveyance Fee?

When you're in escrow, you ought to let the escrow officer handle all the papers involved in the payoff and reconveyance of the loans that are being paid off by funds from new loans. The escrow officer will expedite matters and save you time thereby insuring that your escrow will close promptly.

When you're not in escrow and you have paid off a loan, either by making all the payments as specified in the note or by making a lump sum payoff out of some windfall, you can avoid paying a reconveyance fee by handling the paperwork yourself. It's quite easy, especially because the money has already been paid and no lender has to worry about signing papers before the money has all been paid. There's only one form, too, and it will cost only the amount required to have the form notarized ($5, more or less) and recorded ($7).

Here's what you do:

1. Find your original deed of trust; note the names of the beneficiary (lender), the trustor (borrower), and the trustee (usually an escrow or title insurance company or a bank) as they are written there. If there has been an assignment of the deed of trust, then find the assignment of deed of trust form as well.

2. Make a copy of the *substitution of trustee and full reconveyance* form in the back of this book.

3. Type your name beneath the words "RECORDING REQUESTED BY." Type your name and address beneath the words "WHEN RECORDED, MAIL TO."

4. Type the name of the trustor on the first line and the name of the trustee on the second line where indicated. They should be exactly as shown on the original deed of trust or on a subsequently recorded assignment.

5. Type the recording information on the lines where indicated. You will find this information somewhere on the deed of trust. If any of it is missing, call the county recorder's office and ask someone there for help in identifying your particular deed of trust.

6. Then contact the beneficiary directly and ask for some cooperation in completing the balance of the form in the presence of a notary public. Offer to pay the notary's fees. Also ask the beneficiary to return to you the note that is secured by this deed of trust with "paid in full" and the beneficiary's signature written on it.

7. Take the completed substitution of trustee and full reconveyance form to the recorder's office, pay the recording fee, and leave the form there to be recorded in the county's official records. Within two to three weeks, it will be returned to you, and you as the borrower will have official proof that the loan has been paid off.

RECORDING REQUESTED BY

Secure Title Company

ORDER NO.
ESCROW NO. 12345

WHEN RECORDED MAIL TO

Name Samuel P. Seller
Street Address 4 Evelyn Ct.
City State Zip Sydney, Ill. 50010

RECEIVED AUG 10 20XX

302208

RECORDED AT REQUEST OF
SECURE TITLE CO.

AT 8 O'CLOCK A. M.
BARRETT COUNTY RECORDS
FEE $ 5⁰⁰   V. L. GRAVES
COUNTY RECORDER

302208

RECORDERS USE ONLY

REQUEST FOR COPY OF NOTICE OF DEFAULT

In accordance with Section 2924b, Civil Code, request is hereby made that a copy of any Notice of Default and a copy of

any Notice of Sale under the Deed of Trust recorded _____ August 10 _____, 20XX

as Instrument No. 302206 , in book 3502 at Page 45

_____, Official Records of Barrett _____ County, California,

executed by BRUCE B. BUYER AND BARBARA A. BUYER, HIS WIFE

, as Trustor,

to Independent Trustee Company , as Trustee,

in which FIRST SAVINGS AND TRUST COMPANY

is named as Beneficiary,

be mailed to: Samuel P. Seller

at 4 Evelyn Ct.   Sydney   Ill.   50010
(Street and Number)   (City)   (State)   (Zip)

Dated: August 10, 20XX

Samuel P. Seller

(If Assignment is executed by a corporation, the following corporation form of Acknowledgment must be used.)

STATE OF CALIFORNIA }
COUNTY OF } ss.

On _____, 20_____
before me, the undersigned, a Notary Public in and for said
County and State, personally appeared _____

known to me to be the _____ President, and

known to me to be the _____ Secretary of
the corporation that executed the within instrument, and
known to me to be the persons who executed the within
instrument on behalf of the corporation therein named, and
acknowledged to me that such corporation executed the
within instrument pursuant to its By-Laws or a Resolution
of its Board of Directors.
WITNESS my hand and official seal.

_____
Notary Public in and for said County and State.

— Notary Seal —

STATE OF CALIFORNIA }
COUNTY OF Barrett } ss.

On August 10 , 20XX
before me, the undersigned, a Notary Public in and for said
County and State, personally appeared

Samuel P. Seller

known to me to be the person_____ whose name is
subscribed to the within instrument and acknowledged that
he _____ executed the same.

WITNESS my hand and official seal.

Edna Edwards
Notary Public in and for said County and State.

— Notary Seal —

OFFICIAL SEAL
EDNA EDWARDS
Notary Public

RPF-1   2/79

Chart 7-7. Example of substitution of trustee and full conveyance form

Above all, remember to secure a reconveyance whenever you pay off a loan, whether you do it yourself or seek assistance. Many people forget about it, only to find out later, when they want to dispose of the property, that they face delays and difficulties because the former note holder has died or can't be found.

Is There Anything I Can Do to Avoid Paying a Prepayment Penalty?

As a matter of fact, there are some things you can do to avoid paying a prepayment penalty. Insist as a seller that your buyer obtain a loan from the same lender you used for your loan. In that case, the lender will usually waive the penalty. If you have a government-insured FHA or VA loan, this penalty is now automatically waived by a recent federal law covering prepayments.

If a prepayment penalty is written into your mortgage and the lender insists that you pay it, you cannot simply refuse. If you do, the lender will not allow the mortgage to be cleared from the title to your property and you will not be able to give clear title to your buyer.

Almost all lending institutions will waive the penalty if you obtain a new loan at a higher interest rate. For example, when you want to borrow additional money from the same lender (refinance your loan) and the rate on your old loan is 8% while the interest rate on your new loan will be 10%, your lender will most likely forgo the prepayment penalty.

Also, remember that whenever the rate is revised upward on an adjustable rate loan, the borrower has the option to pay off the loan in full without having to pay a prepayment penalty.

Avoiding a prepayment penalty is definitely to the seller's advantage because it could amount to $1,000 or more. The penalty is generally computed as a percentage of the remaining loan amount. Some lenders charge 3%-5% of the balance, while others charge an amount equal to six months' interest. On a loan with a principal balance of $80,000, this penalty could amount to quite a bit of money. For example, 3% of $80,000 is $2,400; six months' interest at 10% would be $4,000—either way it's calculated, it's no small sum. Generally, through the first five years of the loan, no more than 20% of the principal may be paid in any one year without incurring a prepayment penalty. In other words, on an $80,000 loan, you could make only a $16,000 principal payment in any one year without penalty. Prepayment penalties are burdensome enough for borrowers, but when lenders enforce due-on-sale provisions and charge prepayment penalties, they're really being greedy. Because some lenders had been hitting borrowers with this "double whammy," the Federal Home Loan Bank Board finally issued a regulation prohibiting the practice as of December 13, 1985. The regulation prohibits lenders from imposing prepayment penalties whenever a loan has to be paid off because of a sale or transfer. The regulation applies to all lenders, state and federal, institutional and private, but it applies only to loans secured by owner-occupied, one-to four-unit residential property. Other loans are governed by whatever state laws exist on the subject.

What Does a Prepayment Clause Look Like?

Here's an example of how a prepayment clause might look in a note:

> The indebtedness created hereby may be prepaid at any time, provided that if the aggregate amount prepaid in any 12-month period exceeds 20% of the original amount of this note, I agree to pay the holder hereof an amount equal to six month's advance interest, at the interest rate then in effect, on the amount prepaid in excess of 20% of the original principal amount. However, the charges and limitations contained in this paragraph are not applicable to any prepayment made more than five years after the date of execution of the deed of trust securing this note if the real property covered by said deed of trust is a single-family, owner-occupied dwelling.

How Do I Get the Payoff Information?

To obtain the information necessary to compute what's owed on your old loan, your escrow officer will write your lender a *demand letter* and ask for a *demand statement*. The lender will in turn send her a *payoff or beneficiary's demand statement*, giving her all the information she needs to pay off your loan in full, together with documents necessary for reconveyance. Your escrow officer must allow ample time for the lender to furnish her with this information. Be sure to tell her as soon as possible whether the old loan will be paid off (if you're the seller) or whether you will be assuming it (if you're the new buyer). This payoff or demand request letter should be written at least 10 days prior to the close of escrow.

If you're assuming the existing loan, your escrow officer will write the lender a *request for statement of condition* or *beneficiary's statement letter*, requesting the current status of the loan, the sums left owing, the interest rate, delinquencies, etc. Because lenders are sensitive about subject-to agreements and might try to prevent a takeover or raise the interest rate or make the new buyer qualify as if seeking a new loan or even call the loan due if a due-on-sale clause exists, your escrow officer must be careful to ask for a request only and not for a demand payoff statement.

How May I Obtain Short-Term Financing to Help Me Through Escrow?

Whenever you have to buy a new home before you sell the old one, you'll probably need to arrange some short-term financing. You need what's called a *swing* or *bridge loan*—nothing more, really, than another mortgage placed on your old home for as long as 36 months. You will have to qualify for the swing loan just as you would for a conventional loan.

Usually you can borrow up to 80% of the appraised value of your old home with a swing loan. If your old first mortgage is the only mortgage you have on the house, for example, and it equals 50% of the appraised value, then you should be able to get a swing loan equal to 30%, for a total indebtedness of 80% of the appraised value.

Another short-term financing arrangement, the *assignment loan*, may come in handy when you have sold your old home and haven't been able to get enough cash out of it to purchase a new home because you had to carry back a note to get the old home sold. In that situation, you could ask a lender for an assignment loan, a loan usually written for 70% of the face value of the note you carried back. That note and its mortgage or deed of trust would be the collateral for the assignment loan, which would then give you the cash you need to buy a new home.

Chapter Eight

Title Insurance

Now that I've reviewed loans and financing, it is time to talk about title insurance. Insurance on your title is necessary to guarantee that you are actually buying what you think you are buying. In this chapter I'll explain what title insurance is, why it is so important, and the different types of title insurance available.

What Is Title Insurance?

Title insurance is a guarantee that you are getting something for your money when you buy real estate. Title insurance guarantees that the ownership of the property you are buying is just as it's stated in recorded documents.

Whenever you buy any real property, you expect to acquire use of the property as well as its *title* or legal ownership and you want to be absolutely certain that the owner had clear title to it in the first place and consequently was legally entitled to sell it to you. He might say that he owns the Brooklyn Bridge and you might want to buy it from him on his terms, but unless you determine that he has clear title to it and unless you secure a title insurance policy to protect yourself, you will be giving him money for nothing and he will have the last laugh.

A Typical Misunderstanding: Donald is buying a house directly from an honest, reputable friend. The preliminary report that he orders gives no evidence of title problems, so Donald decides not to waste any money on title insurance.

The Way Things Really Are: Donald's friend may be honest and may have told Donald everything he knows about the house, but what about the previous owners? Did they have a valid claim to the property? Maybe they did and maybe they didn't.

Many kinds of title defects are so serious that they can render a title unmarketable. It is the title insurance you purchase when you acquire real property that protects you against most of these defects.

Real property refers to land and all the things that are either attached to it or considered as part of it, including such things as buildings and minerals below the surface. Title insurance does not cover personal property, including movables like furniture, draperies, washers, or refrigerators.

Title insurance protects the buyer and lender involved in a real property transaction against incompetent past action, clerical errors, an insane person having signed off an earlier deed, incorrect marital status, undisclosed heirs, improper interpretation of wills, signing by anyone without authority, a minor's signing, or any possible forgery in the entire past chain of title signatures. In sum, it insures against claims made by third parties against the title. Like other types of insurance policies, title insurance affords protection to the insured by guaranteeing that the insurer, that is, the title insurance company, will reimburse him for actual loss or damage under the conditions specified in the policy. Unlike other insurance policies, title insurance insures against conditions that already exist rather than against those that may occur in the future.

Why Should I Buy Title Insurance?

The property you are buying may have a past fraught with shady dealings, forgeries, divorce claims, or other peculiarities. There's no way you can be absolutely certain that this seller or any of the previous sellers ever held clear title to the property and could legally transfer it over to you, for even though an owner has a deed and the right to possess the land, he might not have clear title because there may be a defect or cloud on the title that even he doesn't know about. To protect yourself from many such claims out of the past, you should secure title insurance, which is available in every state except Iowa and for almost every conceivable kind of interest in real estate, including leaseholds, rights under a contract of sale, airspace, rights and easements, and mineral rights. (In Iowa, attorneys and others who do title work must participate in the Iowa Title Guaranty program. If there's a title error, the state fund provides coverage.)

In addition, you must have title insurance if you intend to borrow any money on your property. Your lender, wanting to protect his interest in the property that secures his loan to you, will require a policy for his own protection, to insure himself against any previous claims made by legitimate or illegitimate claimants. You need a policy to protect yourself, too. You don't want to learn after the sale that you have no rights to the property at all, that you have, in effect, bought the Brooklyn Bridge in disguise, and neither does your lender. He knows that you won't repay the money he has lent you to buy a property unless you are legally entitled to that property.

But even if your real estate transaction is an all-cash deal, you should obtain title insurance, for a grant deed by itself does not necessarily give clear title to a property. There may be outstanding claims and rights that cannot possibly be determined from the deed alone.

Remember, too, that although you are protected under your purchase agreement against certain damages, only the seller is liable to you for the damages, whereas under a title insurance policy, the title company assumes this liability. If you are not insured and you have to proceed against the seller for any defect in title or any breach of the purchase agreement, you will have to pay the legal expenses yourself prior to a judgment. Even if you win a judgment, you might not be able to collect it, for you might not be able to locate the seller or he might not have the money to pay you; you could be left holding worthless paper. If, on the other hand, you have a title insurance policy, it will pay your legal costs and provide you with coverage for any losses included in the policy. Such insurance is essential to you as a property buyer.

If you were really determined to do so, however, you could insure yourself. In that case, you'd certainly want to try to trace your property's ownership and complete chain of title to get some idea about whether the seller had clear title. When you did, you'd find soon enough that a title search is both time-consuming and tedious. Were you to make the same investigation as the title examiner, you would have to review information from the following sources:

■ Public records at the county recorder's office (In Los Angeles County, there are 9,000 instruments recorded every single day; even in tiny San Francisco County, there are some 900 recorded every day. Searching through just those records for one year would take a long, long time, and you'd have to go back through many years to be safe, back to the original land grants in some cases. In Los Angeles County, for instance, land can be traced back to the rancho days in 1850, when the Los Angeles Recorder's Office opened.)

■ Certain taxing authorities that levy taxes and assess real property

■ Documents in the general index (bankruptcy, divorce, name changes, judgments, trust agreements, probate proceedings, etc.)

■ Bankruptcy proceedings of the United States District Court

Moreover, after going through all those records, you'd have to interpret the effects of such information on ownership. You might have to request documents and additional information. You might even have to initiate court proceedings to clear the title in order to be relatively certain that it was indeed clear. Even if you or your attorney did feel qualified to make a title search, examine the records, and evaluate the effects of those records, a prudent buyer or lender would still want assurance to protect himself against loss or damage in the event of an error, because overlooking just one judgment or lien could be very costly.

The cost of title insurance is minimal when you consider the protection it provides. A title insurance policy for a $100,000 property, for example, costs less than $600.

How Long Does Title Insurance Remain in Effect?

The protection provided by an owner's policy continues until the interest of the insured is transferred, that is, as long as you own the property. Even when an insured dies, his heirs or devisees remain protected under the terms of the policy. A title policy is not assignable or transferable to subsequent purchasers of the property, however. For instance, a seller cannot transfer his policy to you. Each new buyer must purchase a completely new policy regardless of how recently the seller had a title search conducted.

Who Obtains Title Insurance?

Either the buyer or the lender or both of them may obtain title insurance. In many states, both the buyer and the lender are covered in one policy. In California, there are five distinct title insurance possibilities: the California Land Title Association (CLTA) Standard Owner's Policy, the CLTA Owner's and Lender's Joint Protection Policy, the CLTA Lender's Policy, the American Land Title Association (ALTA) Lender's Policy, and the ALTA Owner's Policy.

Most often, the buyer pays for the policies. In some areas, however, the seller pays for the owner's policy and the buyer pays for the lender's policy. Your escrow officer can tell you who pays the various premiums in your area (also see Appendix B). You may, of course, negotiate splitting the costs with the seller, because it is only local practice that determines who pays the premiums and not local laws.

You might like to know, just in case you ever carry back a loan on a property you're selling, that a lender's policy is for the benefit not only of the lender who was insured originally, but also of anyone who might acquire the note at a later time. Liability under the policy doesn't end until the loan is finally paid off.

What Is a CLTA Title Insurance Policy?

The California Land Title Association policy, as the name implies, was issued initially only in California, but other states, notably Nevada and Arizona, have now adopted it. Also referred to as the *standard coverage policy*, it insures owners and/or lenders. It is a limited policy because it will insure against only those matters that are disclosed in public records and will not cover any defects that are concealed from the title company. "Off-record" items—such as an encroachment, an unrecorded easement, a discrepancy in boundary lines, or an interest of parties in possession of the property—that are discovered only by a survey or inspection of the property itself are not covered by a CLTA standard policy.

When issued to insure a lender, a CLTA policy provides coverage against a loss sustained because the deed of trust proved to be invalid (there are some exceptions), because the deed of trust proved to be in a worse position than shown, or because an assignment in the policy proved to be invalid.

A CLTA policy may be issued in any of these three ways:

- An owner's policy, covering the owner only

- A non-institutional lender's policy, covering the private lender only or an institutional lender if he wants it (institutional lenders generally prefer the broader coverage of an ALTA policy)

- A joint-protection policy, covering both the owner and the lender in the same policy (used most often when a seller takes back a second note and deed of trust and wants to be named as an additional insured party)

In order to obtain insurance coverage on the items not covered in the standard policy, you may order added endorsements. Two of these owner's endorsements are included by most title insurers as a matter of course.

The inflation endorsement, which is issued automatically at no additional charge, makes an upward adjustment in the amount of insurance provided in an owner's policy. In other words, if your $100,000 house is worth $110,000 next year and there's a claim against the title, your title insurance policy will cover the inflated price of the house rather than just the sales price.

The homeowner's endorsement, issued only on owner-occupied dwellings with four or fewer units (fourplex or smaller), insures against limited off-record risks involving certain matters related to access, encroachments, restrictions, zoning, taxes, mechanic's and material supplier's liens, as well as the exercise of the right to take minerals. If these are not included in your policy of title insurance, you may order them for a nominal fee so long as the title company will make such endorsements. Your escrow officer will tell you which endorsements are available.

What Is an ALTA Title Insurance Policy?

The American Land Title Association (ALTA) policy was primarily designed to meet the demands of the large national lending institutions for uniform title insurance protection across the country and for increased protection against risks that can be ascertained only by an inspection of the property. In effect, it extends the scope of the basic owner's policy to cover various matters not on record.

In California, any lender, institutional or private, may obtain an American Land Title Association policy to insure against the same items as in the standard CLTA owner's policy, as well as against any of the following: mechanic's liens not yet recorded, claims to water and mineral rights, unrecorded easements, unrecorded tax and assessment liens, and certain other matters. To determine whether a title company will insure against any other matters, the company will inspect public records and, for a fee, the property itself. These off-record investigations sometimes reveal a wide variety of encroachments: overhanging structures or architectural details, common walls, boundary fences, community driveways, etc., that will be shown by the title company as exceptions in the policy and not normally insured against. In states not offering a CLTA policy, an ALTA owner's policy is issued.

An ALTA policy provides a lender with some important protection few people ever think about— protection against the lender's mortgage or deed of trust having been recorded other than when requested. This protection can become very important because the date, time, and order of recording determine a trust deed's priority, that is, whether it becomes a first, second, third, or lesser trust deed. The security a lender seeks most is a valid lien with priority over other claims and interests, plus some assurance that the borrower and the owner of record are one and the same and that this borrower has valid title to the property that secures the loan.

Sometimes, however, a lender may require protection beyond that afforded by an ALTA policy. He may order that an endorsement or a special coverage be added to his policy, the most common of which are those covering violations of covenants, conditions, and restrictions (CC&Rs) limiting the use of land and regulating the type and location of improvements; encroachment of property improve-

SECURE TITLE   Policy No.:___CAS-223346____

SUBJECT TO THE EXCLUSIONS FROM COVERAGE, THE EXCEPTIONS CONTAINED IN SCHEDULE B AND THE CONDITIONS AND STIPULATIONS HEREOF, SECURE TITLE INSURANCE CORPORATION, a California corporation, herein called the Company, insures the insured, as of Date of Policy shown in Schedule A, against loss or damage, not exceeding the amount of insurance stated in Schedule A, and costs, attorneys' fees and expenses which the Company may become obligated to pay hereunder, sustained or incurred by said Insured by reason of:

1. Title to the estate or interest described in Schedule A being vested other than as stated therein;

2. Any defect in or lien or encumbrance on such title;

3. Unmarketability of such title; or

4. Any lack of the ordinary right of any abutting owner for access to at least one physically open street or highway if the land, in fact, abuts upon one or more such streets or highways; and in addition, as to an insured lender only:

5. Invalidity of the lien of the insured mortgage upon said estate or interest except to the extent that such in validity, or claim thereof, arises out of the transaction evidenced by the insured mortgage and is based upon

   a. usury, or

   b. any consumer credit protection or truth in lending law;

6. Priority of any lien or encumbrance over the lien of the insured mortgage, said mortgage being shown in Schedule B in the order of its priority; or

7. Invalidity of any assignment of the insured mortgage, provided such assignment is shown in Schedule B.

This Policy shall not be valid or binding until Schedule B is countersigned by an authorized officer or agent of the company.

IN WITNESS WHEREOF, THE SECURE TITLE INSURANCE CORPORATION has caused its corporate name and seal to be hereunto affixed by its duly authorized officers as of the date shown in Schedule A.

SECURE TITLE INSURANCE CORPORATION

By: *Jack Harper*
                President

Attest: *Russell Kennedy*
                 Secretary

Chart 8-1. Example of a title insurance policy

SCHEDULE A

PREMIUM___432.50_____   Case No.

Amount of Insurance: Date of Policy   Policy No.
$___100,000.00___   August 10, 20XX at   CAS-223346
                         8:00 A.M.

1. Name of Insured:

   BRUCE B. BUYER AND BARBARA A. BUYER

2. The state or interest in the land described herein and which is covered by this policy is:

   A FEE

3. The estate or interest referred to herein at Date of Policy vested in:

   BRUCE B. BUYER AND BARBARA A. BUYER, his wife as
   Joint Tenants

4. The land referred to in this policy is situated in the County of _Barrett_, State of
   _California___, and is described as follows:

   Lot 142, as shown upon that certain map entitled, "Map of
   Barrett Bay Unit One, Boonville, California," filed for record
   September 22, 1960 in Volume 10 of Maps, at page 78, Barrett
   County Records.

This policy is valid only if Schedule B is attached.

Chart 8-2. Example of title policy, schedule A

ments that might extend onto a neighbor's property; damage from the exercise of mineral rights; and mistaken location and dimensions of the property as disclosed in county records. These endorsements expand the coverage of the title insurance policy and are usually added without charge. Any other endorsements requested by the lender in his escrow instructions will be added by the title company, if they are insurable, and their costs will be charged to the borrower.

There are many other endorsements available, each suited to a particular situation or occurrence. As an example, say a zoning ordinance requires all houses to be set back 10 feet from the property boundary at the street and then, after escrow closes, the city discovers that your house is built only eight feet from the street. Should the city require this violation of its zoning ordinance be corrected, resulting in either moving the house two feet or cutting two feet off the front of the house, the situation would be covered if the lender had requested an endorsement to cover it. Another example would be unrecorded mechanic's liens filed after the homeowner has moved in. While the previous owner is responsible for paying the lien, there would be legal expenses involved in finding the previous owner and serving him with the papers. Special policy endorsements may be written to cover numerous situations where an insured desires special insurance against a particular risk, whether based on recorded or unrecorded matters.

Owners may insure themselves with extended coverage policies, too, the most common of which is the ALTA Owner's Policy. This policy insures against off-record matters, but it doesn't come cheap because it requires additional work, likely a physical inspection and maybe even a licensed surveyor's report.

How Much Insurance Will I Need?

You, the buyer, should have a policy for the full amount of the purchase price, whereas the lender needs a policy only for the amount of the loan. In other words, the buyer and lender need enough insurance to cover their individual financial commitments on the property.

Where a multi-policy insurance system is available, your lender will require you to obtain for them an ALTA policy for the amount of their loan, and you as buyer should obtain a CLTA policy for the amount of the purchase price of the property. If the purchase price were $100,000 and the loan amount were $80,000, then you would want a CLTA policy based on your purchase price of $100,000 and an ALTA policy based on your loan of $80,000. If the title company should later have to defend you in a court action, it would be responsible for bearing costs up to the amount paid for the property plus the allowable inflation percentages provided for in the policy.

A Typical Misunderstanding: The Hatfields bought a house for $100,000 and made a down payment of $20,000. Their lender required them to get a title insurance policy for $80,000, which they dutifully bought, but they decided against getting any coverage for themselves because they were trying to save some money and thought they'd never need title insurance themselves anyway.

The Way Things Really Are: When a relative of the previous owner showed up and presented a valid claim to their house only a month after the Hatfields moved in, the title company had to reimburse the lender for its loss. In the aftermath, the lender delivered the mortgage note to the title company and the Hatfields lost both their home and their equity and, because they hadn't covered themselves for the loss, they still owed the mortgage holder $80,000.

How Are Title Insurance Premiums Determined and How Frequently Is the Premium Paid?

Title insurance premiums are based strictly on the amount of coverage provided. The premium is paid only once, when the property is purchased or when its mortgage is refinanced.

Are All Rates Alike?

Title insurance fees are not all alike. They are not set by law. Each title company sets its own and then files them with the state insurance commissioner. Once they're filed, the company must adhere to those fees. Each state varies as to the amount of regulation involved with enforcing title insurance rates. You can look up the filing requirements for your state in the state-by-state guide to rate type and filing requirements located in Appendix B.

You will find by shopping around and making comparisons that fees vary up to $150 for exactly the same coverage from company to company, county to county, and state to state. Most buyers don't bother to shop for the best title insurance rates, however, because they are too busy shopping around for a favorable loan, rearranging their personal finances, or worrying about termite repairs. They don't even think about looking for a better title insurance rate. Try comparing rates the next time you have to pay for title insurance and you'll be amazed at the savings possible. You should also be aware that most title insurance companies offer a discounted rate (usually 20%) on property that has been sold or been insured within the previous two to five years. Check with your closing officer to see if your property qualifies for this discounted or "short-term" rate. If, for example, the basic rate for your title insurance is $550, the short-term, discounted rate would be $440, a savings of $110.

Are Title Insurance Rates the Same on New Construction?

Many title companies have a special rate for new construction. This rate is typically limited to builders only. When the builder applies for the ALTA Owner's Policy and it is to be issued in the amount of the full purchase price at the same

	Owners	Mortgage	Closing Fee	Title Exam	Update	Courier
$50,000	287.50	25.00	150.00	150.00	75.00	50.00
$55,000	318.25	25.00	150.00	150.00	75.00	50.00
$60,000	345.00	25.00	150.00	150.00	75.00	50.00
$65,000	373.75	25.00	150.00	150.00	75.00	50.00
$70,000	402.50	25.00	150.00	150.00	75.00	50.00
$75,000	431.25	25.00	150.00	150.00	75.00	50.00
$80,000	460.00	25.00	150.00	150.00	75.00	50.00
$85,000	488.75	25.00	150.00	150.00	75.00	50.00
$90,000	517.50	25.00	150.00	150.00	75.00	50.00
$95,000	548.25	25.00	150.00	150.00	75.00	50.00
$100,000	575.00	25.00	150.00	150.00	75.00	50.00
$105,000	625.00	25.00	175.00	175.00	75.00	50.00
$110,000	675.00	25.00	175.00	175.00	75.00	50.00
$115,000	725.00	25.00	175.00	175.00	75.00	50.00
$120,000	775.00	25.00	175.00	175.00	75.00	50.00
$125,000	825.00	25.00	175.00	175.00	75.00	50.00
$130,000	875.00	25.00	175.00	175.00	75.00	50.00
$135,000	925.00	25.00	175.00	175.00	75.00	50.00
$140,000	975.00	25.00	175.00	175.00	75.00	50.00
$145,000	1,025.00	25.00	175.00	175.00	75.00	50.00
$150,000	1,075.00	25.00	200.00	200.00	75.00	50.00
$155,000	1,200.00	25.00	200.00	200.00	75.00	50.00
$160,000	1,325.00	25.00	200.00	200.00	75.00	50.00
$165,000	1,575.00	25.00	225.00	225.00	75.00	50.00

Chart 8-3. Sample title insurance rate chart

time as the issuance of a lender's policy, the loan policy is charged at the full published rate, and not at the *simultaneous issue* or discounted rate, which is common practice in the purchase of an existing home. The buyer purchasing a home from a builder pays the full rate for the loan policy and the builder pays a special rate, typically $25.00 for the ALTA Owner's Policy.

Is There Any Other Way to Save on Title Insurance?

There is still another way to save on title insurance that you ought to know about. If you expect to resell your property within a few years following your purchase, you may have the entire CLTA title insurance premium refunded to you, so long as you choose to buy a *binder* policy of title insurance when you buy the property. The cost of this binder policy is 10% of the basic title insurance rate, but you will have to pay for both the binder and the standard policy when you buy the property and, if you fail to sell within the time limit specified in the binder, usually two to five years, you will lose the amount you have paid for the binder.

If the basic title insurance premium for a property were $550, for example, you would have to pay an extra $55 for the binder, or a total of $605. You would then receive a refund of $550 when you sold the property and the title insurance company would keep only the $55. Should you keep the property longer than the binder period, though, you would not qualify for a refund. So, if you stayed you would lose only 10% of the amount of the title insurance policy, but if you sold you would gain 100% of the amount of the policy—a pretty good gamble if you think you would qualify.

Use of a binder does not dilute the policy in any way, but your buyer would have to buy a title insurance policy from the same company you used.

What Should I Look for in My Title Insurance Policy?

Be certain you check to see that the policy amount is correct and that the date given on the policy is, in fact, the escrow's actual closing date, for this is the date when the policy becomes effective. Verify that the policy describes all of the property and all of the interests being acquired. If the buyer thought, for example, that he were buying two lots but the deed covered only one and the title policy described only that one, the title insurer would have no liability.

What Is the Torrens Title System?

A few parts of the country, fewer than 1%, use a different system of guaranteeing title to real property. Under this system, called the Torrens Title System, the county recorder maintains a record of all encumbrances that exist on the title to each piece of property in the county. Before a piece of land can be sold or mortgaged, the buyer and seller must go to court for a hearing. The county recorder sends a notice of the hearing to anybody who, according to the county records, could possibly have a claim against the title. Anybody with a claim must sue to have his claim settled before title is passed to the buyer. The court dismisses or settles all the claims, orders the title to be registered in the buyer's name, and issues the new owner a Torrens certificate, which lists any liens and encumbrances against the title. Once a Torrens certificate is issued, the title is declared marketable and no undisclosed defects can be used later to cause a loss of title.

Grant Deeds and Quitclaim Deeds

In most states, deeds are either *grant* or *quitclaim*. In a grant deed, the seller (grantor) states that he owns the property and that there are no liens, loans, or easements on the property other than those that he has told you about. In a quitclaim deed, the grantor conveys whatever interest he may have in a property without making any guarantees regarding liens, loans, or easements. If the seller has full title, the buyer will get full title. If he has nothing, the buyer will get nothing.

Whenever you buy real property, never accept a quitclaim deed as the sole transfer device. Someone could legally sell you his nonexistent interest in the Brooklyn Bridge, the Golden Gate Bridge, or the Pacific Ocean with such a deed. These deeds are commonly used only to eliminate a minor interest in a property.

Although most community-property states do have quitclaim deeds, not all states do. In community property states (Arizona, California, Idaho, Louisiana, Nevada, New Mexico, Texas, and Washington), husband and wife jointly own all assets acquired during marriage regardless of whose name is on the grant deed. If you want to hold property as your *sole and separate property* in any of these eight states, you should always obtain a quitclaim deed from your spouse to prevent a claim from being made later by your spouse.

Don't become as confused about quitclaim deeds as those many people who have asked me to execute a "quick-claim" deed for them, believing it to be a sort of hurry-up deed. It may be quick, but that has nothing to do with its name. "Quitclaim" simply means to be quit or rid of any claim on a property. That's all.

What Is a Warranty Deed?

Warranty deeds, widely used in the Eastern and Midwestern states (see Appendix B), define their warranties in explicit terms rather than implying them according to prevailing law. The grantors warrant that they have the lawful authority to sell and that the property is free of all encumbrances. They also agree that they will "defend the title against the just and lawful claims of all persons." Title insurance is available under a warranty deed in the same manner as any other type of deed.

How Do Condominiums and Cooperatives Differ and Do Co-Op Shareholders Buy Title Insurance?

Because co-op shareholders do not have deeds to their individual units, they do not buy title insurance nor do they generally go through escrow, although they could certainly go through escrow if they wanted to.

For income tax purposes, the IRS treats co-op owners just like the owners of condos and single-family homes. Co-op owners may deduct their portion of the property taxes and mortgage interest paid by the corporation as a whole.

TIP Many condominium developments require an approval by the condominium board before the transfer from seller to buyer can take place. Oftentimes, the new buyer must be interviewed by the board and the purchase agreement approved. Your closing agent may require a *resale certificate* or copy of the board's approval.

Is Title Insurance Available for Mobile Homes?

Title insurance is not available for mobile homes. Even though they may be on the property tax rolls and sell for more than so-called "stick-built" single-family dwellings, mobile homes are still considered *personal* property rather than *real* property.

In California, the Department of Housing and Community Development (HCD) looks after mobile home titles. Once this department searches the title and finds it clear, and it will do so for a fee of $25, the title is considered clear and marketable.

Whereas buyers and sellers can handle mobile home ownership transfers themselves, increasingly they call upon escrow companies to do the work for them, especially when the mobile homes are of any consequential value. Escrow companies charge a basic fee of approximately $300 for their services plus $25 for the HCD title search. For this sum they will order the title search, get a valid Certificate of Title and a Certificate of Retail Value, insure that all the taxes and fees are paid, and handle the transfer of funds and paperwork between the buyer and seller.

Incidentally, new mobile homes are all on the property tax rolls. Older ones may or may not be. Owners of those that are on the property tax rolls pay local property tax based upon the sales price of the mobile home. Owners of mobile homes not on the property tax rolls pay annual registration fees based upon the "shell" or Blue Book value, rather than on the actual purchase price. To find out which kind of taxation arrangement applies to a particular mobile home, look at the serial number on the mobile home's decal. Those beginning with the letter "L" are on the property tax rolls; those beginning with the letter "A" are not.

Here's a final item of some interest to anyone buying or selling a mobile home. Although mobile homes on the property tax rolls tend to have slightly higher annual tax bills than those that aren't on the rolls, they are not subject to *use tax* upon transfer of ownership. Sellers of mobile homes that are not on the property tax rolls should weigh the consequences of shifting their mobile homes to the property tax rolls just prior to selling, so the buyers can avoid having to pay a steep use tax on the transaction. Let's say that somebody is selling a 20-year-old mobile home for $10,000, with an annual registration fee of $78. The use tax due upon sale would be $825 (in areas where the sales tax is 8.25%). If transferred to the tax rolls, the mobile home would incur an annual property tax bill of $100, but there would be no use tax due upon sale!

What Is Time-Share Ownership and How Does the Time-Share Buyer Get Legal Claim?

Time-sharing or interval ownership, as it is also called, is a means for purchasing a portion of a house or condominium together with other people. Each owner buys a share based upon time.

Commonly, each time-share unit has 52 shares, corresponding to the 52 weeks in a year, each share being for one specific week per year. The price of each share is determined by the type of dwelling and by the demand for a particular time; in Palm Beach, Florida, and Palm Springs, California, for example, shares during

January and February are more desirable than those during July and August and hence command premium prices.

Just as with ordinary real estate, the time-share buyer gets a grant deed and may obtain title insurance. The time-share buyer may also finance the unit with a down payment, typically 30%, and a loan for the balance and, if he or she should default on the loan, the lender would have the right to foreclose. Sounds familiar, doesn't it?

Each time-share owner becomes a member of an interval ownership association, such as Resort Condominiums International. RCI maintains a database of time-share properties throughout the world and assists in time-share exchanges, travel services, and hotel arrangements. You can visit RCI at their Web site, **www.rci.com**, or call them at 1-800-338-7777.

Should you be inclined to become a time-share buyer, remember that time-shares are not investments. The properties involved, if sold as a whole, would not be worth nearly as much as the sum of the 52 shares. Very few buyers ever sell their shares at a profit. Sometimes they cannot resell their shares at all. Essentially what you are doing when you buy a time-share is something quite different from what you would be doing if you were buying an ordinary piece of real estate. As a time-share buyer, you are locking in a price for your future vacations. That's all, pure and simple.

Chapter Nine

Adjustments to the Final Selling Process: Debits, Credits, and Prorations

By now you should have a reasonable grasp of what's involved in obtaining financing, searching the title, and securing title insurance, as well as how to distinguish the four basic ways of taking title. If so, you have acquired the basics of escrow.

If you should happen to forget what you've learned here or if you should ever have any questions or doubts about your own closing, do see your escrow or closing officer. She is there to help you and, besides, you are paying for her services through part of your escrow fees, whether you use her help or not.

How Can I Figure Out Who Owes What at Closing?

You might think that you would have to be an accountant or at the very least a bookkeeper to understand all the calculations used in a closing, but you don't have to be. You just need to have a basic comprehension of the various charges you will be obliged to pay. You should know why you have to pay each charge, how much you have to pay, and when you will have to pay it.

These most important figures are in your closing instructions and will appear as columns of numbers related to *debits*, *credits*, and *prorations*—three words that are important to a full understanding of closing. They are important because, whether you're a buyer or a seller, you will be asked to sign various documents, such as closing escrow instructions, loan documents, and deeds and, when you sign them, not only are you agreeing with your escrow officer's instructions for disbursing the monies, but you are agreeing with the correctness of her escrow figures as well. Therefore, it's doubly important to understand those three words.

■ *Debit* is money you owe, an amount you will be charged in escrow; it's an item you must pay for; it's money that's coming out of your pocket.

■ *Credit* is money owed to you, an amount paid to your account in escrow; it's a sum that the other party must pay you for something; it's money that's going into your pocket.

■ *Proration* is a division of a debit or a credit, that is, to divide a charge that has been paid in advance or is due to be paid in arrears.

Whenever you look at a closing statement instruction sheet, be sure to glance at the bottom and make sure that the debit and credit totals equal each other. If they don't, there's something wrong, for the two must balance to the penny. It's a good idea to do your own addition and subtraction of the columns, too, for escrow officers have been known to force a balance.

Buyer's Scale		Seller's Scale	
Debits	**Credits**	**Debits**	**Credits**
▪ purchase price ▪ title insurance ▪ escrow fee ▪ fire insurance ▪ prorations ▪ termite inspection fee ▪ recording fees	▪ deposits ▪ loans ▪ prorations ▪ miscellaneous	▪ old loan payoffs ▪ escrow fees ▪ prorations ▪ reconveyance fees ▪ transfer tax ▪ sales commission ▪ home warranty insurance premium	▪ sales price ▪ proration ▪ miscellaneous

Chart 9-1. Possible closing costs

Remember that the party who pays the various fees and taxes will vary from state to state and from geographical area to geographical area (see Appendix B). Local custom determines who pays for which items at the day of closing.

> Remember that many closing costs associated with your purchase or sale may be negotiable. Refer to the chart of "Negotiable and Non-Negotiable Closing Costs" in Chapter 6.

Before signing your closing instructions, be sure to verify that what you have been charged is what you were told in the beginning that you would have to pay. If the termite report was originally quoted at $100, see that it is, in fact, $100. Take the checklist at the end of Chapter Eleven and check off each item to be sure that the charges are what you expected and that everything else is as agreed upon before. You should know before escrow closes how much you will be expected to pay and you should check that you actually receive what you are paying for.

How Do Prorations Work?

While debits and credits are pretty straightforward and understandable, prorations tend to confuse people. Yet, prorations are not as complex as they may seem at first. They're really not difficult to understand or to compute either, so long as you think of them merely as dividing up an item of expense according to some definite date.

Prorations apply to any charges that one party or the other may have incurred in advance of the property's sale, charges that cover a period of time following the sale. Such things as property taxes, fire insurance premiums, rents, maintenance charges on condominiums, interest on loans, and impound accounts all might be prorated in escrow in the interest of fairness to both parties. They are either paid in advance by the seller, necessitating a credit due him for the period the buyer will own the property from close of escrow to the date of the next payment due, or paid after the sale by the buyer, thus necessitating a credit due him for the period of time the seller owned the property. Those sums have to be adjusted; prorations do the adjusting.

After you have mastered one proration, you will be able to use the same formula for any item you want to prorate. Let's try one involving taxes.

For any proration, you will have to know two dates, the date you will prorate from and the date you will prorate to. (Be sure you check the instructions. Which word do they use—"to" or "through"? There's an important difference. If the instructions say to prorate "from January 1 to January 10," the prorations would cover nine days. If they say prorate "from January 1 through January 10," the prorations would cover 10 days.) The most common date used for computing prorations is the date of close of escrow (COE), which is usually the date when documents are recorded and the actual change of ownership occurs.

All escrow prorations are normally based on a 30-day month, except for interest, which is based instead on the actual number of days you are using to compute your calculations.

Let's say in our example that you are assuming ownership of a property on August 10 and the first property tax installment is $130.56 and you want to figure out the prorations for both the buyer and the seller.

To begin with, we should take a look at property taxes as a whole, as they are commonly figured in one state, say California. When we do, we find that taxes become an outstanding debt against property on the first day of January, even though they are not payable until considerably later. The full fiscal year for property taxes runs from July 1 to June 30 and it is divided into halves so that payments may be made in two installments. The first tax installment covers the six-month period from July 1 to December 31; it is due on November 1 and is delinquent on

December 10, after which time a penalty is added. The second installment covers the six-month period from January 1 to June 30; it is due on February 1 and becomes delinquent on April 10.

Property taxes have priority over any mortgage or deed of trust or any lien or encumbrance except other taxes. Most mortgages and deeds of trust, therefore, have provisions to the effect that the failure to pay taxes when due can cause a default and give grounds for foreclosure. Assessment bonds and other taxes create a lien or encumbrance against a property also and, like property taxes, have priority over any deed of trust.

Should an owner fail to pay property taxes by the delinquent dates (December 10 or April 10), the property will be given a tax sale number and placed on the delinquent tax roll published once a year on June 30. After publication of this list, the owner has five years in which to pay the delinquent taxes, including penalties and interest. If he doesn't pay after five years, the state will auction off the property.

Now let's get back to our example. The first property tax installment is $130.56 and the close of escrow is August 10. The first thing we must do to determine the buyer's and seller's tax prorations is figure how much the taxes are per day and, to do that, we figure out the taxes per month by dividing $130.56 (six months' taxes) by six. That figure is $21.76. Then we divide $21.76 by 30 days, and get $0.72. Those math whizzes who liked to do word problems when they were in school and who want to skip steps can use another, more direct, way to calculate the taxes per day by dividing $130.56 by 180, which is the accepted number of days in a half year for calculating tax prorations. Either way you figure it, the answer is still the same, $0.72, after you round down to the nearest cent.

Using that figure, you can calculate the property tax proration as follows. Since you, the buyer, take ownership on August 10, you are liable for property taxes until the date they're due and you will be making the payment for those taxes sometime between November 1 and December 10, but the seller is liable from July 1 through August 10, a period of 40 days or one month and 10 days. The seller must therefore credit you, the buyer, with that much in taxes, a total of $28.80. It will be credited to you on the escrow instructions and debited to him, the seller. On the escrow instructions, it looks like this:

	DEBIT	CREDIT
Buyer - Prorata Taxes 7/1 - 8/10	$28.80	
Seller - Prorata Taxes 7/1 - 8/10		$28.80

Note that often the prior year's tax bill has to be used as a basis for prorating the next fiscal year's taxes because there is no new tax bill available. When such is the case, it will be stated on your escrow instructions. Also, if the tax bill has already been mailed out, be sure to ask the seller or your escrow officer to get it for you, because as the new owner you will be responsible for paying the property taxes whether you receive the bill or not. In some states it is common to collect an extra amount from the sellers in order to provide for any rise in property taxes that may have occurred after closing, due to the fact that the exact amount for the next tax bill may not be known at the time of closing. Instead of collecting the daily prorated fee, the buyer may ask that the seller place 100% of the daily fee to cover any increase.

How Is Interest Prorated?

Interest generally is not paid in advance, but in arrears, that is, an August 1 mortgage payment pays for July's interest. This means that when you, the buyer or new owner, make the payment due September 1, you are actually paying interest for the month of August. Should a buyer take over the seller's existing loan either as an assumption or a subject-to, the interest must be prorated. Since interest is usually paid monthly as it accrues, the buyer will be credited and the seller debited for that portion of the month when the seller owned the property and paid the interest on it.

Now, if escrow closes on the August 10, you (the buyer) didn't own the house for the first 10 days of the month, so you should be credited for those 10 days. The interest is prorated, meaning that the seller must pay you for those 10 days. A seller can conserve his cash if the closing is scheduled before a monthly mortgage payment falls due because the buyer will pay it all for him at closing. On the closing instructions, a proration would look like this:

	DEBIT	CREDIT
Buyer - Interest on Existing Loan 8/1 - 8/10	$XXX.XX	
Seller - Interest on Existing Loan 8/1 - 8/10		$XXX.XX

How Are Rents Prorated?

If you are buying an income property that already has tenants, the seller must credit you for the rents that he has collected or should have collected for the month. If the rents are all due August 1, the seller must credit you (the buyer), whether or not he has collected those rents by the time escrow closes, for rents covering the period August 10 through August 30, assuming once again that escrow is closing August 10. In addition, all the advance rent and security/cleaning deposits the seller has collected from his tenants must be credited to you as well and you become responsible for them. Make sure there is a *rent and deposit schedule* attached to your escrow instructions that shows the unit number, amount of rent and when last paid, rental due date, and deposits paid.

The seller of an income property should provide you, the buyer, with all the leases or rental agreements currently in force along with a written assignment assigning the rents to you, the new owner. Get these papers, through your escrow officer or directly from the seller, and you will save yourself considerable grief later.

You should know that in an income property transaction the buyer has an advantage in closing escrow on a date after most of the rents are due because the buyer does not then have to bother collecting those rents and the amount of cash the buyer needs to close escrow will be reduced by the amount of rent credited. In most cases, what this means is that the buyer has an advantage in closing escrow a few days after the first of the month, whereas the seller has an advantage in closing escrow a few days before the first of the month.

Here is an example of one rent schedule:

Rent Statement In order that rents for the property I am conveying may be correctly prorated, I hereby state that the rentals as to amounts and dates to which they are paid are as follows:						
				Credit Buyer		
House/Apt No.	**Tenant's Name**	**Monthly Rent**	**Date Paid to**	**Last Mo Rent**	**Deposits**	**Pro-Rata Amount**
1	Smith	$300	Sept. 1		$150	$200.00
2	Jones	$200	Sept. 5		$200	$166.67
3	Appleby	$375	Aug. 15		$250	$52.50
			Totals:		$600	$429.17

Chart 9-2. Example of rent statement

How Is Fire Insurance Prorated?

Fire insurance policies are usually written for either a one-year or a three-year period. They may be paid in full in advance, on a percentage basis spread out over three years, or monthly. However they are paid, they are usually ahead when a property is being sold and goes through escrow, so the seller is entitled to be compensated for the prepayment, either directly from his insurance company or through escrow. Because most buyers prefer to secure their own fire insurance policies, it is not all that often that a buyer assumes the existing policy; however, if that happens, the premium must be prorated.

Prorate fire insurance premiums as you prorate property taxes. You must first figure the cost of the insurance per day before you can calculate each party's share. Let's figure an example where the policy's inception date is August 1, the policy period is 36 months, the premium was paid last year for the entire 36 months, and the premium is $235 per year. We first divide $235 by 12 months, to get $19.58, and then divide $19.58 by 30 days, to get the per-day rate of $0.65. If escrow closes August 10 and the policy is paid for almost two more years, the buyer would credit the seller for two years (2 x $235) less 10 days ($6.50), for a total of $463.50. That's all there is to it.

Naturally you should be sure to get an assignment from the fire insurance company, naming you as an insured party on the policy.

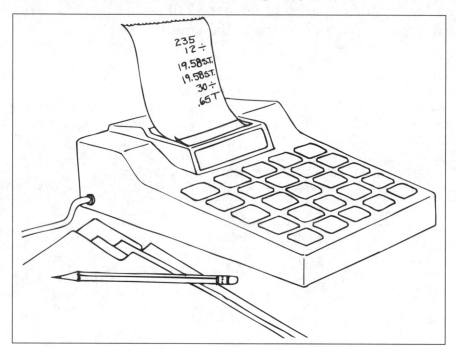

How Are Maintenance Charges and Homeowner's Dues Prorated?

This kind of proration applies generally if you are buying a unit in a planned development, condominium, or cooperative that has a homeowners' association that collects assessments from each unit to cover common expenses, such as maintaining parking lots, grounds, and swimming pools.

These association dues are usually paid monthly, so they, too, will have to be adjusted to debit or credit the buyer and seller according to the period for which they were last paid. For example, if the monthly maintenance dues are $65 and they are due on the first of each month and the seller has already paid them, then when escrow closes on August 10, the buyer, who will own the property 20 days during that month, will be debited for $43.20 (20 days at $2.16 per day) and the seller will be credited for a like amount on his escrow instructions.

How Is an Impound Account Adjusted?

An *impound account* is a sum collected in advance by some lenders and held as a deposit for such things as property taxes and fire insurance premiums. Any existing balance is normally refundable when the loan is paid off. If there is an impound account involved in a transaction, it is adjusted if the new buyer is assuming both the existing loan and the impound account balance as well. If the seller has paid these advance deposits to the lender and they have not been used for taxes or insurance, the seller must be reimbursed because the buyer is also assuming the responsibility to provide an impound account. Strictly speaking, this is not a proration, since it doesn't divide something that has been partly used up. It is more like a savings account, which transfers ownership along with the property. The seller is simply credited for the amount of the impound account and the buyer is debited for that same amount.

What Is a Documentary Transfer Tax and How Is It Calculated?

In many areas the seller must pay a *transfer tax*. Years ago this tax was evidenced by actual stamps affixed to the grant deed. Today, although the stamps themselves are no longer used, the term *documentary stamps* is still used for the tax. Nowadays the transfer tax is generally stated on the deed by the dollar amount only.

The transfer tax is a percentage of the sales price. It varies widely, not only from city to city and county to county, but also from state to state, and it may range from a low of $50 to a high of $300 or even sometimes more. Your escrow officer can tell you what the rate is in your area.

When Are Real Estate Commissions Earned and How Are They Handled in the Closing?

As a general rule, an agent has earned his commission when he has found a buyer who is ready, willing, and able to buy a property on the exact terms of the listing agreement or on terms acceptable to the seller. The agent is usually entitled to his commission regardless of whether the sale is ever completed. Once the agent has found that willing and able buyer, he may sue the seller to get his commission if the seller changes his mind and decides not to sell the property.

A Typical Misunderstanding: Tom and Evelyn decide that their real estate agent really didn't do that much work to sell their house. The day after they listed it, the agent brought someone over to look at it, who then bought the place for the asking price. They decide that they just won't pay him his full commission because he didn't really do much to earn it.

The Way Things Really Are: Tom and Evelyn's agent has the legal right to collect his full commission so long as he has met the terms of the listing and purchasing agreements. They should be happy that he sold their house so quickly and got the full price they wanted for it.

Fortunately for them, agents seldom have to sue to get their commissions. They get paid through escrow, whether the commission is a stipulated dollar amount or a percentage of the sales price.

Most real estate firms charge a standard percentage of the purchase price as their commission, usually 6% for houses and 10% for raw land, and they use the same percentage for every similar property no matter what it sells for. Don't be afraid to discuss this commission percentage with your agent because some agents are flexible. The right time to discuss it, however, is not when escrow is about to close and the agent has already done most of his work. The right time to discuss it is when the property is listed, though you might want to negotiate who's going to pay the commission when you and the buyer are still talking price and terms, that is, before you open escrow. Typically, the seller pays the entire real estate commission, but sometimes seller and buyer each pay half.

If there's only one agent representing both seller and buyer, often referred to as a *transactional broker* or a *dual agent*, you might want to ask the agent whether he will reduce his commission somewhat, say, by 1%. Some will. Some won't. You won't know unless you ask.

When two agents are involved, one representing the buyer and one representing the seller, and they are splitting the commission right down the middle, you can't expect any concessions unless there are some pretty unusual circumstances. Here's an example. Let's say your listing was about to expire and the listing agent had done little but put your house in the multiple-listing book. You found the buyer yourself by telling a fellow church member you were trying to sell your house. You showed it to him after church and he made an acceptable offer through his brother-in-law, who's a real estate agent. That's unusual enough for you to expect a commission concession.

Remember that agents are not compelled by law to charge any specific commission percentage. They can be flexible, and sometimes they will be. Just don't expect them to be flexible late in the game. Settle on their commission before you ever open escrow. To avoid any confusion, explain the exact terms of the commission to your closing officer when you open escrow. The escrow officer needs to know precisely who is to be paid what, when, and how.

By the way, whenever you sign a listing agreement with a real estate agent, be sure you understand all the terms and conditions with which you must comply. They are legally binding.

 Under no circumstances will your closing officer pay the sales commission to the real estate agent before the close of escrow. When it is paid, it will be paid to the agent's office, not to the agent directly.

Chapter Ten

Handling Tax-Deferred Exchanges

I n this chapter I'll discuss the details of exchanges, where the buyer and seller transfer property between them, sometimes with the help of a mediator or *accommodator*. I'll address third-party exchanges, delayed exchanges, and the tax benefits of these transactions.

How Do Exchanges Work? Who Benefits from Exchanges? And How Are Their Escrow Closing Instructions Drafted?

Whereas a *sale* is the transfer of property for money or the promise to pay money, an *exchange* is the transfer of property in return for other property, with perhaps some money changing hands to balance the exchange. These balancing funds are called *boot*.

An exchange may be a simple transfer of properties between two parties as follows. Appleby is tired of all the hassles in running an apartment building and wants to trade it for some raw land, and Bartleby is tired of holding onto his raw land, which yields no income, and wants to trade his equity for an apartment building that does yield income, so the two parties arrange to trade their properties.

Two-way exchanges such as this occur sometimes, but far less frequently than exchanges involving three or more parties, because locating a property owner who wants to trade his property for yours can be very difficult. Therefore, the parties who want to do an exchange often agree to participate in a three-way exchange, with three or more parties involved, one of whom brings cash into the exchange and one of whom takes cash out.

Here's the way a three-way exchange works. Abbott wants to exchange his property for a property owned by Barnes, but Barnes doesn't want Abbott's property. Barnes wants to get cash out of his property, although he says that he will participate in a three-way exchange in order to get the cash he wants. Cole wants Abbott's property and he can meet all of the terms specified by Abbott.

They put the exchange together in three steps: Abbott deeds his property to Barnes, Barnes deeds his property to Abbott, and Barnes deeds Abbott's property to Cole in exchange for cash and/or a promise of money. As a result of this three-way exchange, Abbott gets Barnes' property, Barnes gets cash and/or notes, and Cole gets Abbott's property. Everyone achieves his objective.

Sellers are the ones who really benefit from exchanges, because they can avoid having to pay tax on whatever capital gain results from the sale of their property. IRS Section 1031, Tax-Free Exchanges, keeps sellers' capital intact for further investment. (Some people insist upon calling these exchanges tax-*deferred*. However, because the exchanger never pays any capital gains taxes, so long as he receives no boot and he continues exchanging his equity until he dies, exchanges really are tax-*free*.)

> **A Typical Misunderstanding:** Tom is delighted. He bought a fancy duplex six years ago for $200,000 and now he's selling it for $600,000. He's planning to do a 1031 exchange into another nice duplex, which is costing him $450,000. He's going to take his $150,000 profit, buy himself a Porsche, and take a leisurely tour of Europe.

> **The Way Things Really Are:** If Tom chooses to take the $150,000 cash (boot) out of the exchange, he had better not spend all of it because he's going to have to pay taxes on it. Before you dispose of any real estate, consult an accountant or tax attorney about your options and the tax consequences of each. Make sure that one of those options is exchanging, for whenever you move equity from one investment property to another, you can realize a significant tax advantage by exchanging.

Your accountant or attorney can explain the conditions that must be met in order for either a principal residence or an income property to qualify in an exchange. For escrow purposes, though, we are concerned about only two things:

- Make sure that the properties are of like kind, that is, that you are exchanging real property for real property and not personal property for real property. (An apartment house may be exchanged for an office building, but a piece of machinery may not be exchanged for an office building.) You are allowed to exchange real property for a 30-year or longer lease on another piece of property.

- Close and record the transactions on the same day or within a reasonable time span. (Often the properties involved in an exchange are located in different counties, even in different states, and closing the escrows concurrently, which is the general escrow practice, takes a fair amount of coordination. However, concurrent closing is generally necessary for the exchange to qualify under Section 1031, unless the exchange is specifically set up to be delayed. More about delayed exchanges in a moment.)

The closing for a three-way exchange involves some extra paperwork. Here's how it works. Abbott signs a set of exchange instructions in which he relinquishes title to his property and acquires title to Barnes' property, Barnes signs exchange instructions relinquishing title to his property and receives money or a note and the deed to Abbott's original property, Barnes also signs seller's instructions deeding Abbott's property to Cole, and Cole signs buyer's instructions and acquires title to Abbott's former property.

This method of handling a three-way exchange is called *serial deeding* and up until April 1991, it was the only safe way to structure the deeding. Now there's another method, called *direct deeding*, which enables the seller to deed directly to the exchanger or buyer. Direct deeding originated as a method to circumvent certain complications of serial deeding, such as double transfer taxes and hazardous materials liability assumed by every owner of record.

Direct deeding is becoming more widespread, but it has some exacting requirements. All parties must agree to the direct deeding method. The escrow instructions must state that direct deeding is being used. If there's an institutional lender involved, it must approve the direct deeding method before the escrow instructions are drawn up. To sort out which method would work best for your exchange, ask your escrow officer for help.

> **TIP**
>
> For income tax purposes, real estate is divided into four classifications: real estate held for personal use, real estate held for use in a trade or business, real estate held for investment, and real estate held primarily for sale to customers in the ordinary course of business. Real estate held for both business and investment qualifies for a 1031 tax-deferred exchange. Real estate held for personal use would not qualify. To qualify for 1031 treatment, both the property you trade and the replacement property must qualify. To qualify for 1031 exchange benefits, you must actually own the relinquished property and you must acquire ownership of the replacement property. For example, a partnership-owned building could not be exchanged for a building that is to be deeded directly to only some of the limited partners.

Can Any Closing Officer Handle an Exchange?

By now many closing officers have had experience handling exchanges and should be able to handle one competently. Exchanges are pretty commonplace nowadays, especially in the Western U.S.

Nonetheless, you should ask your closing officer whether she has ever handled an exchange before and whether she has any doubts about her ability to handle yours. If she hesitates, ask to talk with someone who has the experience you feel you need. Most every title and escrow company has somebody who specializes in exchanges.

A Typical Misunderstanding: Adele is exchanging a property in Los Angeles for one in Sacramento and she figures that, because an exchange is so complex, she'd better hire an attorney to draft the escrow instructions and help her sort out all the details.

The Way Things Really Are: Escrow companies have preprinted exchange instruction forms that will fit almost any property exchange. They also have an escrow officer who is proficient in handling exchanges. If the escrow officer believes that Adele needs an attorney, the officer will recommend that she secure one.

What's a Delayed Exchange? What's the Starker Case?

A *delayed exchange* is a three-way exchange in which the properties close at different times. Delayed exchanges occur when an exchanger hasn't found a property to exchange into but still wants the tax advantage of exchanging. He must leave the proceeds of the first part of his exchange in escrow as he continues looking for his exchange property. He doesn't have the right to touch those funds. If he were to touch them, that is, get what the tax law calls *constructive receipt* of the sales proceeds, it would automatically disqualify the tax-free exchange.

A Typical Misunderstanding: Gary and Lyndy want to exchange their rental property in Lompoc for a rental property in Santa Barbara. They have found a buyer for the Lompoc house, but they haven't yet been able to find a suitable Santa Barbara property. They feel they can't put their buyer off any longer. Either they'll have to cancel the deal or they'll have to try getting their buyer to wait until they can find another property.

The Way Things Really Are: Gary and Lyndy may leave their sales proceeds from the Lompoc house in a special escrow while they look for another property. They have 45 days after closing on the house to identify the new property and they have 180 days to close escrow on it.

The Starker decision, the Tax Reform Act of 1984 (yes, there was a Tax Reform Act of 1984; it put time limits on delayed exchanges and gave them legal recognition), and the IRS regulations issued in 1991 gave guidelines for legally acceptable delayed exchanges. Year after year, such exchanges have become more formalized and more commonplace.

The case of T.J. Starker v. United States involved a taxpayer who agreed in 1967 to convey certain of his real property to Crown Zellerbach Corporation in exchange for certain other properties that hadn't yet been identified. The parties agreed on the value of Starker's property in April 1967 and he conveyed the property to Crown at that time. Instead of getting any cash for his property, though, Starker accepted credits on Crown's books with the proviso that he would have until April 1972 to accept properties from them of equivalent value. If any balance remained in his account then, he would receive it in cash. Over a three-month period, Crown conveyed properties to Starker that were of equivalent value and he received no proceeds in cash. Although the parcels Starker selected were not owned by Crown when they originally entered into their agreement, the court determined that Starker never received any cash in lieu of property and therefore the transaction did indeed qualify as an exchange under Section 1031. Thus the court found delayed exchanges, or what it called "non-simultaneous," qualified for tax deferral.

This decision has had a profound and substantial effect on the real estate market and on the tax planning involved in disposing of investment property. And, wonder of wonders, the dreaded Tax Reform Act of 1986, which dealt some brutal body blows to real estate investors, did nothing to diminish the significant tax advantages of the delayed three-way exchange.

There are now formal guidelines that exchanges must follow in order to qualify for 1031 benefits. They're relatively simple, but they must be followed to the letter.

The property to be acquired must be designated within 45 days following the disposition of the other property and must close escrow within 180 days or by the due date (including extensions) of the tax return covering the year of the disposition, whichever comes first. (You will have to file an automatic tax return extension request to get the full 180 days if you close on the old property after mid-October.) The designated replacement property must be submitted in writing and the property unambiguously described. You can choose one of three approved methods:

- The Three Property Rule: three properties, no matter what their value
- The 200% Rule: any number of properties, as long as their combined fair market value does not exceed 200% of the fair market value of all relinquished property
- The 95% Rule: any number of properties no matter what the aggregate fair market value, provided 95% of the identified properties are acquired

The sales proceeds must be held by a third-party intermediary, such as an attorney or a bank trust department or an *accommodator*. You may not put the funds into a separate bank account or take possession of them until the exchange is complete, but you may get funds directly from the buyer to pay the expenses of the sale, such as real estate commissions, third-party guarantees, mortgages, or letters of credit securing the buyer's obligation for transferring the replacement property.

Your closing officer cannot act as your *agent* in a delayed exchange.

Whether your tax-free exchange is delayed or concurrent, the IRS wants you to spell out the details and the *intent* of the parties involved. To do so, include in the various purchase agreements the following statement: "This transaction is intended to be a Section 1031 EXCHANGE."

To learn more about delayed exchanges specifically, see *How to Do a Delayed Exchange*, by John T. Reed (John T. Reed Publishing, 342 Bryan Drive, Alamo, CA 94507, 925-820-7262, **www.johntreed.com**). You may also want to look on the Web sites of Realty Exchangers, Inc., **www.1031help.com**, or National Exchange Service Group, LLC, **www.exchangeservice.com**. Both sites provide general and specific information on the requirements of a 1031 tax-deferred exchange.

TIP

If you choose to take some of the proceeds from your tax-deferred exchange, you may do so only after you have acquired all of the properties identified in your 45-day identification period. If you do not acquire all of the properties identified in the 45 days, then the unused proceeds cannot be released until the earlier of the due date of your tax return, including extensions, or 180 days after the close of the sale of the relinquished or exchanged property. You will be taxed on the amount you don't use in the exchange. These unused proceeds are referred to as *boot* and are taxed on their face value at the capital gains tax rate.

May I Acquire a New Property and Set Up an Exchange Before I Have a Buyer for My Old Property?

You may indeed acquire a new property and set up an exchange before you find a buyer for your old property. Such an arrangement is called a *reverse delayed exchange*. (For specific IRS guidelines, see Revenue Procedure 2000-37.) Make sure that the sales contract you use in this situation refers to a *contemplated exchange* or a *contemplated disposition* of the old property at some future time and that it says the seller of the new property agrees to participate in the exchange.

In order to make a reverse delayed exchange work smoothly; some investors use an *accommodator*. This person or legal entity takes title either to the investor's old property or to the new property until a buyer surfaces for the old property. Here's how each of the two possible scenarios works:

1. The accommodator "buys" the new property and exchanges it for the investor's old property. Then he "sells" the old property whenever possible, without worrying about time limits, and the parties settle up.

2. The accommodator "buys" the new property and holds onto it until the investor finds a buyer for the old property. Then the investor, the buyer, and the accommodator execute the exchange so that the investor gets the new property, the buyer gets the old property, and the accommodator gets a flat-rate fee or a percentage commission for services rendered.

Of course, the accommodator never puts any money into these transactions. He, she, or it uses the investor's money and takes title in name only just to accommodate the investor's exchange. Because the accommodator could sour everything by absconding with funds or going broke, take care to find one that is entirely trustworthy.

What Is an Improvement Exchange?

An improvement exchange may be involved during a construction or custom building project and will allow an investor to use exchange proceeds to either make improvements to an existing property or to build a new replacement property. This regulation allows you to exchange your property for property that has not yet been built. The transfer will still qualify under Section 1031 if the new construction is identified within the 45-day period and received within the 180-day exchange period. The property must be carefully identified; this identification should include the legal description of the ground and as much other description as possible for the property to be constructed.

This exchange technique allows the investor to purchase properties needing renovation or to acquire bare land and to build to the investor's exact specifications. A *qualified intermediary* makes improvements to the replacement property during the exchange period and transfers the improved property back to the exchanger by the 180th day. With an improved exchange, careful planning is necessary to allow for normal construction delays that could occur. The needed improvements or construction must be completed within the 180-day exchange period.

There are two ways in which new construction may be handled in an exchange:

1. You can contract with a builder to purchase a property that will be completed and ready to close prior to the end of the 180-day exchange period. You can purchase the land prior to construction as one of your replacement properties or you can purchase the land and building from the builder at the time of closing. This is generally the least expensive and easiest method for the exchanger.

2. You can contract to do a *build-out exchange*, in which the exchanger finances all or part of the constructions. Using a special agreement with a qualified intermediary, the builder will draw on the exchange proceeds as certain steps of the construction are completed.

In either case, for your protection the purchase and sale agreement should have provisions written into the contract that require the builder to bear responsibility for the exchanger's taxes if the exchange fails due to the completion of the construction after the required 180-day exchange closing period.

How Might I Convert a Conventional Sale Already in Progress into an Exchange?

If you should want to convert a conventional sale into an exchange while everything is still in escrow, you may do so by including an addendum to your deposit receipt or closing instructions.

Ask your closing officer whether he or she has such an addendum, and use it if it is available. If the officer doesn't, ask this person for the name of an attorney who knows exchanges backwards and forwards and pay that attorney to draft the addendum for you.

For more help on this subject and on many other fine points of exchanging, refer to the IRS Publication 544, *Sales and Other Dispositions of Assets*. You can read this publication online at **www.irs.gov**.

> **TIP**
>
> One of the most important provisions of the 1031 tax-deferred exchange rule is that the taxpayer cannot have actual constructive receipt of the proceeds during the exchange period. The funds must be held by a qualified intermediary, who may not be a related party or an agent of the taxpayer. Receiving the proceeds during the exchange could result in the loss of any tax benefits.

How Do I Find Someone Willing to Do an Exchange with Me?

It is generally not difficult to find someone to participate in a three-way tax deferred exchange with you. When you find a property you would like to purchase in exchange for selling a property that you own, you will need to ask the seller of your desired property to cooperate in a tax-deferred exchange. There generally will be no additional cost to the seller. The seller will be required only to sign certain exchange documents and will not actually have to acquire the property that you are exchanging.

You may want to contact a company specializing in tax-deferred exchanges, often called a *qualified intermediary* or an *accommodator*. These companies will initiate the documentation necessary for your delayed exchange and furnish all the paperwork and necessary forms. There is a Federation of Exchange Accommodators that you can call at (916) 388-1031 with further questions (**www.1031.org**). To qualify for a tax deferment under a property exchange, you will qualify by finding *like-kind* property and by not receiving cash or other benefits from the exchange.

A direct exchange, in which you exchange your property for another person's property, is more difficult to arrange. When looking at property to acquire through an exchange, you can ask your real estate agent or the owner of the property about doing a direct exchange. Since 1990, when the IRS issued regulations allowing deferred sale and purchase exchanges, it is no longer necessary to do a direct exchange.

When Must I Report My Tax Deferred Exchange?

Parties involved in a 1031 Tax Deferred Exchange must report their exchange transaction on their tax return for the year in which the exchange begins. You will report the exchange on Form 8824, "Like-Kind Exchanges." You will be asked to provide the dates of the exchange transaction, the date the properties were identified, and any financial information obtained from the closing or settlement statement.

Closing costs may generally be used to reduce the realized gain on the relinquished property, reduce any boot received, and are added to the basis of the replacement property.

Chapter Eleven

Signing Your Paperwork

Signing your paperwork is the final step in the process of purchasing or selling your property. In this chapter I'll go through, step by step, the paperwork that you'll have to sign and what you should know about each document. I've included checklists for both buyers and sellers as well as things that you can do to avoid problems at the closing.

What's Involved in Drawing up Closing Escrow Instructions?

Closing or escrow instructions differ greatly from transaction to transaction, but, whatever they look like, they always result from the closing officer's taking the purchase agreement and other pertinent information out of the opening file and then drawing up actual instructions detailing how the transaction will take place. These instructions are, in essence, the written authorization to the escrow or title company; they usually begin with the statement: "You are hereby authorized and directed to do the following." Of course, the "you" here is the escrow or title company.

Closing instructions specify all the various conditions that must be met prior to close of escrow. They state who will pay for what costs and they authorize the escrow holder to disburse the monies to the proper parties and to record the necessary documents in order to close escrow when the parties involved have met all of the terms specified. Once opened, escrow remains open until the transaction is terminated according to the terms of the instructions.

If you wanted to draw up your own instructions, you could do so, although few people do. But they would have to meet the escrow holder's requirements. They would have to be written, signed by each submitting party, legally binding, and revocable only by mutual consent.

Most closing and escrow companies have standard preprinted escrow-instruction forms that the escrow officer uses to accommodate an individual transaction. Often there is one set of preprinted forms used for a standard real estate transaction between buyer and seller and another somewhat more complicated set used for an exchange. Most escrow companies now use computerized escrow forms and the escrow officer fills in the pertinent information and the computer program makes all the necessary calculations. Should an attorney represent one of the parties, he may want to draft his own escrow instructions, especially if the preprinted forms do not include provisions for a complicated transaction. There is no legal requirement governing the format for escrow instructions and, so long as her company approves them, the escrow officer must receive and follow specially drafted instructions in the same way she does those that are on her company's own forms.

Whether the escrow instructions are entered on a form by the closing officer, drawn up by you, or drafted by an attorney, they should give the escrow holder the following information:

- A listing of documents and/or monies that are to be deposited into escrow and by whom they are to be deposited

- Conditions that must be met prior to close of escrow (loans, termite reports, etc.)

- A listing of items to be prorated, including property taxes, insurance, interest, and rents

- An explanation of the fees to be paid by the buyer and/or seller

The most important thing to remember about escrow closing instructions is that your closing officer must know all the facts of the purchase so that she can carry out the expectations of all the parties concerned to their mutual satisfaction. Information given in the escrow instructions should never contradict those agreements reached between the parties in the purchase agreement.

As a safety measure, however, both documents should indicate that any inconsistency is to be interpreted in favor of the escrow instructions because they are usually drawn up after the purchase agreement. When escrow instructions of buyer and seller are discovered to be materially different, the instructions may not be a contract between them at all, for their individual rights depend upon their mutual agreement.

A Typical Misunderstanding: When Pete comes in to sign his seller's escrow closing instructions, he looks at what he's paying for roof repairs. He can't remember ever agreeing to pay so much. To be fair to himself, he decides to lower the figure and he writes in a new amount. He then signs the instructions and thinks that the escrow officer has to abide by them.

The Way Things Really Are: Pete's closing officer must abide by both parties' closing instructions and those instructions must correspond with each other exactly. A debit of $685 for roof repair on Pete's instructions must show up as a $685 credit on his buyer's instructions. The buyer will have to approve Pete's change before escrow can close.

Although some escrow companies and closing agencies prefer not to keep a copy of the purchase agreement in the escrow file because of the legal complications it might cause, you should submit a copy of your own purchase agreement when you open escrow, so your escrow officer will have the terms of the transaction at her disposal for clarification.

A Typical Misunderstanding: Now that Erik's purchase is in escrow, he decides to delay the close of escrow for another three months because he doesn't want to be penalized for taking his money out of his certificate of deposit (CD) before it matures. He's got the property all tied up anyway. It's in escrow, so he can't possibly lose it.

The Way Things Really Are: Erik's purchase agreement and his bank loan commitment will determine how long he has to close escrow on the property. Both have specific expiration dates. He could easily lose the property.

Closing instructions may be either *unilateral* (buyer signs one set of instructions and the seller signs another) or *bilateral* (buyer and seller sign the same set of instructions). In those areas that follow the unilateral custom, the real estate agent plays a large part in getting information to the escrow company and sees that the escrow instructions are complied with. The instructions are then normally drawn up after all the information is in and escrow is ready to close. Other areas follow the bilateral system, in which case the escrow instructions are generally drawn up and signed when escrow is opened.

Sometimes the buyer and seller have to change the original instructions. Perhaps the actual date of closing is going to differ from the original date used for computing the prorations. Perhaps they want to convert the transaction from an outright sale to an exchange. When such things happen, the escrow officer draws up the appropriate amendments and has all parties sign them.

What Happens After Escrow Has Taken Its Normal Course?

Once your closing has taken its normal course, that is, after you have been notified that the loan has gone through and the termite clearance has been sent in and all the loan documents have been drawn up, you are finally ready for delivery. Generally an escrow's gestation and delivery takes a month or two, but it can take whatever time period the principal parties agree upon.

At this time your real estate agent or closing officer should be telephoning you and saying, "OK, everything's ready. You can come in and sign the escrow instructions." That means your closing officer has taken all of the facts and figures pertinent to your transaction and has compiled them into instructions that apply to both the buyer and the seller. As mentioned before, those instructions may be bilateral or unilateral.

What's most important here is that you are well aware that once you have signed your set of escrow documents, you may be subject to penalties, and perhaps even legal action, if you attempt to cancel the sale for any reason whatsoever. Be certain, therefore, that you can abide by the agreements you are signing. Take time to read and review all the documents carefully. Take them home if necessary and check for mathematical or clerical errors. Never let yourself be rushed through these procedures.

A Typical Misunderstanding: Andrew and Judith don't have time to read all their documents at the escrow company. After all, their visit to the escrow company is eating into their lunch hour. They decide to sign all the papers just as they're presented and to review them later at home.

The Way Things Really Are: If they don't have the time to look over their papers at lunch, Andrew and Judith should take the papers home overnight before signing. Once they have signed, it is too late for them to make any changes.

What Papers Will I Have to Sign as a Buyer?

Although there are certain papers that must always be signed and others that will vary according to the lender's requirements, the answer to this question will depend primarily on the loan you have arranged. Some lenders require more documents than others, especially if there is any bureaucratic agency involved, like the FHA or the VA.

No matter what the real estate transaction, though, a buyer will always sign an original promissory note and an original mortgage or deed of trust. In addition to those two documents, the papers will vary and may include a fire insurance requirement form, a "TIL" or Truth-in-Lending form (disclosure statement), a right of rescission form (right to cancel a refinance loan within three working days), a borrower's statement to the lender, and loan instructions.

Since your escrow officer has probably spelled out the details and conditions of your transaction on each of your escrow documents, you still want to be sure that you understand the intent of the documents you are signing. So let's look at each one of them separately.

■ Original note and mortgage or deed of trust—Your note is your "promise to pay." Read it over very carefully before signing it. Verify the loan amount, the interest rate, the monthly payment, and the due date. They all will affect your life for years to come.

■ Fire insurance requirement form—You might be asked to sign a statement agreeing to comply with the lender's requirements for fire insurance on the property. The lender will specify the kind of insurance (fire, flood, earthquake, etc.) and how much coverage you must have. The lender will normally require you to obtain fire insurance in the amount of his loan and pay for one year's premium in advance, but for your own protection you will want to be sure that the buildings you purchase are adequately covered for their entire replacement value.

■ Truth-in-Lending (TIL) disclosure statement—As a borrower, you will be given an "Estimated Statement of Loan Fees and Closing Costs." This statement is also called a *Regulation Z form* or a *federal Truth in Lending statement* (see Chapter Six). Its purpose is to give you a breakdown of all the loan items you will be charged for, including the total amount you will be paying over the life of the loan. This statement will disclose the annual percentage rate (APR) on your loan. The APR includes the points and many of the fees you are charged on your loan. You will have been given a copy of this document within three business days of applying for your loan.

■ Right of rescission notice—This document allows you as borrower a last opportunity to cancel the loan within three working days (on refinance loans only). Oddly enough, you will probably be asked to sign this document twice, first when you sign your loan documents and then at the end of the three-day waiting period. The first time you are agreeing to the receipt of the notice and the second time you are actually giving up your legal right to cancel the loan. The right of rescission is normally limited to property that the borrower expects to use as his principal residence.

■ Affidavits—There may be affidavits prepared by your lender that you will be asked to sign. There may be an affidavit that states that you will use the property as your principal residence or one that states that the improvements to the property required in the purchase agreement have been completed prior to closing.

■ Lender's escrow instructions—On this statement are the lender's instructions to the escrow company stating the conditions that must be met before the deed of trust can be recorded. You, the borrower, sign a copy of this statement signifying that you have read it and understood it and that you agree with its terms and conditions. Your escrow officer must follow these instructions exactly as they are written. They will direct her to do the following: see that all loan documents are properly executed by the borrower and returned to the lender (except for the deed of trust, which is held until recorded and then returned to the lender); obtain a policy of title insurance; confirm fire insurance coverage for the lender (generally the requirement is that a minimum of one year's coverage be paid in escrow); and close escrow by a certain date or abort it and return all the documents.

■ Bill of sale—When you buy a property, sometimes the seller will include movable items such as a refrigerator, drapes, a stove, and a dog house as part of the deal. If so, you, the buyer, should obtain a bill of sale signed by the seller stating which items he agrees will be part of the property sale. This is a standard operating procedure and avoids the possible confusion later over what belongs to whom, what stays, and what goes along with the seller when he moves out.

■ Statement of information—Title insurance companies usually require a *statement of information* (sometimes called a *statement of identity*) on all individual grantors, grantees, and borrowers. These statements provide pertinent data on individuals. They serve as a safeguard against forgeries and help title companies eliminate such items as judgments and bankruptcies against parties with similar names. Information on these forms is kept strictly confidential, used only by the title company to ensure that you aren't being confused with somebody else who goes by a similar or identical name. You needn't be concerned about your privacy when asked to provide this information.

■ HUD-1 settlement statement—You will be asked to sign a HUD-1 settlement statement, which itemizes the services provided and lists the charges and fees for both buyer and seller. You should have been allowed to review this form prior to your closing day.

At the end of this chapter there are buyer's and seller's checklists that should help you verify everything you need to know before you sign your closing papers. Here is a summary of what both the buyer and the seller will probably be signing:

Documents	Buyer	Seller
Escrow Instructions	Original	Original
Note	Original	
Deed of Trust	Original	
Loan Documents	Original	
Grant Deed		Original
Bill of Sale		Original

Chart 11-1. Documents buyer and seller will sign

When Does Personal Property Become "Real Property"?

Personal property becomes real property when it is nailed, bolted, screwed, plastered, cemented, or built into a structure. A chandelier, for example, is personal property when purchased at a lighting store, but when it is attached to the ceiling it becomes a fixture and is supposed to be included in the sale of a property unless specifically excluded. On the other hand, the chandelier's light bulbs remain personal property because they are not permanently attached to the structure, so a tightwad seller is within his rights in removing the light bulbs before relinquishing possession of the property.

When buyer and seller cannot agree whether something is real property or personal property, five legal tests are brought to bear on the situation.

The first and most important test is the method of *attachment*. If the item has been permanently attached with some sort of fastener, such as nails, screws, or bolts, or with some sort of bonding material, such as glue or cement, then it has become a fixture. Fixtures are real property and must be included in a sale.

The second test is the *adaptability* of a particular item for use with the property. Built-in equipment that requires special wiring, such as an audio speaker or an intercom or a burglar alarm, is personal property that has been adapted to the property. It has become real property.

The third test is the *intention* of the buyer and seller, intention best made known in writing. If the microwave oven mounted over the stove has been mentioned in the listing agreement as "not included in sale," then there's no doubt about the seller's intention. Although it is obviously a fixture and ought to be included in the sale, that microwave oven attached to the wall needn't be left behind by the seller.

The fourth test is the actual *agreement* between buyer and seller. The purchase agreement should list all the items that might cause controversy later on and it should state exactly how each will be handled. Sometime prior to close of escrow, the buyer should ask the seller to prepare a bill of sale for these items, too. There should be no doubt about whose they will be when escrow closes.

The fifth test is the *relationship* of the parties. In determining whose assumptions are correct in any litigation about whether something is personal property or real property, courts tend to favor buyers over sellers, tenants over landlords, and lenders over borrowers.

Don't let some unfortunate misunderstanding about personal and real property spoil what should be a happy occasion for you, the closing of a real property transaction. Get everything in *writing*.

A Typical Misunderstanding: When Esther first looked at the house, she fell in love with the hanging Tiffany lamp, the wooden decorator blinds, and

the oak towel bars. She was pleased that she would be getting all of these extras along with the house.

The Way Things Really Are: Esther never thought about getting a bill of sale for these specific items. The seller took all of them with him when he moved out, the no-good skunk! He installed cheap replacements.

Is There Anything More I Can Do to Protect Myself?

Yes, one last and very important step you should take before authorizing your closing officer to close escrow is to inspect the property personally. You probably haven't seen the property for some time now. How do you know that all the personal property items—refrigerator, stove, drapes, and light fixtures—are the same ones you saw originally and are now in the same condition as they were? When you inspected the property with the intention of buying it, the seller naturally had everything shined and polished to perfection. Everything was as neat as a pin, the lawn was mowed, the crystal chandelier was twinkling, and the dog was out visiting relatives. Who knows what the place looks like now and whether the items you agreed would be included in the bill of sale are still there? Find out for yourself.

Inspect everything again before you ever allow your money to be released to the seller, for once your escrow has closed and the seller has your money, you have little recourse to get any repairs or restitutions made. Whom would you call anyway? The closing officer can't really pressure the seller and the real estate agent proba-

---

Bill of Sale

THIS BILL OF SALE is dated the `10th` day of `August, 20XX`

WITNESSETH:

That `SAMUEL P. SELLER`

herein called the Seller, for good and valuable consideration, hereby sells, assigns, and transfers to

`BRUCE B. BUYER AND BARBARA A. BUYER`

herein called the Buyer, all that certain property which is hereinafter described.

IT IS HEREBY COVENANTED by the Seller, which covenant shall be binding upon the heirs, executors, and administrators of the Seller, that this sale is warranted. The sale of said property will be defended against any and every person who lawfully claims the same.

The property which is hereby sold, assigned, and transferred is described as follows, to-wit [described as precisely as possible and give location, if known]:

```
Hanging Tiffany lamp in breakfast nook
Oak towel bars in master bathroom
Crystal chandelier in dining room
Wooden decorator blinds in den
Frigidaire electric stove, model ES-142 in kitchen
Frigidaire refrigerator, model SF-32 in kitchen
Kemmore washer, model 89131, in garage
Kenmore electric dryer, model 12756, in garage

All items located at 12 Allendale Ct., Boonville, CA 91002
```

Signature of Seller: _*Samuel P. Seller*_____

`SAMUEL P. SELLER`

Chart 11-2. Example of a bill of sale

bly doesn't want to get involved. You may try hassling with the seller yourself by taking him to small claims court or threatening to "make a federal case out of the matter," but who needs that kind of additional aggravation anyway? You will be busy enough just moving in without worrying about having to make repairs and recover missing items.

Avoid the post-escrow closing blues by making one final walk-through inspection just before escrow closes.

Final Walk-Through Checklist

❏ Turn on appliances to be sure they are still in working order.

❏ Look in cabinets and closets. Inspect for leaks, mold, visible signs of pests.

❏ Turn on light switches, check faucets, try garage door opener. Check that garage door opens and closes properly.

❏ If you had a professional inspection made of the property, be sure that all items mentioned in the report have been repaired or negotiated with the seller.

❏ Test heater and air conditioner systems.

❏ Check outside sprinkler systems and faucets.

❏ If there is debris and other unwanted items in the yard, be clear as to who will be removing these items. If the seller had agreed to have the yard cleaned, be sure this is done before signing any of your closing documents.

❏ Look for any damage that may have been caused when the seller moved furniture or other items out of the house. Look for broken windows, doors that do not close properly, chips in the paint or woodwork.

❏ Make a list of everything that does not seem to be in the condition it was when you first inspected the house. Your purchase contract should specify what will happen if the property is damaged or in a different condition than when you initially inspected the property and made your offer to purchase. In the excitement to close, some buyers do not perform a final walk-through inspection. After the tedious 30- to 45-day period of submitting documents to a lender and reading through escrow and closing documents, they are just relieved to finish the whole closing process. Unfortunately, oftentimes you cannot assume that the house will be delivered to you in "move-in" clean condition. Perform the final walk-through and give a list of any items that you find to your broker or attorney, with a copy to the seller. Resolve these issues before you agree to close.

What Happens if One of the Principals Isn't Available to Sign the Papers?

If the closing instructions are ready to sign and suddenly your wife has to go to the hospital or the partner with whom you intend to buy the property must leave town, you will need to get a *power of attorney*, a document your hospitalized wife or departing partner signs to allow someone else—real estate agent, friend, or, most often, the other person signing—to act in his stead and sign the papers for him. The person granted a power of attorney is known as an *attorney-in-fact*.

The power of attorney may be either specific or general. A general power of attorney grants the right to sign all documents, no matter what kind, during a person's absence. A specific power of attorney specifies exactly what may be signed.

If you find that the person with whom you intend to buy a property must be absent, notify your escrow officer as soon as possible and she will obtain the power of attorney for you in advance, inasmuch as it will have to be recorded with the county recorder, either at the close of escrow or before.

There's no need to feel uneasy about using a power of attorney because it cannot possibly be used legally to allow drastic changes to occur. Your house cannot be given away, nor can any property be deeded to the holder of the power of attorney. The holder may not use the power for his personal benefit at all. The power of attorney is simply a document designed to solve a particular problem, namely, someone's necessary absence. When the person returns, he merely records a cancellation of the power at the recorder's office.

> **TIP**
>
> In order to avoid any problems at closing, the power of attorney should be approved by your lender and your title or closing agent. Your lender will require that the power of attorney be specific to the property that you are buying, that it have an expiration date, and that the legal description of the property has been attached.

Which Escrow Papers Should Be Notarized?

As you may know, a *notary public* is simply an official witness, one who acknowledges the signing of documents. This acknowledging is commonly called *notarizing*.

Not all documents relating to an escrow transaction have to be notarized. Only those that are to be recorded need be. For example, neither escrow instructions nor bills of sale have to be notarized. If you have any doubts about whether a certain document should be notarized, ask your officer. She's probably a notary herself.

If you have to sign any of your escrow documents on a weekend or holiday, do be sure you arrange to have your signatures acknowledged. It's a must. You'll find

RECORDING REQUESTED BY

Secure Title Co.

WHEN RECORDED, MAIL TO·
Bruce B. Buyer
12 Allendale Ct.
Boonville, CA 91002

302210

RECEIVED AUG 1 0 20XX

RECORDED AT REQUEST OF
SECURE TITLE CO.

AT 8 O'CLOCK A M·
BARRETT COUNTY RECORDS

FEE $ 5   V L. GRAVES
COUNTY RECORDER
Recorder's Use Only

302210

POWER OF ATTORNEY

Know All Men by These Presents: That _____ BARBARA A. BUYER
the undersigned (jointly and severally, if more than one) hereby make, constitute, and appoint _____
_____ BRUCE B. BUYER
as my true and lawful Attorney for me and in my name place, and stead and for my use and benefit.

(a) To ask, demand, sue for, recover, collect, and receive each and every sum of money, debt, account, legacy, bequest, interest, dividend, annuity, and demand (which now is or hereafter shall become due, owing, or payable) belonging to or claimed by me, and to use and take any lawful means for the recovery thereof by legal process or otherwise, and to execute and deliver a satisfaction or release therefor, together with the right and power to compromise or compound any claim or demand,

(b) To exercise any or all of the following powers as to real property, any interest therein, and/or any building thereon· To contract for, purchase, receive and take possession thereof and of evidence of title thereto, to lease the same for any term or purpose, including leases for business, residence, and oil and/or mineral development, to sell, exchange, grant, or convey the same with or without warranty, and to mortgage, transfer in trust, or otherwise encumber or hypothecate the same to secure payment of a negotiable or non-negotiable note or performance of any obligation or agreement,

(c) To exercise any or all of the following powers as to all kinds of personal property and goods, wares and merchandise, choses in action and other property in possession or in action. To contract for, buy, sell, exchange, endorse, transfer, and in any legal manner deal in and with the same, and to mortgage, transfer in trust, or otherwise encumber or hypothecate the same to secure payment of a negotiable or non-negotiable note or performance of any obligation or agreement,

(d) To borrow money and to execute and deliver negotiable or non-negotiable notes therefor with or without security, and to loan money and receive negotiable or non-negotiable notes therefor with such security as he shall deem proper;

(e) To create, amend, supplement, and terminate any trust and to instruct and advise the trustee of any trust wherein I am or may be trustor or beneficiary; to represent and vote stock, exercise stock rights, accept and deal with any dividend, distribution, or bonus, join in any corporate financing, reorganization, merger, liquidation, consolidation, or other action and the extension, compromise, conversion, adjustment, enforcement or foreclosure, singly or in conjunction with others of any corporate stock, bond, note, debenture, or other security, to compound, compromise, adjust, settle, and satisfy any obligation, secured or unsecured, owing by or to me and to give or accept any property and/or money whether or not equal to or less in value than the amount owing in payment, settlement, or satisfaction thereof,

(f) To transact business of any kind or class and, as my act and deed, to sign, execute, acknowledge, and deliver any deed, lease, assignment of lease, covenant, indenture, indemnity agreement, mortgage, deed of trust, assignment of mortgage or of the beneficial interest under deed of trust, extension or renewal of any obligation, subordination or waiver of priority, hypothecation, bottomry, charter-party, bill of lading, bill of sale, bill, bond, note, whether negotiable or non-negotiable, receipt, evidence of debt, full or partial release or satisfaction of mortgage, judgment, and other debt, request for partial or full reconveyance of deed of trust and such other instruments in writing of any kind or class as may be necessary or proper in the premises.

Giving and granting unto my said Attorney full power and authority to do and perform all and every act and thing whatsoever requisite, necessary, or appropriate to be done in and about the premises as fully to all intents and purposes as I might or could do if personally present, hereby ratifying all that my said Attorney shall lawfully do or cause to be done by virtue of these presents The powers and authority hereby conferred upon my said Attorney shall be applicable to all real and personal property or interests therein now owned or hereafter acquired by me and wherever situated.

My said Attorney is empowered hereby to determine in his sole discretion the time when, purpose for, and manner in which any power herein conferred upon him shall be exercised, and the conditions, provisions, and covenants of any instrument or document which may be executed by him pursuant hereto, and in the acquisition or disposition of real or personal property, my said Attorney shall have exclusive power to fix the terms thereof for cash, credit, and/or property, and if on credit with or without security.

The undersigned, if a married woman, hereby further authorizes and empowers my said Attorney, as my duly authorized agent, to join in my behalf, in the execution of any instrument by which any community real property or interest therein, now owned or hereafter acquired by my spouse and myself or either of us, is sold leased, encumbered, or conveyed.

When the context so requires, the masculine gender includes the feminine and/or neuter, and the singular number includes the plural.

[ ] This is to be considered a general Power of Attorney
[ ] Notwithstanding the aforesaid, this is to be considered a specific power of attorney limited to   that real property
_____ located at 12 Allendale Ct., Boonville, CA 91002 _____ and expiring August 10, 20XX
Witness my hand this 5th day of August , 20 XX .

_____

STATE OF   California   )
). s.s.
COUNTY OF Barrett   )
On _____ August 5th _____, 20 XX ,
before me, the undersigned, a Notary Public in and for said County and State, personally appeared

    Barbara A. Buyer

proved to me on the basis of satisfactory evidence to be the person__ whose name__ is (are) subscribed to the within instrument and acknowledged that _____ she _____ executed the same.

Barbara A. Buyer
BARBARA A. BUYER

WITNESS my hand and official seal.

Edna Edwards
Notary Public in and for said County and State
NOTARY SEAL

OFFICIAL SEAL
EDNA EDWARDS
Notary Public

Chart 11-3. Example of a power of attorney document

that notaries are listed in the Yellow Pages. You'll also find that real estate and insurance offices usually have notaries and are open on weekends.

A Typical Misunderstanding: Mark's wife is busy getting ready to move into a new house some 300 miles away when she's needed to sign over the grant deed for the old house. Mark decides to forge her signature on the deed just as he sometimes endorses checks with her signature. He knows how she signs her name well enough so that nobody could tell the difference.

The Way Things Really Are: Mark may secure a power of attorney from his wife so he can legally sign for her, but otherwise she will have to appear before a notary personally to have her signature on the grant deed acknowledged.

Many people think that notaries can certify just about anything: photographs, paintings, sweepstakes entries, hunting trophies—you name it. That's incorrect. Unless something includes certain wording, a signature, and a notarial certificate, it cannot be notarized.

Some people also think that a person's name may be changed on a whim. It can't be. A notary can accept only legal names as verified by an official identification card. Should a hairy hulk wearing a designer dress and heavy eye makeup want to sign as Harriet even though the ID produced says Harry, the notary must refuse to acknowledge the signature. The person in question must produce a valid driver's license or some other authoritative ID with the name Harriet in order to sign notarized documents as Harriet.

> **TIP** At the closing you must be certain that the terms are just as you have negotiated them. Look for clerical errors and all mathematical figuring. Never let yourself be rushed through these procedures. Never become casual about any part of your purchase—particularly these final and extremely important details.

Buyer's and Seller's Checklists

For your own protection, whether you are the buyer or the seller in a transaction, you might wish to use the checklists on the following pages before you sign your final escrow and loan documents. By using them, you can be reasonably certain that everything meets with your approval. They may save you much grief later, too.

Buyer's Checklist

❏ Is the purchase price correct?

❏ Have you been credited for all the loans and deposits put into escrow?

❏ Is your name correct on the grant deed? Is it spelled correctly, and does it include the correct middle initial? Is the manner in which you will take title stated correctly? Is the legal description of the property correct? Does this description conform with the one given in the preliminary title report? Was the title cleared to your satisfaction?

❏ Are the notes properly filled out? Are the loan amount, interest rate, due date, and prepayment terms all correct?

❏ Is your name correct on the deed of trust? Is it dated correctly? Is the loan amount stated correctly?

❏ If there is any personal property included, are you being given a bill of sale, and do you agree with the items included?

❏ Are you paying for fire insurance yourself outside of escrow or through escrow? If through escrow, is the premium amount correct?

❏ Are the prorations correct?

❏ Is the termite inspection fee correct? Were you credited for any work that was agreed upon between you and the seller?

❏ Is the correct date given for the close of escrow?

Seller's Checklist

❏ Is the sales price correct?

❏ Are the old loans being paid off or assumed? Do you agree with the payoff loan amount?

❑ Is the deed correct? Does it show the correct amount of transfer tax?

❑ If there are any notes in your favor, are they correct?

❑ If there will be a deed of trust recorded in your favor, ask to see a copy. Is it correct?

❑ If you will be signing a bill of sale for any personal property, are all the agreed-upon items listed and correctly described?

❑ If the buyer is assuming your old loan, were you given credit for the existing fire insurance premium and for the impound account?

❑ Are the prorations correct?

❑ Did you agree to credit the buyer for any termite work, structural damage, or other repairs to be done? Do these credits show up on your escrow instructions as debits?

❑ Is the correct date given for the close of escrow?

What Happens if Something Goes Wrong at the Closing?

Despite all your best efforts to diligently read your closing documents, inspect the property, and be certain all the provisions of your purchase agreement have been accurately reflected, repairs have made, and loan documents have been correctly prepared, there are circumstances that can still hold up your closing. Being aware of what can go wrong and making the proper preparations will assure you that nothing will go wrong at your closing.

The first problem that commonly occurs is a delay in the transfer of your down payment, if this is to be done by wire or bank transfer. A delay would hold up the closing, perhaps a day or more. The closing agent or title company will not accept your personal check, so you would then have to scramble to your bank to get a certified or cashier's check. You can avoid this situation by either paying your closing costs with a certified check or being certain that your wire transfer is done several days in advance of the closing. You may not know the exact amount you will be required to put into escrow. In that case, you can give the title company more than the amount they state to you and then you would be refunded any excess.

Incorrect loan documents are not uncommon and can hold up your closing. As far in advance as possible, ask to review the loan documents and carefully check the information contained in them. If any errors are found, the documents may have to be redrawn or the lender may allow the closing agent to make changes at closing. Sometimes the lender may ask you for additional documentation at closing, such as a copy of a canceled deposit check, original fire insurance premium, copies of the purchase agreement on the sale of your previous home, or a rental agreement, if you will be renting out your previous residence. You can prevent this potential problem by staying in close communication with your loan officer or loan broker and asking them if there is anything additional the lender could ask for. You can always bring additional documentation to the closing, just in case. You are better off bringing everything you can think of that pertains to your purchase.

A missing loan package would hold up your closing. It happens that the lender's loan documents do not arrive at the title or closing company by the time scheduled for closing. You can avoid this problem by keeping in close contact with your closing agent, asking them if they have all the documents in their possession prior to the closing. You may even want to call one to two hours before your closing and ask if all the paperwork has been received and is ready for signing.

Oftentimes you will perform a final walk-through of the property on the day before closing. Many buyers wait until closing to bring up items that have not been repaired or are damaged or missing. It is best to bring up any items in dispute before the closing and come to an agreement with the seller prior to the closing day. This would be the time to negotiate with the seller or the seller's attorney or broker for a credit for work to be performed or other arrangements that are satisfactory to you. If negotiations cannot be done before closing, insist that they be handled at the closing. No matter how long it takes, while you have all the parties to the closing gathered in one place, come to an agreement with the seller and have the closing agent or your attorney draw up an appropriate document outlining that agreement.

You can prevent last-minute title problems by carefully reading your title report or abstract well in advance of the closing day. Make sure there are no liens against the title. Insist that all title problems be cleared before you close on your home.

One last thing you can do to ensure a smooth and effortless closing is to be sure that all the parties arrive on time at the closing location. This may seem obvious, but oftentimes a party miscalculates or for other unexpected reasons does not arrive on time. The title company or attorney scheduling your closing may have several closings scheduled for the same day, and if all the parties in your transaction are not available at the appointed time, you may be left waiting until a new time is arranged. Call your attorney and closing agent the morning of your closing, confirm the closing hour with all parties involved, and be certain they will arrive on the correct day and time. I have attended closings that extended well into the late evening, after the title company had closed, and the parties were still at the closing, working out last-minute details.

Chapter Twelve

The Closing and What Happens after Closing

You have gone through all the steps leading up to the actual closing. Now what happens? In this chapter, we'll answer that question as well as look at how to deal with any problems that might come up.

What Happens after I Have Signed All the Necessary Closing Documents?

To begin with, your escrow or closing officer must have the following in hand to close escrow:

- The final escrow closing instructions signed by buyer and seller
- The signed loan documents
- A certified check, money order, wired funds, or pile of currency from the buyer for the full balance of the purchase price
- A signed and acknowledged grant deed and, if applicable, a signed bill of sale
- Instructions from buyer and seller to record the deeds on a specific date

When the closing officer has all of these papers in her possession, then, and only then, may escrow close.

One of the first things the closing officer does next is secure a check from the lender in order to pay off the seller for the balance owed on the property, including any old bills and loans. But institutional lenders are quite strict about disbursing funds. They will release their money only after they have received the entire closing package, especially the loan documents. It is an "I'll give you this when you give me that" situation. Consequently, the closing officer usually hand-delivers the whole package. Moreover, lenders like to have this exchange completed 24 hours in advance of the actual recording time, so they will have plenty of time to check over all the documents to be certain that everything is in order.

Your closing officer drafts a *funding* or cover letter detailing all the documents in the package. This letter, together with the original loan documents, is called the *funding* or *loan package*.

The closing officer must make sure that all the documents sent to the lender are properly filled out and properly executed. Should she find an error, regardless of how small (even a missing initial), she will call the party concerned and have him rectify it. Lenders, in general, require a good deal of specific accuracy for two reasons:

1. They are audited frequently by government agencies and have to show that their paperwork is in order.

2. They might want to sell the loan later and must make sure that it complies with accepted banking guidelines so that it will be marketable.

The lender, upon receiving and checking this package, will then call the closing officer and give her the authorization to record the necessary papers with the county and release the check for the loan proceeds.

What Is "Recording" and Why Is It Necessary?

Throughout this book you have been reading about recording this or that document at the county recorder's office and you've probably had a few questions about this subject that haven't been answered yet.

Over centuries of land ownership, people began to recognize that somehow one had to make known his right to own a certain piece of real property. Because a simple bill of sale is easy to lose or forge and because it might be challenged by the heirs of a long-departed original seller, a bill of sale by itself wasn't enough. So someone decided that making ownership known publicly with a recorded document would solve the problem and ensure that a property belonged to its rightful owner. Over the years, this idea took root and became the accepted practice. Even in the Wild West, where the stakes were high and almost anything could happen, prospectors would make a beeline into town to record their gold claims to ensure that no one else would get the legal rights before they did.

The county recorder's office is now the place where documents are recorded and thus made secure. Once a document is recorded, the public is assumed to have knowledge of its existence. *Constructive notice* has been given.

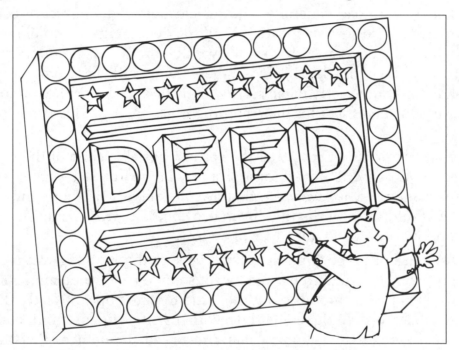

The first written documents showing land transfers eventually evolved into what we now call *deeds*. Whereas *title* represents ownership of property, a deed is the instrument used to transfer title from one person to another. A person holding a deed to a parcel of land holds the title as represented by the writing in the deed.

A deed, remember, is not a contract between a buyer and a seller. Do not confuse a deed, which transfers title, with a deed of trust, which is used to secure a promissory note in some states.

Recording deeds has become essential for the buyer and the lender. In most cases, the recorded instrument carries legal preference over the unrecorded instrument. For example, should a seller give a grant deed to two different buyers, the one holding a recorded deed would have valid claim to the property and the buyer with an unrecorded deed would lose out even if he received his deed from the seller before the recorded deed was given. Likewise, if more than one deed of trust was recorded, the first one on record would get the first opportunity at foreclosure.

To record the deeds and other necessary documents, the title company's *recorder* takes them to the county recorder's office. There she will have the necessary documents recorded to make the purchase official. This time of recording is considered the close of escrow—the day, hour, and minute when the property legally and rightfully changes hands.

Each county recorder sets definite times when documents may be recorded at that office. Escrow and closing agents generally have special recording hours set aside for them, during which time the general public may record a document so long as they do not interrupt a closing agent's series of document numbers. A county with a heavy workload generally requires closing agents to record early in the morning in order to be sure the posting of all the documents is completed by closing time, whereas a county with a small workload may set the hours for closing agents in the middle of the day. Likewise, these hours will vary from place to place. If you wish to find out exactly when escrow will close, check with your local county recorder or closing officer for the recording times set aside for closing agents in your area.

Closing agents prefer to record at the earliest possible time of the day, preferably 8 a.m. Here's why: if a deed for a property is recorded at 10 a.m. and a lien affecting the same property was recorded by someone else an hour and a half earlier, the lien would prevent the title insurance company from being able to ensure clear title and it could delay the close of escrow.

The closing agent's recording clerk must be sure that nothing was recorded on the same property or against the same persons named in her documents. She has to check all documents carefully, run the "title to date" up to exactly the minute she will record. Recording right after the recorder's office opens eliminates the possibility of an intervening document being recorded. Remember that the first to record is the first in right.

A Typical Misunderstanding: Steve's preliminary report doesn't show the latest loan he took out only 12 days ago. If he doesn't say anything about it, he can go ahead and sell the property and nobody will know about the loan.

The Way Things Really Are: The title or escrow company will learn about this new loan when they run the "title to date" just before recording. The close of escrow will be delayed until either Steve has paid off the loan or the new buyer has agreed to assume it.

When there is an exchange of properties that are located in different counties or states, recording the transfer of ownership tends to become more complicated, because each party involved in the exchange wants the properties to record con-

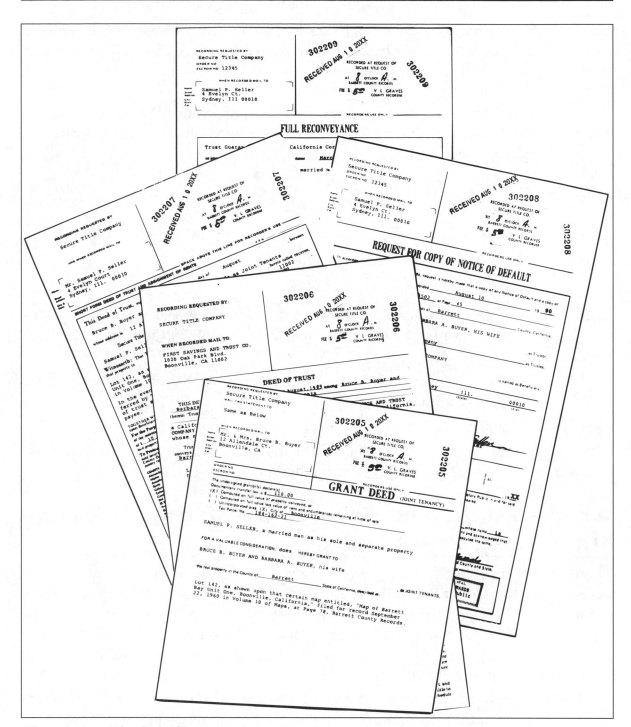

Chart 12-1. Closing documents

currently. The escrow agents involved make special reservations with the county recorders so that the recording times will coincide.

Before county recorders will record any document, they collect a recording fee. This fee is generally $9 for the first page and $3 for each additional page. There is an additional $3 charge for each legal-size document. If you want to determine the recording fees for your area, these fees are posted on your county assessor and recorder's office Web site. Or, if you wish, you can call your local assessor's office and ask for the fees.

The closing officer determines the exact recording sequence by following the order of each document's priority. A sample recording might follow this sequence:

- Grant deed—seller to buyer
- Deed of trust—buyer to first lender
- Deed of trust—buyer to second lender
- Request for notice of default—second lender's request on first loan
- Deed of reconveyance—trustee to seller

The recording itself consists of four steps:

1. The county recorder enters in the upper right corner of each document the filing number, the time of receipt (down to the minute), and the amount of fees collected.

2. She makes a photocopy of the original document and puts it in a large bound book or she microfilms it.

3. She files and indexes her copy.

4. She returns the original document to the party whose name and address appear in the upper left corner of the first page.

What's the Difference Between Transferring Title and Transferring Possession?

The title of real property changes legally at the time of recording, but actual possession may transfer at an earlier date or a later date. Sometimes a buyer wants to move in before close of escrow and pay rent and sometimes a seller wants to remain for a while and rent the property back from the buyer. In either case, the terms should be spelled out on the original purchase agreement, with the monthly or weekly rental charge clearly stated.

Here's an example of a rent-back agreement clause: "If the seller has not vacated the premises upon recordation of the deed, seller agrees to pay purchaser $___ per day (week) from recordation to date of possession by the buyer. This sum is to be prorated in escrow."

How Are the Funds Disbursed?

After all of the documents have been recorded, your closing officer will release the monies that have been held in the escrow account. This involves paying everybody off—the seller, the holders of old loans, the termite companies, the real estate agents, and so on—according to the instructions. The closing officer will issue checks using the figures (debits and credits) stated on the escrow instructions. She will release the escrow funds with great care, being absolutely sure that she has received all the money due in escrow and that all personal checks have cleared the bank. She cannot take the risk of releasing checks without having funds sufficient to cover them.

In California, the law requires that all funds be drawn on a California bank and that all personal funds be in escrow one day prior to recording. This law was enacted because so many savings institutions were tied in with Eastern banks and the funds were not available on the day of close of escrow.

I remember well one buyer who stopped payment on his check several days after escrow had closed because he was unhappy that the seller had left the kitchen dirty and wanted to get back at the "dirty dog." The buyer thought that by stopping payment on his check the seller would suffer and not get his money from the sale. The buyer failed to understand that on the day escrow closes, the escrow officer

disburses all of the monies held in escrow, so the seller had already been paid.

Precisely to avoid problems of this sort, most escrow and closing companies require a cashier's check for money presented near or at the time of closing. Those companies that do accept personal checks will hold up the close of escrow until the personal checks have cleared, two or three days for local banks and longer for out-of-town banks. If you want to use a personal check, deposit it with your closing officer well ahead of the close of escrow to prevent any delay in closing.

A Typical Misunderstanding: Dan doesn't quite have enough funds in the bank on Friday to cover his personal check needed to close escrow, but he knows he'll have the money there first thing Monday morning. He goes ahead and gives his check to the escrow company on Friday.

The Way Things Really Are: Before she deposits his personal check into the escrow account, the escrow officer calls the bank to verify that the check is good. Escrow cannot close until Dan's check has cleared.

Prodded by the California Land Title Association, California finally enacted a law governing the holding periods for escrow deposits. It makes the holding periods dependent upon the nature of the funds when they're deposited into escrow. Funds deposited into escrow in the form of cash or an electronic transfer become available immediately for escrow disbursements. Funds deposited in the form of a cashier's check, a teller's check, or a certified check become available for escrow disbursements on the first business day following the deposit. Funds deposited in the form of personal or business checks become available for disbursements according to the holding periods set by the Federal Reserve Board.

The Federal Reserve Board allows local checks to be held for up to three business days and non-local checks to be held for up to seven business days. Generally, "local" checks are those drawn on a bank in the same metropolitan area as the escrow office. San Francisco and Los Angeles are certainly not in the same metropolitan area, while San Francisco, San Jose, and Oakland are. Should you wonder whether your check is local or non-local, ask the escrow officer for a determination and ask her how long the check will be held before the funds that it brings into escrow are made available for disbursement. An escrow company does have some leeway under the law. Local checks may be held for up to three business days; non-local checks may be held for up to seven business days. Your escrow company may hold them for less time but not for more.

Often the closing officer uses a worksheet or disbursement form that shows exactly who gets paid what. By totaling the disbursements according to the closing statement, she can check that the money she took in equals the money she will pay out.

By now you probably think that the closing of escrow is a complex operation. It is, to a degree. Fortunately for you, though, all of this behind-the-scenes work is done for you. It is explained here simply to keep you informed. Besides, it's useful information. The more you know about the inner workings of the curious rite of escrow, the better protected you are.

SECURE TITLE COMPANY
1220 Oak Park Blvd.
Boonville, CA 91002

Office: _____
Address: _____

Date: August 10, 20XX
Escrow No. 12345

CREDITS	Debits	CREDITS
Deposit July 5, 20XX		1 0 0 0 0 0
Deposit August 9, 20XX		1 1 7 6 2 5 4
Deposit		
Deposit		
Funds to Hold in Escrow Termite Repair Fees	2 5 0 0 0	
Transfer of Funds		
Billing		
Loan Proceeds to Come From First Federal Trust		7 8 2 1 0 9 5

COMPANY

1. Policy Charge 432.50 + 96.50=	529.00
2. Escrow Fees	160.00
3. Recording Fees	25.00
4. Transfer Tax	110.00
5. Other Notary Fee + Inspection Fee	26.00

CHECKS TO BE DRAWN	CHECK NO.	Debits	Credits
Title Company – Escrow Fees		8 5 0 0 0	
Insurance Company – One Year Premium		2 3 5 0 0	
Termite Company – Termite Report Fee		8 5 0 0	
Real Estate Company – Commission		6 0 0 0 0 0	
Existing First Lender – Payoff in Full		4 7 1 7 5 7 0	
Existing Second Lender – Payoff in Full		5 0 1 3 8 0	
Trust Company – Trustee Fees		3 0 0 0	
Seller – Sales Proceeds		3 1 3 3 3 9 9	
TOTALS:		9 0 9 7 3 4 9	9 0 9 7 3 4 9

Chart 12-2. Escrow disbursement table

What Happens after the Recording of Documents and Disbursements of Funds?

At this point, your closing or escrow officer considers the escrow closed and she will proceed to draw up the final closing statements, tending to any last-minute adjustments and additional details. She will then mail out the title insurance policies, fire insurance policies, promissory notes, and any other pertinent documents, along with her closing letters, one to the buyer, one to the seller, and one to the lender.

What Documents Does Everyone Receive?

The table below can best answer this question.

Document	Buyer	Seller	Lender
CLTA Policy	Original		
ALTA Policy			Original
RESPA Statement	Copy	Copy	Original
Bill of Sale	Original		
First Insurance Policy	Copy	Old One	Original
Promissory Note	Copy		Original
Grant Deed	Original		
Deed of Trust			Original

What Is the HUD-1 Statement or "RESPA"?

"RESPA" is an acronym for the Real Estate Settlement Procedures Act of 1974, which was passed to control real estate settlement costs nationally. This act provides for a uniform settlement statement of closing costs, called a *HUD-1 statement*, to be given to the borrower within three days of the loan application; it requires that the booklet titled *Buying Your Home: Settlement Costs and Information* be given to the borrower; and prohibits kickbacks and fees for services that are not provided. "RESPA" and "HUD-1" are frequently used interchangeably for the same document used in escrow. ("HUD" is another acronym, for the Department of Housing and Urban Development.) The form is a consumer-protection-act form, and your closing officer must fill one out if there is an institutional lender with federally insured deposits involved in the escrow. Unlike the Regulation Z Truth-in-Lending form, which is given to a borrower before his loan is completed, the HUD-1 form is given to a borrower after the loan is processed.

Everyone involved in a property transaction—buyer, seller, and lender—receives a HUD-1 statement. This form shows all the final debits and credits used to compute and close the escrow. These itemized statements are mandatory when there is a loan involved and when that loan is used, in whole or in part, to finance the purchase or transfer of title to dwellings housing one to four families, that is, for single-family dwellings through fourplexes. Most institutional lenders are obligated to comply with this 1974 act, so they issue a HUD-1 statement through the escrow company, which completes and mails out the form for them.

The only transactions exempt from this act, which applies to all federally insured lenders, are those involving loans used to finance or purchase property consisting of 25 acres or more, loans on vacant land, assumptions, all-cash transactions, and sales made subject to an existing loan.

Which Items on the HUD-1 Statement Are Tax-Deductible?

The items given on your HUD-1 statement actually fall into three categories relative to your income taxes, and they are very important to you: *tax-deductible* in the current year, *capitalized* (added to the price paid for the property and thereby becoming part of your base for capital gains tax purposes when you sell), or *neither* (personal expense). The tax-deductible items are interest, points, loan-origination fees, any prepayment penalty, and property taxes. The capitalized items are the termite clearance costs, title insurance premiums, attorney's fees, appraisal fees, recording fees, notary fees, escrow fees, transfer taxes, and the ALTA inspection fee. The personal expense items are the fire insurance premium, private mortgage insurance, and any money put into an impound account.

What Happens When Escrow Has to Be Canceled?

Occasionally a deal won't close and escrow must be canceled. The biggest concern, of course, is how the monies already held in escrow will be released. The funds could remain in escrow for a year or more unless you make proper provisions for their disposition.

A Typical Misunderstanding: After his offer has been accepted, Nick finds out that the house he's buying, which is only 15 miles from work, is really a two-hour commute each way during rush hour. He also realizes that he'll have to eat a lot more beans and spaghetti in order to meet the monthly payments. Even though he'd like to back out of the deal, he feels he has to go through with it now because it's already in escrow.

The Way Things Really Are: Nick can always ask the seller to release him from the deal before escrow closes. By mutual consent, buyer and seller may cancel escrow.

When you signed your original purchase agreement with the seller, you probably agreed upon a time limit for closing, after which time penalties could be charged to the party responsible for the delay, or the escrow could be canceled altogether. In other words, if escrow closes within the time limit, all is well, but if it has to be scheduled to close after that date, one of you will have to pay more or you might agree to cancel the whole deal.

An escrow closing may be terminated by mutual consent of the buyer and the seller for any number of reasons—inability to obtain financing, tight money, extensive structural damage to the property—or it may be terminated by a failure on the part of one party or another to satisfy certain of the escrow conditions within a specified time.

If your purchase agreement does not include a clause providing for a time limit within which to close escrow, say 30 or 60 days, the closing could drag on for months, waiting for the buyer and/or the seller to sign his papers and deliver his money.

Many times I have seen a closing delayed by a buyer who gets "cold feet" and just can't sign all those loan documents or by a seller who has been offered more money by another buyer and tries to get the first buyer to back out of the agreement. Generally, however, once the closing process has gone to the point that all the legal documents are drawn and signed, the parties eventually agree to close.

Most escrow and closing instructions include a clause for cancellation that enables the buyer and the seller, by mutual agreement, to cancel escrow by giving notice to the escrow holder.

Here's how it works if both parties are agreeable to canceling. The party deciding not to go through with the agreement writes or telephones the closing officer and informs her of his reasons for requesting a cancellation. She then makes copies of this communication, either the letter or a cancellation agreement she has drawn up to reflect the telephone conversation, and she forwards these copies to the other parties involved so that everyone knows what's going on and so that any questions or disagreements may be resolved satisfactorily. In addition to reasons for the cancellation, this letter should state what is to happen to the monies already held in escrow, who gets the buyer's deposit, who pays any accumulated bills such as the termite report, and so on.

The escrow company or closing agent may charge a cancellation fee to cover the cost of preparing the preliminary report and any legwork that the company has already completed on the property, but that's all.

If you believe a cancellation of your escrow will be necessary, try to cancel before signing your closing escrow instructions. Once they are signed, cancellation is much more complicated. Escrow and closing instructions may be considered legally binding contracts and aren't revocable like purchase agreements because they generally do not have escape clauses.

Canceling escrow is relatively simple when both buyer and seller agree to end the transaction, but what if they should disagree? What happens when either the buyer or the seller does not live up to the original purchase agreement? Suppose the buyer continually stalls the close of escrow or decides at the last minute not to buy at all. What recourse does the seller have?

The purchase agreement and closing instructions, like a rental agreement, are legally binding contracts and their provisions are enforceable in a court of law. If the *seller* defaults on the contract, the buyer may sue the seller for *specific performance*, which means that the court can order the seller to live up to his or her part of the contract and deliver the property to the buyer. The buyer also has the option of recording a lis pendens to prevent the seller from selling the property to another buyer or refinancing the property. If the *buyer* defaults, however, the seller sues for monetary damages only. In other words, a seller usually cannot force a buyer to buy. His or her only recourse is to retain the deposits, but to do so he or she must show that out-of-pocket expenses have been incurred. Many purchase agreements contain a *liquidated damages* clause, which outlines the maximum default damages the buyer would incur in case of default.

If a seller refuses to release a buyer's deposits, he may be held liable for a penalty equal to three times the amount withheld, not less than $100 or more than $1,000, plus attorney's fees. In order to qualify to keep a portion of the deposits, the seller must provide the buyer with a written accounting of his monetary losses in withdrawing the property from the market.

Should the other principal in your real estate transaction wish to cancel the escrow or closing, consult your closing officer, your attorney, and/or someone who specializes in real estate matters. You may have some remedies—and, then again, you may not.

A Typical Misunderstanding: The day before close of escrow, Bruce decides he doesn't want to buy the Danielsons' property after all and he instructs the escrow agent to return his entire deposit. The Danielsons refuse to sign amended escrow instructions that would cancel escrow and return Bruce's deposit because they believe that they should get the deposit as compensation for taking the property off the market for two months. Although they have incurred no actual monetary losses and can sell the property now for more than what Bruce would have paid them, they instruct the closing agent to release the deposit to them under the liquidated damages/forfeiture provision in the purchase agreement.

The Way Things Really Are: The Danielsons' real estate agent warns them that they should not interfere with Bruce's efforts to get his good-faith deposit back because they can't come up with any actual out-of-pocket expenses resulting from their dealings with Bruce. If they interfere with the return of Bruce's deposit, they could be liable for a monetary penalty. He's entitled to get his deposit back within 30 days after he demands it.

How Can the Buyer and Seller Avoid Losing Interest on Deposits Held in Escrow When a Dispute Arises?

With the mutual consent of both buyer and seller, the closing officer will draw up closing instructions authorizing that funds held in escrow be put into an interest-bearing account. These instructions specify the amount of money to be deposited, the type of account, the name and address of the financial institution, the method used for distributing the interest, and a statement disclosing any restrictions and penalties for early withdrawal. Once the dispute is resolved and the funds are needed to settle the accounts, the escrow officer will redeposit the funds into the escrow account as directed.

Is There Anything Special About Buying Property from a Foreigner?

The Foreign Investment in Real Property Tax Act of 1980 (FIRPTA) requires that anyone who buys non-residential property for more than $400,000 from a foreigner set aside 10% of the purchase price for the IRS. According to IRS Code 1445, the term "foreign persons" refers to foreign nationals who do not hold permanent resident visas.

Buyers and real estate agents are held liable if this 10% is not withheld, agents to the extent of their commission and buyers for the balance. Buyers are responsible for determining a seller's citizenship status and should require the seller to sign an affidavit of this status. If the seller is a foreigner, if the property's sales price exceeds $400,000, and if the property is not used as a residence, then the 10% must be withheld at closing.

What Is CAL-FIRPTA?

CAL-FIRPTA is California's version of the federal FIRPTA. It is a tax act which became effective in 1988 and was amended in 2002. It requires Buyers of California real estate to withhold 3 1/3% of the sales price for certain transactions. The law applies to California residents and non-residents.

The act requires the withholding tax on any property transaction, except: 1) property in which the sales price is less than $100,000, 2) property which is the principal residence of an individual seller, 3) property which is transferred to a corporate beneficiary by a foreclosure, 4) property transferred by an individual and placed in a 1031 tax deferred exchange, 5) property in which the seller is a tax-exempt or a California corporation or partnership, 6) irrevocable trusts with a California trustee, estates with a California decedent and banks or banks acting as a fiduciary for a trust, and 6) sales in which the seller is an individual and the transaction will result in a loss.

For questions contact the Franchise Tax Board, Withholding-at-Source Unit, P.O. Box 651, Sacramento, CA 95812, (888) 792-4900, **www.frb.ca.gov.**

How Does the Tax Reform Act of 1986 Affect Closings?

The Tax Reform Act of 1986 requires that all real estate transactions be reported to the Internal Revenue Service.

Whoever handles the closing—escrow company, title company, financial institution, or attorney—must report the necessary information using IRS Form 1099. This form calls for the following on each seller or exchanger: name, taxpayer identification number (TIN), and forwarding address. In addition, it calls for the closing date, the sales price, the type of transaction, the real estate broker's name, address, and TIN, the property's address, assessor's parcel number, and legal description.

Where Can I Go to Complain About My Escrow or Title Insurance Company?

Direct your escrow closing or title insurance complaints to the commissioner of corporations, to the state department of real estate, or to your local district attorney.

If you used an independent escrow company, as is customary in Southern California, direct your complaint to the commissioner of corporations. The commissioner imposes strict regulations on independent escrow agents to ensure their impartiality and competence. Also make your complaint about an independent escrow agent known to the state escrow association, if there is one. (There is a California Escrow Association, which is devoted to better escrow practices and public relations.)

If you used a bank or savings and loan escrow department, direct your complaint to your state's bank or savings and loan commissioner or to whatever federal agency regulates the institution.

If you have a complaint about a title insurance company, direct it to the insurance commissioner. Title insurance companies have to file their rates, policies, and endorsement forms with the state insurance commissioner, so that office should be knowledgeable enough to help you.

What if I Have a Complaint Against My Lender?

If your lender is a state-chartered bank that is a member of the Federal Reserve System, you should address your complaint to the Federal Reserve member bank in your district. (If you're unsure which is your district, consult the map on the Federal Reserve Web site: **www.federalreserve.gov/otherfrb.htm**.)

Federal Reserve Bank of Boston
600 Atlantic Avenue
Boston, MA 02106
(617) 973-3000

Federal Reserve Bank of New York
33 Liberty Street
New York, NY 10045
(212) 720-5000

Federal Reserve Bank of Philadelphia
10 Independence Mall
Philadelphia, PA 19106-1574
(215) 574-6000

Federal Reserve Bank of Cleveland
1455 East Sixth Street
Cleveland, OH 44114
(216) 579-2000

Federal Reserve Bank of Richmond
701 East Byrd Street
Richmond, VA 23219
(804) 697-8000

Federal Reserve Bank of Atlanta
1000 Peachtree Street, NE
Atlanta, GA 30309-4470
(404) 498-8500

Federal Reserve Bank of Chicago
230 South LaSalle Street
Chicago, IL 60604
(312) 322-5322

Federal Reserve Bank of St. Louis
411 Locust Street
St. Louis, MO 63102
(314) 444-8444

Federal Reserve Bank of Minneapolis
90 Hennepin Avenue
P.O. Box 291
Minneapolis, MN 55401-0291
(612) 204-5000

Federal Reserve Bank of Kansas City
925 Grand Boulevard
Kansas City, MO 64198
(816) 881-2000

Federal Reserve Bank of Dallas
2200 North Pearl Street
Dallas, TX 75201
(214) 922-6000

Federal Reserve Bank of San Francisco
101 Market Street
San Francisco, CA 94105
(415) 974-2000

If your lender is a state-chartered bank that is not a member of the Federal Reserve System, you should address your complaint to the Federal Deposit Insurance Corporation, an independent federal agency that supervises "state non-member banks."

Federal Deposit Insurance Corporation
Division of Compliance and Consumer Affairs
550 17th Street, NW
Washington, DC 20429
(877) 275-3342 (ASK-FDIC)
Web: **www.fdic.gov**

If your lender is a national bank (a bank with "national" in the name or "N.A." after the name), you should address your complaint to the Office of the Comptroller of the Currency, an agency of the United States Department of the Treasury.

Comptroller of the Currency
Customer Assistance Unit
1301 McKinney Street, Suite 3710
Houston, TX 77010
(800) 613-6743
Web: **www.occ.treas.gov/customer.htm**

If your lender is a federal savings and loan or a federal savings bank, you should address your complaint to the Office of Thrift Supervision, a bureau of the

Department of the Treasury that is the primary regulator of all federally chartered and many state-chartered thrift institutions, which include savings banks and savings and loan associations.

Office of Thrift Supervision
Consumer Programs
1700 G Street, NW
Washington, DC 20552
(202) 906-6237 or (800) 842-6929
Web: **www.ots.treas.gov**

If your lender is a federally chartered credit union, you should address your complaint to the National Credit Union Administration, an independent federal agency that charters, regulates, examines, and supervises federal credit unions (identified by the word "federal" in their names and the NCUA logo).

National Credit Union Administration
Office of Public and Congressional Affairs
1775 Duke Street
Alexandria, VA 22314-3428
(703) 518-6330
Web: **www.ncua.gov**

If your lender is a mortgage company, you should address your complaint to the Federal Trade Commission, which enforces federal consumer protection laws that prevent fraud, deception, and unfair business practices.

Federal Trade Commission
Consumer Response Center
6th and Pennsylvania, NW
Washington, DC 20580
877-FTC-HELP (382-4357) (toll-free)
Web: **www.ftc.gov**

Laws That Protect Individuals in Their Dealings with Financial Institutions

These are the major laws that govern financial institutions and protect individuals in their financial dealings:

- *Truth in Lending Act* requires a lender to tell you how much it will cost to borrow money so that you can compare the terms of credit offered by different lenders.

- *Fair Credit and Charge Card Disclosure Act* requires a lender offering you a credit card to tell you the annual percentage rate (APR), the amount of any annual fee, and whether you have a grace period to pay your bill before a finance charge is added.

- *Fair Credit Reporting Act* controls how your credit history (how you pay your bills) is kept by credit bureaus and used by lenders.

- *Equal Credit Opportunity Act* prohibits lenders from discriminating against you in a credit transaction on the basis of certain personal characteristics, such as race, color, religion, national origin, sex, marital status, age, because you receive public assistance, or because you've exercised your rights under the Consumer Credit Protection Act.

- *Fair Debt Collection Practices Act* lays out the rules a debt collector must follow when trying to collect a debt from a consumer.

- *Home Equity Loan Consumer Protection Act* requires a lender to give you complete information about the home equity loan plan it offers—first when you receive an application and again before you first use the line of credit.

- *Home Ownership and Equity Protection Act* requires disclosures and imposes substantive limitations on mortgage transactions having rates or fees above a certain percentage or amount. It also requires disclosures about the potential costs for reverse mortgages.

- *Fair Housing Act* prohibits lenders from discriminating against you in real estate mortgage or home improvement loans on the basis of race, color, religion, national origin, sex, familial status, or handicap.

- *Real Estate Settlement Procedures Act (RESPA)* states that lenders must give purchasers information about the costs required to close a mortgage loan. It also protects consumers from unnecessarily high real estate settlement costs by prohibiting certain business practices. This applies when you take out or refinance a loan secured by real estate such as a mortgage loan or a home equity loan.

- *Fair Credit Billing Act* requires that a lender promptly correct a mistake on your credit card bill.

- *Expedited Funds Availability Act* limits how long a bank may delay your use of the funds you deposit in an account.

- *Truth in Savings Act* requires lenders to disclose the terms of their deposit accounts in a uniform way.

Who Regulates the Escrow Impound Accounts Collected by My Lender?

Escrow impound accounts are regulated by the Department of Housing and Urban Development under the Real Estate Settlement Procedures Act (RESPA).

RESPA sets the limits on the amounts that your lender may require you to pay into the escrow account each month. This amount may be no more than one-twelfth of the total of all disbursements payable during the year, plus an amount necessary to pay for any shortage in the account. Your lender is allowed to collect an amount equal to one-sixth of the total disbursements of the year, to provide for any increases in the charges during the year. Your lender will be required to perform an analysis of your escrow account once a year and to notify you of any shortage in the account. An excess of any amount over $50 that they have collected must be returned to you.

You are entitled to file a complaint if you have a problem with your escrow account. You should first contact your loan servicer in writing, who is required to answer your complaint in writing within 20 business days after receipt of your complaint. The loan servicer must resolve the complaint within 60 business days or give you a statement of the reason for its position. In addition, HUD has the authority to impose penalties on loan servicers who do not give you an annual escrow account statement. If you have a complaint you should contact the HUD Office of Consumer and Regulatory Affairs:

Director, Interstate Land Sales/RESPA Division
Office of Consumer and Regulatory Affairs
U.S. Department of Housing and Urban Development
451 7th Street, SW, Room 9146
Washington, DC 20410.
(202) 708-0502

Are There Any Other Questions That Might Be of Concern to Me as a Buyer or Seller after the Closing?

There certainly are. After your purchase or sale has closed, after the monies have been disbursed, and after the closing statements and documents have been distributed, you should take one last look at your new obligations to be certain you understand exactly what they are.

- Do you clearly understand when your loan payments are due? Get the loan payment book from the seller if you are assuming his loan and verify when the next payment is due and where it is to be made.

- Do you know when the property taxes come due? Get the old tax bill from the seller and also contact the tax collector if you don't get a new tax bill by mail when it is due. Ignorance of the dates and amounts owed is no acceptable excuse for missing a property tax payment. The tax collector has heard them all. Be aware that in states that peg property taxes to sales prices the tax collector will be sending you at least one and sometimes two supplemental property tax bills. These bills cover the increase in property taxes from the old figure to the new one.

- Do you know when the next fire insurance premium falls due?
- Do you know, if you bought a condo or co-op, when the homeowners' association fees must be paid?

If you have any uncertainties about these matters, even after escrow has closed, be sure you discuss them with your escrow officer. She will go over your new commitments with you and explain anything you don't understand.

One last and very important item to remember, one you should write in big red letters on your calendar, is that you should inquire about any monies that have been held in escrow after the close. More often than not, in the relief and joy of closing escrow, buyers and sellers forget that they still have money held back in their account. They think, since this amount has been stated on the closing instructions, that the matter is over and done with. It's not.

Some time ago I spent one entire week, eight hours a day, trying to release money that was held in various escrow accounts. I had a stack of more than a hundred old escrow files on my desk, each one with from $1.20 to $15,000 still in the escrow account. Many files were a year or more old and most of the people involved had completely forgotten about the money! They, of course, were delighted to hear of their windfall checks that I would be sending them. They hadn't realized that they could have rightfully claimed their money long before if they had only advised me that certain conditions had been met.

The reasons for holding their money were all different, ranging from money held for lawn repair and roof repair to money held for termite clearance and receipt of a new property assessment bill.

One of these files actually held $15,000. This was a deposit made on a large land purchase, which, believe it or not, was still pending after three years. I reminded the buyer about his $15,000 earnest money held in escrow and suggested that we put it into an interest-bearing savings account until the escrow closed. He replied that he had never thought of doing that. Had he requested three years before that we put his $15,000 into a bank account yielding a mere 6% interest, his escrow account would have been worth a whopping $17,700!

How Do I Begin Looking after My Property Investment?

You should begin looking after your property investment by keeping all of the property's papers organized. If you don't already keep a separate file folder for your monthly bills, now is a good time to begin. As each is paid, file it in that month's section and put the bills ahead to the next month when they are to be paid. Keep a master list of all your bills in a special folder; transfer this list each month with your other bills so you can't possibly overlook a payment.

Because you want to protect your credit and avoid having to pay late fees, you'll want to make your loan payments on time. To remind yourself of your obligations, you might want to write their due dates on your calendar over the next 12 months or make up a master list of the periodic bills. It might be similar to the one shown here. It lists when the bills are due, when they are delinquent, how much they are, and to whom they are to be paid.

Master List for Property Located at: 12 Allendale Ct., Boonville			
To Whom Payable	**Due Date**	**Delinquent After**	**Amount Paid**
Lender	First	Tenth	792.24
Seller	Tenth	Twentieth	212.48
Tax Collector	Nov 1	Dec 10	326.30
	Feb 1	Apr 10	326.30
Fire Insurance Co.	Aug 12		243.88

Chart 12-4. Example of master list for payments

An institutional lender will usually give you a 10- to 15-day grace period in which to make your loan payment, but after that you'll have to pay a very costly penalty, in some cases as much as $150. Be sure to mail your check to your lender well ahead of its delinquent date, though, because they expect to have received your payment by this date. If you have an adjustable rate loan, you will be notified ahead of time of any payment increase or decrease. Be aware what index your adjustable rate loan is based on and where the index is published so you can keep track of it.

Property taxes, on the other hand, must be postmarked, not actually received, on or before the delinquent date given on the tax bill.

TIP Don't be alarmed if you are notified shortly after closing that your loan will be serviced by an agency other than your original lender. The rights to service your loan may change several times before your loan is paid off. Servicing transfers are so common that borrowers are now protected by RESPA against unlawful loan servicing practices. Under this law, you must be notified by both your old and new lenders of any change in servicing your loan. You are entitled to be notified where your loan payments are to be sent and who is responsible for collecting monthly escrow payments for payment of taxes and hazard insurance. At closing, you will have received a *service disclosure statement* that provided information about servicing procedures, transfer practices and complaint resolution. Look through your closing documents for a copy of this form.

Problems can occur if, for example, you accidentally send your loan payment to your previous lender and the new lender charges you late fees and penalties when your payment arrives after the due date. Luckily, you are protected under a 60-day grace period provision that states that you cannot be charged a late fee if you send your mortgage payment to the old mortgage servicer instead of the new one. Even if the new servicer receives your payment late, it cannot report that to a credit bureau.

If you encounter a problem with your loan servicing company, you should first contact the company. The servicer is required to respond to you within 20 business days of receiving your letter and must correct the mistake within 60 days. If a telephone call and a letter detailing the problem do not correct the mistake, you can register a complaint with the Department of Housing and Urban and Development:

Office of Inspector General Hotline
Assistant Inspector General for Investigations
451 7th St., SW, Room 8270
Washington, DC 20410-4500
800-347-3735
e-mail: hotline@hudoig.gov

What Important Things Should I Remember About Escrow and Closing?

Remember that escrow means simply to involve a disinterested third-party holder in a specialized process to protect all the parties in a transaction. Escrow may be referred to as *closing* or *settlement* in different parts of the country, but the process is the same.

Remember that the escrow or closing officer is there to help you, whether you are the buyer or the seller or even the lender, so don't hesitate to ask her about anything related to your escrow.

A Typical Misunderstanding: Two months after their escrow has closed, Max and Gertrude are talking with a new neighbor about one of their common fence lines. Later they begin to feel that the old owner may have misled them and they begin looking more carefully into their title insurance policy. With certain questions in mind, they try to contact their real estate agent, but learn that he is off visiting relatives. They decide to wait until he returns rather than bother their escrow officer. After all, she's been paid off and probably won't have any record of the matter anyway.

The Way Things Really Are: Max and Gertrude should not hesitate to contact their escrow officer with their questions about title insurance, no matter whether it's days or years after escrow has closed.

Remember that your own escrow closing is never the only one in the office and that your escrow or closing officer is usually dealing with 15 to 20 files at once. She can't possibly remember your escrow number. So whenever you call your escrow officer, always identify yourself by name and escrow number and you'll get the prompt service you want.

Remember that anyone with a qualifying document may record it at the county recorder's office, so if a situation should arise that does not necessitate the purchase of title insurance, a situation such as changing the manner of holding title or correcting a name on a deed, you can do the paperwork yourself. If you should happen to encounter any difficulties doing it, you might even ask the escrow officer who last handled a real estate transaction for you to help you out.

My Final Closing Statement

I do hope that the information in this book has been of help to you. I have always believed that escrow and closing can be made simple and understandable and that people involved in a closing should know much more about what they're doing. In the same way that a well-insulated house conserves energy and saves on utility bills, so, too, does knowledge insulate. It conserves energy and saves grief and labor. The knowledge you have gained here should insulate you well from many of the problems people encounter at closing.

I welcome any replies that might help make this a better book. If you have any suggestions, please write me at: Sandy Gadow, P.O. Box 2165, Palm Beach, Florida 33480, or contact me via e-mail at:sandygadow@escrowhelp.com. For the latest escrow and closing information and help, visit me on the internet at **www.escrowhelp.com**.

Escrow and Closing Forms You Can Use

Some of the forms shown in the text appear here as blanks so that you may copy and use them. Before you copy them, cover the bottom of the page so the page number doesn't show. Below is a list of these forms together with page numbers where they were first introduced in the text.

	Blank Form on Page No.	Introduced on Page No.
Worksheet for Opening Escrow	208	17
Quitclaim Deed	209	47
Agreement to Change Title	210	50
Loan Shopper	211	70
Cash-to-Close Worksheet	212	82
Straight Note	213	103
Installment Note	214	104
Assignment of Deed of Trust	215	106
Substitution of Trustee and Full Conveyance	216	128
Bill of Sale	217	175
Power of Attorney	218	178

Permission to Reprint

The author hereby grants permission to the purchaser of this book to copy any of these forms for personal use. Their reproduction for sale or distribution shall constitute an infringement of copyright. The author assumes no responsibility for the legality or currency of these forms. Before using them, check with your escrow agent, real estate attorney, or closing agent to determine whether they are appropriate for your use.

Worksheet for Opening Escrow

Date_____

Person opening escrow_____

  Address_____

  Telephone_____

Property Address_____

Owner_____

  Address_____

  Telephone_____

Buyer_____

  Address_____

  Telephone_____

Sales Price_____Deposit_____

Total down payment (including deposit)_____

Commission_____

_____Paid to_____

_____Paid to_____

1st deed of trust—lender_____

  Amount_____Terms_____

2nd deed of trust—lender_____

  Amount_____Terms_____

Termite Report Company_____

  Termite report copies sent to_____

Bill of Sale (personal property)_____

_____

Closing date_____

Closing costs_____

  Title insurance paid by_____

  Escrow fees paid by_____

  Transfer taxes paid by_____

Title_____

  Purchaser to take title as_____

Miscellaneous_____

RECORDING REQUESTED BY:

MAIL TAX STATEMENT TO:

WHEN RECORDED, MAIL TO:

Recorder's Use Only

ORDER NO.

ESCROW NO.

QUITCLAIM DEED

DOCUMENTARY TRANSFER TAX $_____

_____COMPUTED FULL VALUE OF PROPERTY CONVEYED, OR

_____COMPUTED ON FULL VALUE LESS LIENS & ENCUMBRANCES

REMAINING THEREON AT TIME OF SALE

_____Unincorporated Area_____City of_____

Tax Parcel No._____

FOR A VALUABLE CONSIDERATION,   HEREBY QUITCLAIM to:

the real property in the County of_____, State of_____, described as

Witness my hand this _____ day of _____, 20___.

_____   _____

STATE OF   )   WITNESS my hand and official seal:

) s.s.

COUNTY OF   )

On_____, 20____,   _____

before me, the undersigned, a Notary Public in   Notary Public in and for said County and State

and for said County and State, personally

appeared   NOTARY SEAL

proved to me on the basis of satisfactory evidence

to be the person__ whose name__ is (are) sub-

scribed to the instrument and acknowledge

that _____ executed the same.

AGREEMENT TO CHANGE TITLE FROM JOINT TENANCY TO COMMUNITY PROPERTY

1. PARTIES:

Parties to this agreement are_____
and_____.

2. RECITALS:

a) The parties hereto are husband and wife, residing in the
County of_____ State of_____.

b) They have heretofore held property in their common or separate names, and may hereafter do so.

c) They hold portions of their property in joint tenancy only as a matter of convenience of transfer.

d) This agreement is entered into with the full knowledge on the part of each party of the extent and probable value of all of the property and estate of the community, and of the separate and joint property of each other, ownership of which would be conferred by law on each of them in the event of the termination of their relationship by death or otherwise.

e) It is the express intent of the parties hereto that all their common properties are and shall be their community property.

3. AGREEMENT THAT ALL PROPERTY SHALL BE COMMUNITY:

Each party hereby releases all of his or her separate rights in and to any and all property, real or personal and wherever situated, which either party now owns or has an interest in, and each party agrees that all property or interest therein owned heretofore or presently or hereafter acquired by either from common funds shall be deemed to be community property of the parties hereto, whether held in their separate names, as joint tenants, as tenants in common, or in any other legal form. The parties understand that this agreement will automatically, without other formality, transfer to the other a one-half interest in any separate property now owned and that such transfer could constitute a taxable gift under Federal and State law.

4. AGREEMENT MODIFIABLE IN WRITING ONLY:

This agreement shall not be modified except in writing signed by both parties, or by the mutual written surrender or abandonment of their said community interest in accordance with the laws of said State pertaining to the management of community property, or by the termination of their marriage by death or otherwise.

DATED:_____, 20____

_____

_____

LOAN SHOPPER			
	Lender One	**Lender Two**	**Lender Three**
Initial interest rate on note			
Fixed, variable, graduated, other			
Amortization due date			
Points and other fees (total)			
Prepayment penalty			
Assumability (specific requirements)			
Interest rate cap			
Index used			
Interest rate adjustments			
Co-borrowers allowed			
Maximum negative amortization			

CASH-TO-CLOSE WORKSHEET

ANALYSIS OF CASH TO CLOSE

Full amount of price of new house	$_____	A
Loan amount requested	$_____	B
Down payment needed (without closing costs)	$_____	C=A-B
Closing cost estimate (3-5% of loan amount)	$_____	D

TOTAL AMOUNT NEEDED TO CLOSE $_____ E=C+D

ANALYSIS OF CASH TO CLOSE

Amount from sale of present house	$_____	F
Amount of cash deposit	$_____	G
Amount from savings and checking accounts	$_____	H
Amount from gifts	$_____	I
Amount from stocks and other securities	$_____	J
Amount from other sources (secondary financing, etc.)	$_____	K

_____

_____

_____

TOTAL CASH AVAILABLE FOR CLOSING $_____ L=F+G+H+
I+J+K

NOTE: "L" must be equal to or greater than "E."

STRAIGHT NOTE

$_____ _____(city)

_____(state), _____ , 20____

_____after date for value received,

I promise to pay to_____

_____or order, at

_____

the sum of_____DOLLARS

with interest from_____, until paid at the

rate of_____percent per annum, payable_____

_____

Principal and interest payable in lawful money of the United States of America. Should default be made in payment of interest when due, the whole sum of principal and interest shall become immediately due at the option of the holder of this note. If action be instituted on this note, I promise to pay such sum as the Court may fix as Attorney's fees. This note is secured by a Mortgage Deed or a Deed of Trust of even date herewith.

_____   _____

_____   _____

_____   _____

When paid, this Note, if secured by a Deed of Trust, must be surrendered to Trustee for cancellation before reconveyance will be made.

DO NOT DESTROY

INSTALLMENT NOTE

$_____ _____(city)

_____(state), _____, 20____

FOR VALUE RECEIVED, I promise to pay in lawful money of the United States of

America to _____

or order, at _____

the principal sum of _____DOLLARS

with interest in like lawful money from _____, 20_____

at _____percent per annum of the amounts of the principal sum remaining

unpaid from time to time. Principal and interest payable in installments of _____

_____DOLLARS, or more each, on the _____

day of each and every _____

beginning _____

_____

_____

_____

Each payment shall be credited first to the interest then due, and the remainder to the principal sum; and interest shall thereupon cease upon the amount so paid on said principal sum. AND I agree that in case of default in the payment of any installments when due, then the whole of said principal sum then remaining unpaid, together with the interest that shall have accrued thereon, shall forthwith become due and payable at the election of the holder of this note, without notice. AND I agree, if action be instituted on this note, to pay such sum as the Court may fix as Attorney's fees. This note is secured by a Mortgage Deed or a Deed of Trust of even date herewith.

_____   _____

_____   _____

_____   _____

When paid, this Note, if secured by a Deed of Trust, must be surrendered to Trustee for cancellation before reconveyance will be made.

DO NOT DESTROY

RECORDING REQUESTED BY:	
WHEN RECORDED, MAIL TO:	Recorder's Use Only

ASSIGNMENT OF DEED OF TRUST

FOR A VALUABLE CONSIDERATION, the undersigned hereby grants, assigns, and transfers to:

all beneficial interest under that certain Deed of Trust dated _____, 20____

executed by_____, as Trustor,

to_____, as Trustee,

and recorded as Instrument Number_____ on_____, 20____

in Book_____ at Page_____

of Official Records in the office of the County Recorder of_____
together with the Promissory Note secured by said Deed of Trust and also all rights accrued or to accrue under said Deed of Trust.

Witness my hand this _____ day of _____, 20___.

_____   _____

STATE OF   )
) s.s.   WITNESS my hand and official seal:
COUNTY OF   )
On_____, 20___,   _____
before me, the undersigned, a Notary Public in   Notary Public in and for said County and State
and for said County and State, personally
appeared   NOTARY SEAL

proved to me on the basis of satisfactory evidence
to be the person__ whose name__ is (are) subscribed to the instrument and acknowledge
that _____ executed the same.

NOTE: This Assignment should be kept with the Note and Deed of Trust hereby assigned.

RECORDING REQUESTED BY:	
WHEN RECORDED, MAIL TO:	Recorder's Use Only

ASSIGNMENT OF DEED OF TRUST

THE UNDERSIGNED, PRESENT BENEFICIARY under that certain Deed of Trust executed by:

_____, as Trustor

_____, as Original Trustee

and recorded as Instrument Number_____ on_____, 20____

in Book_____ at Page_____of Official Records, in the office of the County

Recorder of_____ County, State of_____
hereby appoints and SUBSTITUTES the Undersigned as the new and substituted Trustee
thereunder in accordance with the terms and provisions contained therein; AND

as such duly appointed and substituted Trustee thereunder, the Undersigned DOES HEREBY
RECONVEY to the person or persons legally entitled thereto, without warranty, all the estate,
title, and interest acquired by the Original Trustee and by the Undersigned as the said substituted Trustee under said Deed of Trust.

Wherever the text of this document so requires, the singular includes the plural.

Witness my hand this _____ day of _____, 20___.

Beneficiary and Substituted Trustee

_____

STATE OF _____)

) s.s.

COUNTY OF _____)

On_____, 20___,
before me, the undersigned, a Notary Public in
and for said County and State, personally
appeared

_____

WITNESS my hand and official seal

NOTARY SEAL

proved to me on the basis of satisfactory evidence
to be the person__ whose name__ is (are) subscribed to the instrument and acknowledge
that _____executed the same.

BILL OF SALE

THIS BILL OF SALE is dated the _____ day of _____, 20_____
WITNESSETH:

That _____

herein called the Seller, for good and valuable consideration, hereby sells, assigns, and transfers to

herein called the Buyer, all that certain property which is hereinafter described.

IT IS HEREBY COVENANTED by the Seller, which covenant shall be binding upon the heirs, executors, and administrators of the Seller, that this sale is warranted. The sale of said property will be defended against any and every person who lawfully claims the same.

The property which is hereby sold, assigned, and transferred is described as follows, to-wit [described as precisely as possible and give location, if known]:

Signature of Seller: _____

RECORDING REQUESTED BY:	
WHEN RECORDED, MAIL TO:	Recorder's Use Only

POWER OF ATTORNEY

Know All Men by These Presents: That _____
the undersigned (jointly and severally, if more than one) hereby make, constitute, and appoint _____
as my true and lawful Attorney for me and in my name, place, and stead and for my use and benefit:

(a) To ask, demand, sue for, recover, collect, and receive each and every sum of money, debt, account, legacy, bequest, interest, dividend, annuity, and demand (which now is or hereafter shall become due, owing, or payable) belonging to or claimed by me, and to use and take any lawful means for the recovery thereof by legal process or otherwise, and to execute and deliver a satisfaction or release therefor, together with the right and power to compromise or compound any claim or demand;

(b) To exercise any or all of the following powers as to real property, any interest therein, and/or any building thereon: To contract for, purchase, receive and take possession thereof and of evidence of title thereto; to lease the same for any term or purpose, including leases for business, residence, and oil and/or mineral development; to sell, exchange, grant, or convey the same with or without warranty; and to mortgage, transfer in trust, or otherwise encumber or hypothecate the same to secure payment of a negotiable or non-negotiable note or performance of any obligation or agreement;

(c) To exercise any or all of the following powers as to all kinds of personal property and goods, wares and merchandise, choses in action and other property in possession or in action: To contract for, buy, sell, exchange, endorse, transfer, and in any legal manner deal in and with the same; and to mortgage, transfer in trust, or otherwise encumber or hypothecate the same to secure payment of a negotiable or non-negotiable note or performance of any obligation or agreement;

(d) To borrow money and to execute and deliver negotiable or non-negotiable notes therefore with or without security; and to loan money and receive negotiable or non-negotiable notes therefor with such security as he shall deem proper;

(e) To create, amend, supplement, and terminate any trust and to instruct and advise the trustee of any trust wherein I am or may be trustor or beneficiary; to represent and vote stock, exercise stock rights, accept and deal with any dividend, distribution, or bonus, join in any corporate financing, reorganization, merger, liquidation, consolidation, or other action and the extension, compromise, conversion, adjustment, enforcement or foreclosure, singly or in conjunction with others of any corporate stock, bond, note, debenture, or other security; to compound, compromise, adjust, settle, and satisfy any obligation, secured or unsecured, owing by or to me and to give or accept any property and/or money whether or not equal to or less in value than the amount owing in payment, settlement, or satisfaction thereof;

(f) To transact business of any kind or class and, as my act and deed, to sign, execute, acknowledge, and deliver any deed, lease, assignment of lease, covenant, indenture, indemnity, agreement, mortgage, deed of trust, assignment of mortgage or of the beneficial interest under deed of trust, extension or renewal of any obligation, subordination or waiver of priority, hypothecation, bottomry, charter-party, bill of lading, bill of sale, bill, bond, note, whether negotiable or non-negotiable, receipt, evidence of debt, full or partial release or satisfaction of mortgage, judgment, and other debt, request for partial or full reconveyance of deed of trust and such other instruments in writing of any kind or class as may be necessary or proper in the premises.

Giving and granting unto my said Attorney full power and authority to do and perform all and every act and thing whatsoever requisite, necessary, or appropriate to be done in and about the premises as fully to all intents and purposes as I might or could do if personally present, hereby ratifying all that my said Attorney shall lawfully do or cause to be done by virtue of these presents. The powers and authority hereby conferred upon my said Attorney shall be applicable to all real and personal property or interests therein now owned or hereafter acquired by me and wherever situated.

My said Attorney is empowered hereby to determine in his sole discretion the time when, purpose for, and manner in which any power herein conferred upon him shall be exercised, and the conditions, provisions, and covenants of any instrument or document which may be executed by him pursuant hereto; and in the acquisition or disposition of real or personal property, my said Attorney shall have exclusive power to fix the terms thereof for cash, credit, and/or property, and if on credit with or without security.

The undersigned, if a married woman, hereby further authorizes and empowers my said Attorney, as my duly authorized agent, to join in my behalf, in the execution of any instrument by which any community real property or interest therein, now owned or hereafter acquired by my spouse and myself, or either of us, is sold leased, encumbered, or conveyed.

When the context so requires, the masculine gender includes the feminine and/or neuter, and the singular number includes the plural.

[ ]This is to be considered a general Power of Attorney.
[ ]Notwithstanding the aforesaid, this is to be considered a specific power of attorney limited to_____
_____and expiring _____
Witness my hand this _____ day of _____, 20_____.

_____   _____

STATE OF _____)	WITNESS my hand and official seal
) s.s.	
COUNTY OF _____)	
On _____, 20_____	
before me, the undersigned, a Notary Public in and for said County and State personally appeared	_____
	Notary Public in and for said County and State
	NOTARY SEAL
proved to me on the basis of satisfactory evidence to be the person whose name__ is (are) subscribed to the within instrument and acknowledge that _____executed the same.	

State-by-State Guide to Real Estate Closing Practices in the U.S.

This reference guide contains summary information. Contact a local title company, closing agent, or real estate attorney for more detailed information.

Alabama

Attorneys handle closings. Conveyance is by warranty deed. Mortgages are the customary security instruments. Foreclosures are non-judicial. Foreclosure notices are published once a week for three weeks, county by county. The foreclosure process takes a minimum of 21 days from the date of first publication. After the sale, there is a one-year redemption period. Alabamans use ALTA policies to insure titles. Buyers and sellers negotiate who's going to pay the closing costs and usually split them equally. Property taxes are due and payable annually on October 1.

Consumer Complaints:
Banking Department
401 Adams Avenue, Suite 680
Montgomery, AL 36130-1201
334-242-3452
Fax: 334-242-3500
Web: www.bank.state.al.us
David Parsons, Acting Commissioner
Alabama Department of Insurance
201 Monroe Street, Suite 1700
P.O. Box 303351
Montgomery, AL 36104
334-269-3550
Fax: 334-241-4192

E-mail: insdept@insurance.state.al.us
Web: www.aldoi.org
Alabama Real Estate Commission
1201 Carmichael Way
Montgomery, AL 36106-4350
334-242-5544, TTY: 334-396-0064
Fax: 334-270-9118
E-mail: arec@arec.state.al.us
Web: www.arec.state.al.us

Rate filing statute: File and use
Customary title fee splits:
Owner's policy: Negotiable
Lender's policy: Buyer
Title search: Negotiable
Transfer taxes: Buyer
Closing fees: Negotiable
Recording fees: Buyer
Real estate transfer disclosure required? No
Agency relationship disclosure required:
Required by time of purchase offer.

Alaska

Title companies, lenders, and private escrow companies all handle real estate escrows. Conveyance is by warranty deed. Deeds of trust with private power of sale are the customary security instruments. Foreclosures take 90-120 days. Alaskans use ALTA owner's and lender's policies with standard endorsements. There are no documentary or transfer taxes. Buyer and seller usually split the closing costs. Property tax payment dates vary throughout the state.

Consumer Complaints:
Division of Banking, Securities, and
  Corporations
Department of Community and Economic
  Development
150 Third Street, Suite 217
Juneau, AK 99801
P.O. Box 110807
Juneau, AK 99811-0807
907-465-2521, TTY/TDD: 907-465-5437
Fax: 907-465-1231
Web: www.dced.state.ak.us/bsc
Department of Community and Economic
  Development
Division of Insurance
P.O. Box 110805
Juneau, AK 99811-0805
State Office Building, 9th Floor
333 Willoughby Avenue
Juneau, AK 99801
907-465-2515, TDD/TTY: 907-465-5437
Fax: 907-465-3422
550 W. 7th Avenue, Suite 1560
Anchorage, AK 99501-3567
907-269-7900
Fax: 907-269-7910
E-mail: insurance@dced.state.ak.us
Web: www.dced.state.ak.us/insurance
Division of Occupational Licensing
Real Estate Commission
Frontier Building
3601 C Street, Suite 722
Anchorage, AK 99503-5986
907-269-8160
Fax: 907-269-8196
E-mail: license@dced.state.ak.us
Web: www.dced.state.ak.us/occ/prec.htm

Rate filing statute: File and use
Customary title fee splits:
Owner's policy: Seller
Lender's policy: Buyer
Title search: Included in premium
Closing fees: Divided equally
Real estate transfer disclosure required? Yes
Agency relationship disclosure required? Yes

Arizona

Title companies and title agents both handle closings. Conveyance is by warranty deed. Whereas deeds of trust are the security instruments most often used, mortgages and "agreements for sale" are used approximately 20% of the time. Foreclosure depends upon the security instrument. For deeds of trust, the foreclosure process takes about 91 days. Arizonans use ALTA owner's and lender's policies, standard or extended, with standard endorsements. The seller customarily pays for the owner's policy and the buyer pays for the lender's policy. They split escrow costs otherwise. There are no documentary, transfer, or mortgage taxes. The first property tax installment is due October 1 and delinquent November 1; the second half is due March 1 and delinquent May 1. Arizona is a community property state. Right of survivorship is permitted when holding title as community property.

Consumer Complaints:
State Banking Department
2910 N. 44th Street, Suite 310
Phoenix, AZ 85018
602-255-4421
Fax: 602-381-1225
E-mail: consumeraffairs@azbanking.com
Web: www.azbanking.com
Department of Insurance
2910 N. 44th Street, Suite 210
Phoenix, AZ 85018-7256
Toll-free in AZ: 800-325-2548, 602-912-8444
Fax: 602-954-7008
Web: www.state.az.us/id
Department of Real Estate
2910 N. 44th Street
Phoenix, AZ 85018
602-468-1414 ext 100
Fax: 602-955-6284
E-mail: ICSD@re.state.az.us
Web: www.re.state.az.us

Rate filing statute: File and use
Customary title fee Splits:
Owner's policy: Seller
Lender's policy: Buyer
Title search: Included in premium
Closing fees: Divided equally
Recording fees: Seller pays for recording any documents required to remove encumbrances. Buyer pays to record deed and mortgage.

Arkansas

Title agents handle escrows, and attorneys conduct closings. Conveyance is by warranty deed. Mortgages are the customary security instruments. Foreclosure requires judicial proceedings, but there are no minimum time limits for completion. Arkansans use ALTA policies and endorsements and receive a 40% discount for reissuance of prior policies. Buyers and sellers pay their own escrow costs. The buyer pays for the lender's policy; the seller pays for the owner's. The buyer and seller split the state documentary tax. Property taxes come due three times a year as follows: the third Monday in April, the third Monday in July, and October 10.

Consumer Complaints:
Arkansas State Banking Department
Sedgwick Center
400 Hardin Road
Little Rock, AR 72211
501-324-9010
E-mail: asbd@banking.state.ar.us
Web: www.state.ar.us/bank
Department of Insurance
1200 W. 3rd Street
Little Rock, AR 72201-1904
Toll-free in AR: 800-282-9134, Toll-free nationwide: 800-282-5494, 501-371-2640
Fax: 501-371-2749
E-mail: insurance.consumers@mail.state.ar.us
Web: www.state.ar.us/insurance
Real Estate Commission
612 S. Summit Street
Little Rock, AR 72201-4740
501-683-8010
E-mail: arec@mac.state.ar.us
Web: state.ar.us/arec/arecweb.html

Rate filing statute: File and use
Customary title fee splits:
Owner's policy: Seller
Lender's policy: Buyer
Title search: Seller
Transfer taxes: Seller
Closing fees: Divided equally
Real estate transfer disclosure required: No
Agency relationship disclosure required: Yes

California

Not only do escrow procedures differ between Northern and Southern California, they also vary somewhat from county to county. Title companies handle closings through escrow in Northern California, whereas escrow companies and lenders handle them in Southern California. Conveyance is by grant deed. Deeds of trust with private power of sale are the security instruments used throughout the state. Foreclosure requires a three-month waiting period after the recording of the notice of default. After the waiting period, the notice of sale is published each week for three consecutive weeks. The borrower may reinstate the loan at any time prior to five business days before the foreclosure sale. All in all, the procedure takes about four months. Californians have both ALTA and CLTA policies available. In Southern California, sellers pay the title insurance premium and the transfer tax. Buyer and seller split the escrow costs. In the Northern California counties of Amador, Merced, Plumas, San Joaquin, and Siskiyou, buyers and sellers share title insurance and escrow costs equally. In Butte County, sellers pay 75%; buyers pay 25%. In Alameda, Calaveras, Colusa, Contra Costa, Lake, Marin, Mendocino, San Francisco, San Mateo, Solano, and Sonoma counties, buyers pay for the title insurance policy, whereas sellers pay in the other Northern California counties. Each California county has its own transfer tax; some cities have additional charges. Property taxes may be paid annually on or before December 10, or semiannually by December 10 and April 10. California is a community property state. Right of survivorship is allowed when holding title as community property.

Consumer Complaints:
Department of Corporations
320 W. 4th Street, Suite 750
Los Angeles, CA 90013-2344
800-622-0620, 213-576-7500
1515 K Street, Suite 200
Sacramento, CA 95814
916-445-7205
Web: www.corp.ca.gov
(CDC regulates independent escrow companies.)
Insurance Commissioner, Department of Insurance
300 Capitol Mall, Suite 1500
Sacramento, CA 95814
916-492-3500
Web: www.insurance.ca.gov

(DI regulates title and title company escrow divisions.)
Department of Real Estate
2201 Broadway
Sacramento, CA 95818
916-227-0931
Web: www.dre.ca.gov

Rate filing statute: File and use
Customary fee splits:
Owner's policy: Buyer or Seller
Lender's policy: Buyer
Title search: Included in premium
Transfer taxes: Seller
Closing fees: Varies by region
Real estate transfer disclosure required? Yes
(Real Estate Transfer Disclosure Statement)
Agency relationship disclosure required? Yes
Obtain disclosure forms:
Real Estate Business Services, Inc.
525 S. Virgil Avenue
Los Angeles, CA 90020
213-739-8200 (within California), 888-750-3343 (outside California)
Fax: 213-480-7724

Colorado

Title companies, brokers, and attorneys all may handle closings. Conveyance is by warranty deed. Deeds of trust are the customary security instruments. Public trustees must sell foreclosure properties within 45-60 days after the filing of a "notice of election and demand for sale," but they will grant extensions up to six months following the date of the originally scheduled sale. Subdivided properties may be redeemed within 75 days after sale; properties described by metes and bounds may be redeemed within six months after sale. The public trustee is normally the trustee shown on the deed of trust, a practice unique to Colorado. Foreclosures may be handled judicially. Coloradoans have these title insurance policy options: ALTA owner's, lender's, leasehold, and construction loan; endorsements are used, too. Although they are negotiable, closing costs are generally paid by the real estate agent. Sellers pay the title insurance premium and the documentary transfer tax. Property taxes may be paid annually at the end of April or semiannually at the ends of February and July.

Consumer Complaints:
Department of Regulatory Agencies, Division of Banking

1560 Broadway, Suite 1175
Denver, CO 80202
303-894-7575
Fax: 303-894-7570
E-mail: banking@dora.state.co.us
Web: www.dora.state.co.us/banking
Commissioner, Division of Insurance
1560 Broadway, Suite 850
Denver, CO 80202
303-894-7499 ext 4311
Fax: 303-894-7455
Web: www.dora.state.co.us/Insurance
Department of Regulatory Agencies, Division of Real Estate
1900 Grant Street, Suite 600
Denver, CO 80203
303-894-2166 or 303-894-2185
Fax: 303-894-2683
E-mail: real-estate@dora.state.co.us
Web: www.dora.state.co.us/real-estate

Rate filing statute: File and use
Customary fee splits:
Owner's policy: Seller
Lender's policy: Buyer
Title search: Included in premium
Transfer taxes: Buyer
Closing fees: Divided equally
Recording fees: Buyer
Real estate transfer disclosure required? No
Agency relationship disclosure required? Yes

Connecticut

Attorneys normally conduct closings. Most often conveyance is by warranty deed, but quitclaim deeds do appear. Mortgages are the security instruments. Judicial foreclosures are the rule, either by a suit in equity for strict foreclosure or by a court decree of sale. Court decreed sales preclude redemption, but strict foreclosures allow redemption for three to six months, depending upon the discretion of the court. There are lender's and owner's title insurance policies available with various endorsements. Buyers customarily pay for examination and title insurance, while sellers pay the documentary and conveyance taxes. Property tax payment dates vary by town.

Consumer Complaints:
Consumer Credit Division
Department of Banking
260 Constitution Plaza

Hartford, CT 06103-1800
Toll-free 800-831-7225, 860-240-8200
Fax: 860-240-8178
E-mail: michael.buchas@po.state.ct.us
Web: www.state.ct.us/dob/pages/ccdiv.htm
Consumer Affairs
Department of Insurance
P.O. Box 816
Hartford, CT 06142-0816
Toll-free: 800-203-3447, 860-297-3984
Fax: 203-297-3872
Web: www.state.ct.us/cid
Department of Consumer Protection
Real Estate and Professional Trades Division
165 Capital Avenue
Hartford, CT 06106
860-713-6135 or 800-842-2649

Rate filing statute: File and use
Customary fee splits:
Owner's policy: Buyer
Lender's policy: Buyer
Title search: Buyer
Transfer taxes: Seller
Closing fees: Negotiable
Real estate transfer disclosure required? Seller must complete a property disclosure form
Agency relationship disclosure required? Yes

Delaware

Attorneys handle closings. Although quitclaim and general warranty deeds are sometimes used, most conveyances are by special warranty deeds. Mortgages are the security instruments. Foreclosures are judicial and require 90-120 days to complete. ALTA policies and endorsements are prevalent. Buyers pay closing costs and the owner's title insurance premiums. Buyers and sellers share the state transfer tax. Property taxes are on an annual basis and vary by county.

Consumer Complaints:
Office of the Bank Commissioner, Compliance Staff
555 E. Loockerman Street, Suite 210
Dover, DE 19901
302-739-4235
Fax: 302-739-2356
Web: www.state.de.us/bank
Department of Insurance
841 Silver Lake Boulevard, Rodney Building
Dover, DE 19904
Toll-free in DE: 800-282-8611, 302-739-4251

Fax: 302-739-6278
Web: www.state.de.us/inscom
Department of Administrative Services
Division of Professional Regulation
Real Estate Commission
861 Silverlake Boulevard, Cannon Building, Suite 203
Dover, DE 19904
302-739-4522 ext 219
Fax: 302-739-2711
Web: www.professionallicensing.state.de.us/ boards /realestate/index.shtml

Rate filing statute: File and use
Customary fee splits:
Owner's policy: Buyer
Lender's policy: Buyer
Title search: Buyer
Transfer taxes: Divided equally
Closing fees: Negotiable
Recording fees: Buyer
Real estate transfer disclosure required? Yes
Agency relationship disclosure required? Yes

District of Columbia

Attorneys, title insurance companies, or their agents may conduct closings. Conveyances are by bargain-and-sale deeds. Though mortgages are available, the deed of trust, containing private power of sale, is the security instrument of choice. Foreclosures require at least six weeks and start with a 30-day notice of sale sent by certified mail. ALTA policies and endorsements insure title. Buyers generally pay closing costs, title insurance premiums, and recording taxes. Sellers pay the transfer tax. Property taxes fall due annually or, if they're less than $100,000, semiannually, on September 15 and March 31.

Consumer Complaints:
Department of Insurance and Securities Regulation
810 First Street, NW
Washington, DC 20002
202-727-8000
Fax: 202-535-1196
E-mail: disr@dcgov.org

Rate filing statute: No direct filing provisions
Customary fee splits:
Owner's policy: Buyer
Lender's policy: Buyer
Title exam: Buyer
Transfer taxes: Buyer pays recordation tax, sell-

er pays transfer tax
Closing fees: Buyer
Recording fees: Buyer
Real estate transfer disclosure required? Only
of underground storage tanks
Agency relationship disclosure required? Yes

Florida

Title companies and attorneys handle closings.
Conveyance is by warranty deed. Mortgages are
the customary security instruments. Foreclosures
are judicial and take about three months. They
involve service by the sheriff, a judgment of foreclosure and sale, advertising, public sale, and
finally issuance of a certificate of sale and certificate of title. ALTA policies are commonplace.
Buyers pay the escrow and closing costs, while
county custom determines who pays for the title
insurance. Sellers pay the documentary tax.
Property taxes are payable annually, but the due
and delinquent dates are months apart,
November 1 and April 1.

Consumer Complaints:
Division of Financial Investigations
Department of Banking and Finance,
101 E. Gaines Street, Suite 516
Tallahassee, FL 32399-0350
Toll-free in FL: 800-848-3792, 850-410-9286
E-mail: fldbf@mail.dbf.state.fl.us
Web: www.dbf.state.fl.us
Department of Insurance
State Capitol, Plaza Level 11
Tallahassee, FL 32399-0300
Toll-free in FL: 800-342-2762, TDD toll-free:
    800-640-0886, 850-922-3130
Web: www.doi.state.fl.us
Division of Real Estate
Department of Business and Professional
    Regulation
P.O. Box 1900
Orlando, FL 32802-1900
400 W. Robinson, Suite N308
Orlando, FL 32801
407-423-6053
Fax: 407-245-0800
E-mail: callcenter@dbpr.state.fl.us
Web: www.state.fl.us/dbpr/re/frec_welcome.
    shtml

Rate filing statutes: Promulgated rate
Customary fee splits:
Owner's policy: Seller

Lender's policy: Buyer
Title search: Seller
Transfer taxes: Buyer pays mortgage tax, seller
pays deed tax
Closing costs: Buyer
Recording fees: Buyer
Real estate transfer disclosure required? No
Agency relationship disclosure required? Yes

Georgia

Attorneys generally take care of closings. Conveyance is by warranty deed. Security deeds
are the security instruments. Foreclosures are
non-judicial and take little more than a month
because there's a power of attorney right in the
security deed. Foreclosure advertising must
appear for four consecutive weeks prior to the
first Tuesday of the month; that's when foreclosure sales take place. Georgians use ALTA title
insurance policies, including owner's and
lender's, and they use binders and endorsements. Buyers pay title insurance premiums
and also closing costs usually. Sellers pay transfer taxes. Property tax payment dates vary
across the state but generally are due by
December 20. Some counties have an earlier
deadline for payment and some require the
taxes to be paid in two installments. Specific
information about payment deadlines may be
found at www2.state.ga.us.

Consumer Complaints:
Department of Banking and Finance
2990 Brandywine Road, Suite 200
Atlanta, GA 30341-5565
770-986-1633
Fax: 770-986-1654 or 770-986-1655
Web: www.ganet.org/dbf/dbf.html
Georgia Real Estate Commission
International Tower, Suite 1000
229 Peachtree Street, NE
Atlanta, GA 30303-1605
404-656-3916
Fax: 404-656-6650
E-mail: grecmail@grec.state.ga.us
Web: www2.state.ga.us/ga.real_estate
Insurance and Safety Fire Commissioner
2 Martin Luther King, Jr. Drive, West Tower,
    Suite 704
Atlanta, GA 30334
Toll-free in GA: 800-656-2298, 404-656-2070,
TDD/TTY: 404-656-4031
Fax: 404-657-8542

Web: www.inscomm.state.ga.us

Rate filing statute: No direct rate filing provisions
Customary fee splits:
Owner's policy: Negotiable
Lender's policy: Buyer
Title search: Buyer
Transfer taxes: Seller
Closing fees: Negotiable
Recording fees: Buyer
Real estate transfer disclosure required? Yes
Agency relationship disclosure required? Yes

Hawaii

By law, only attorneys may prepare property transfer documents, but there are title and escrow companies available to handle escrows and escrow instructions. Conveyance of fee-simple property is by warranty deed; conveyance of leasehold property, which is common throughout the state, is by assignment of lease. Condominiums are everywhere in Hawaii and may be fee simple or leasehold. Sales of some properties, whether fee simple or leasehold, are by agreement of sale. Mortgages are the security instruments. Hawaiians use judicial foreclosures rather than powers of sale for both mortgages and agreements of sale. These foreclosures take six to 12 months and sometimes more, depending upon court schedules. Title companies issue ALTA owner's and lender's policies and make numerous endorsements available. Buyers and sellers split escrow fees. Sellers pay the title search costs and the conveyance tax. Buyers pay title insurance premiums for the owner's and lender's policies. Property taxes come due twice a year, on February 20 and August 20.

Consumer Complaints:
Division of Financial Institutions
Department of Commerce and Consumer
  Affairs
P.O. Box 2054
Honolulu, HI 96805
1010 Richards Street, Room 602-A
Honolulu, HI 96813
808-586-2820
Fax: 808-586-2818
E-mail: dfi@dcca.state.hi.us
Web: www.state.hi.us/dcca/dfi
Hawaii Real Estate Commission

250 South King Street, Room 702
Honolulu, HI 96813
808-586-2643
Web: www.hawaii.gov/hirec
Department of Commerce and Consumer
  Affairs, Insurance Division
250 South King Street, 5th Floor
Honolulu, HI 96813
P.O. Box 3614
Honolulu, HI 96811-3614
808-586-2790, 808-586-2799
Fax: 808-586-2806
Web: www.state.hi.us/dcca/ins

Rate filing statute: No direct rate filing provision
Customary fee splits:
Owner's policy: Varies based on value
Lender's policy: Buyer
Title exam: Included in premium
Transfer taxes: Seller
Closing fees: Divided equally
Recording fees: Divided equally
Real estate transfer disclosure required? Yes
Agency relationship disclosure required? Yes

Idaho

Closings are handled through escrow. Conveyance is by warranty deed or corporate deed, though often there are contracts of sale involved. Either mortgages or deeds of trust may be the security instruments. Deeds of trust which include power of sale provisions are restricted to properties in incorporated areas and properties elsewhere which don't exceed 20 acres. After the notice of default has been recorded, deed-of-trust foreclosures take at least 120 days and there's no redemption period. Judicial foreclosures for mortgages take about a year, depending upon court availability, and there's a six- to 12-month redemption period after that, depending on the type of property involved. Idahoans use ALTA policies and various endorsements. Buyers and sellers split escrow costs in general and negotiate who's going to pay the title insurance premiums. There are no documentary taxes, mortgage taxes, or transfer taxes, but there are property taxes, and they're due annually in November and delinquent on December 20 or semiannually on December 20 and June 20. Idaho is a community property state.

Consumer Complaints:
Department of Finance
700 W. State Street, 2nd Floor
P.O. Box 83702
Boise, ID 83702-0031
208-332-8004
Web: finance.state.id.us/home.asp
Consumer Assistance
Department of Insurance
700 W. State Street
P.O. Box 83720
Boise, ID 83720-0043
Toll-free in ID: 800-721-3272, 208-334-4250
Fax: 208-334-4398
Web: www.doi.state.id.us
Idaho Real Estate Commission
P.O. Box 83720
Boise, ID 83720
208-334-3285

Rate filing statute: Prior approval
Customary fee splits:
Owner's policy: Seller
Lender's policy: Buyer
Title exam: Included in premium
Closing fees: Divided equally
Recording fees: Buyer
Real estate transfer disclosure required? Yes
Agency relationship disclosure required? Yes

Illinois

Title companies, lenders, and attorneys may conduct closings, but only attorneys may prepare documents. Lenders generally hire attorneys and have them prepare all the paperwork. Conveyance is by warranty deed. Recorded deeds must include a declaration of the sales price. Mortgages are the customary security instruments. Judicial foreclosure is mandatory and takes at least a year from the filing of the default notice to the expiration of the redemption period. Illinoisans use ALTA policies. Buyers usually pay the closing costs and the lender's title insurance premiums; sellers pay the owner's title insurance premiums and the state and county transfer taxes. Property tax payment dates vary: larger counties typically schedule them for March 1 and September 1; smaller counties schedule them for June 1 and September 1.

Consumer Complaints:
Office of Banks and Real Estate

500 East Monroe
Springfield, IL 62701-1509
Toll-free: 877-793-3470, 217-782-3000, TDD: 217-524-6644
Fax: 217-524-5941
310 S. Michigan Avenue, Suite 2130
Chicago, IL 60604-4278
Toll-free: 877-793-3470, 312-793-3000, TDD: 312-793-0291
Fax: 312-793-7097
E-mail: consumer@bre.state.il.us
Web: www.obre.state.il.us
Department of Insurance
320 W. Washington Street
Springfield, IL 62767-0001
217-782-4515, TDD: 217-524-4872
Fax: 217-782-5020
100 W. Randolph Street, Suite 15-100
Chicago, IL 60601-3251
312-814-2427, TDD: 312-814-2603
Fax: 312-814-5435
E-mail: director@ins.state.il.us
Web: www.state.il.us/ins/

Rate filing statute: No direct rate filing provisions
Customary fee splits:
Owner's policy: Seller
Lender's policy: Buyer
Title search: Seller
Transfer taxes: Seller
Closing fees: Divided equally
Recording fees: Buyer
Real estate transfer disclosure required? Yes
Agency relationship disclosure required? Yes

Indiana

Title companies, lenders, real estate agents, and attorneys handle closings. Conveyance is by warranty deed. Mortgages are the customary security instruments. Judicial foreclosures are required; execution of judgments varies from three months after filing of the complaint in cases involving mortgages drawn up since July 1, 1975, to six months for those drawn up between January 1, 1958, and July 1, 1975, to 12 months for those drawn up before that. Immediately following the execution sale, the highest bidder receives a sheriff's deed. Hoosiers use ALTA policies and certain endorsements. Buyers usually pay closing costs and the lender's title insurance costs, while sellers pay for the owner's policy. There are no documentary, mortgage, or transfer taxes. Property taxes fall due on May 10 and November 10.

Consumer Complaints:
Department of Financial Institutions
402 W. Washington Street, Room W-066
Indianapolis, IN 46204
317- 232-3955
Fax: 317- 232-7655
Web: www.dfi.state.in.us
Department of Insurance
311 W. Washington Street, Suite 300
Indianapolis, IN 46204-2787
Toll-free in IN: 800-622-4461, 317-232-2385
Fax: 317-232-5251
E-mail: doi@state.in.us
Web: www.state.in.us/idoi

Rate filing statute: No direct rate filing provisions
Customary fee splits:
Owner's policy: Seller
Lender's policy: Buyer
Title exam: Included in premium.
Closing fees: Negotiable
Recording fees: Buyer
Real estate transfer disclosure required? Yes
Agency relationship disclosure required? Yes

Iowa

Attorneys may conduct closings, and so may real estate agents. Conveyance is usually by warranty deed. Mortgages and deeds of trust are both authorized security instruments, but lenders prefer mortgages because deeds of trust do not circumvent judicial foreclosure proceedings anyway. Those proceedings take at least four to six months. Since Iowa is the only state that does not authorize title insurance, Iowans who want it must go through a title company in another state. Buyers and sellers share the closing costs; sellers pay the documentary taxes. Property taxes are due July 1, based upon the previous January's assessment.

Consumer Complaints:
Department of Commerce
Division of Banking
200 E. Grand Avenue, Suite 300
Des Moines, IA 50309-1827
515-281-4014
Web: www.idob.state.ia.us/
Insurance Division
330 Maple Street

Des Moines, IA 50319-0065
Toll-free: 877-955-1212, 515-281-5705
Fax: 515-281-3059
E-mail: consumer.affairs@iid.state.ia.us
Web: www.iid.state.ia.us/
Professional Licensing & Regulation Division
Iowa Real Estate Commission
1918 SE Hulsizer Road
Ankeny, IA 50021-3941
515-281-7393
Fax: 515-281-7411
E-mail: irec@max.state.ia.us
Web: www.state.ia.us/government/com/prof/
    realesta

Rate filing statute: Title insurance is not permitted in Iowa
Customary fee splits:
Owner's policy: Negotiable
Lender's policy: Buyer
Title search: Seller pays pre-closing and abstract charges, buyer pays post-closing charges.
Transfer taxes: Seller
Closing fees: Split
Recording fees: Buyer
Real estate transfer disclosure required? Yes
Agency disclosure required? Yes

Kansas

Title companies, lenders, real estate agents, attorneys, and independent escrow firms all conduct closings. Anyone who conducts a title search must be a licensed abstracter, a designation received after passing strict tests and meeting various requirements. Because many land titles stem from Indian origins, deeds involving Indians as parties to a transaction go before the Indian Commission for approval. Conveyance is by warranty deed. Mortgages are the customary security instruments. Judicial foreclosures, the only ones allowed, take about six months from filing to sale. Redemption periods vary, the longest being 12 months. Kansans use ALTA policies and endorsements. Buyers and sellers divide closing costs. Buyers pay the lender's policy costs and the state mortgage taxes; sellers pay for the owner's policy. Property taxes come due November 1, but they needn't be paid in a lump sum until December 31. They may also be paid in two installments, the first on December 20 and the second on June 20.

Consumer Complaints:
Office of the State Bank Commissioner
700 SW Jackson, Suite 300
Topeka, KS 66603
785-296-2266
Fax: 785-296-0168
Kansas Real Estate Commission
3 Townsite Plaza, Suite 200
120 SE 6th Avenue
Topeka, KS 66603-3511
785-296-3411
Fax: 785-296-1771
Web: www.accesskansas.org/krec
Insurance Department
420 SW 9th Street
Topeka, KS 66612-1678
800-432-2484, 785-296-7801
Fax: 785-296-2283
Web: www.ksinsurance.org

Rate filing statute: File and use
Customary fee splits:
Owner's policy: Varies by county
Lender's policy: Buyer
Title search: Varies by county
Closing fees: Divided equally
Recording fees: Buyer
Real estate transfer disclosure required? No
Agency relationship disclosure required? Yes

Kentucky

Attorneys conduct closings. Conveyance is by grant deed or by bargain-and-sale deed. Deeds must show the name of the preparer, the amount of the total transaction, and the recording reference by which the grantor obtained title. Mortgages are the principal security instruments because deeds of trust offer no power-of-sale advantages. Enforcement of any security instrument requires a decree in equity, a judicial foreclosure proceeding. Kentuckians use ALTA policies and endorsements. Sellers pay closing costs; buyers pay recording fees. Responsibility for payment of title insurance premiums varies according to locale. Property taxes are payable annually; due dates vary from county to county.

Consumer Complaints:
Department of Financial Institutions
1025 Capital Center Drive, Suite 200
Frankfort, KY 40601
502-573-3390, 800-223-2579
Fax: 502-573-8787

Web: www.dfi.state.ky.us/
Real Estate Commission
10200 Linn Station Road, Suite 201
Louisville, KY 40223
502-425-4273, toll-free 888-373-3300
Fax: 502-426-2717
Web: www.krec.net
Department of Insurance
Public Protection and Regulation
P.O. Box 517
Frankfort, KY 40602-0517
215 W. Main Street
Frankfort, KY 40601
Toll-free: 800-595-6053, 502-564-3630, TTY
    toll-free: 800-462-2081
Fax: 502-564-1650
Web: www.doi.state.ky.us/

Rate filing statute: File and use
Customary fee splits:
Owner's policy: Buyer
Lender's policy: Buyer
Title search: Buyer
Transfer taxes: Seller
Closing fees: Buyer
Recording fees: Buyer
Real estate transfer disclosure required? Yes, when a real estate agent is involved
Agency relationship disclosure required? No

Louisiana

Either attorneys or corporate title agents may conduct closings, but a notary must authenticate the documentation. Conveyance is by warranty deed or by act of sale. Mortgages are the security instruments generally used in commercial transactions, while "vendor's liens" and "seller's privileges" are used in other purchase money situations. Foreclosures are swift (60 days) and sure (no right of redemption). Successful foreclosure sale bidders receive an "adjudication" from the sheriff. Louisianans use ALTA owner's and lender's policies and endorsements. Buyers generally pay the title insurance and closing costs. There are no mortgage or transfer taxes. Property tax payment dates vary from parish to parish (parishes are like counties). Louisiana is a community property state.

Consumer Complaints:
Office of Financial Institutions
Post Office Box 94095

Baton Rouge, LA 70804-9095
8660 United Plaza Boulevard, 2nd Floor
Baton Rouge, LA 70809-7024
225-925-4660
Fax: 225-925-4548
Web: www.ofi.state.la.us/
Real Estate Commission
9071 Interline Avenue
Baton Rouge, LA 70809
P.O. Box 14785
Baton Rouge, LA 70898-4785
504-925-4771
Department of Insurance
950 N. Fifth Street
Baton Rouge, LA 70804-9214
Toll-free: 800-259-5300, 225-343-4834
Fax: 254-342-5900
Web: www.ldi.state.la.us

Rate filing statute: File and use
Customary fee splits:
Owner's policy: Buyer
Lender's policy: Buyer
Title search: Buyer
Closing fees: Split by buyer and seller
Real estate transfer disclosure required? No
Agency relationship disclosure required? Yes

Maine

Attorneys conduct closings. Conveyance is by warranty or quitclaim deed. Mortgages are the security instruments. Foreclosures may be initiated by any of the following: an act of law for possession; entering into possession and holding the premises by written consent of the mortgagor; entering peaceably, openly, and unopposed in the presence of two witnesses and taking possession; giving public notice in a newspaper for three successive weeks and recording copies of the notice in the Registry of Deeds, and then recording the mortgage within 30 days of the last publication; or by a bill in equity (special cases). In every case, the creditor must record a notice of foreclosure within 30 days. Judicial foreclosure proceedings are also available. Redemption periods vary from 90 to 365 days depending on the method of foreclosure. Mainers use ALTA owner's and lender's policies and endorsements. Buyers pay closing costs and title insurance fees; buyers and sellers share the documentary transfer taxes. Property taxes are due annually on April 1.

Consumer Complaints:
Office of Consumer Credit Regulation
Department of Professional and Financial
   Regulation
36 State House Station
August, ME 04333-0035
Toll-free in ME: 800-332-8529, 207-624-8527,
   TTY: 207-624-8563
Fax: 207-624-8690
Web: www.state.me.us/pfr/pfrhome.htm
Bureau of Insurance
Department of Professional and Financial
   Regulation
34 State House Station
Augusta, ME 04333
Toll-free in ME: 800-300-5000, 207-624-8475
Fax: 207-624-8599
Web: www.state.me.us/pfr/ins/ins_index.htm

Rate filing statute: File and use
Customary fee splits:
Owner's policy: Buyer
Lender's policy: Buyer
Title search: Buyer
Transfer taxes: Divided equally
Closing fees: Buyer
Recording fees: Buyer
Real estate transfer disclosure required? Yes, when agent is involved.
Agency relationship disclosure required? Yes

Maryland

Attorneys conduct closings, and there has to be a local attorney involved. Conveyance is by grant deed, and the deed must state the consideration involved. Although mortgages are common in some areas, deeds of trust are more prevalent as security instruments. Security instruments may include a private power of sale, so it naturally is the foreclosure method of choice. Marylanders use ALTA policies and endorsements. Buyers pay closing costs, title insurance premiums, and transfer taxes. Property taxes are due annually on July 1. Water bills may become a lien against the house if not properly paid. Water bill will be transferred from seller to buyer at closing.

Consumer Complaints:
Consumer Credit Unit
Division of Financial Regulation
500 N. Calvert Street, Room 402
Baltimore, MD 21202

410-230-6097
E-mail: finreg@dllr.state.md.us
Web: www.dllr.state.md.us/finance
Insurance Administration
525 St. Paul Place
Baltimore, MD 21202-2272
Toll-free: 800-492-6116, 410-468-2000,
TTY: 800-735-2258
Fax: 410-468-2020
Web: www.mdinsurance.state.md.us
Real Estate Commission
Division of Occupational and Professional
   Licensing
Department of Licensing and Regulation
500 N. Calvert Street, Room 308
Baltimore, MD 21202-3651
Toll-free: 888-218-5925, 410-230-6230
Fax: 410-333-0023
E-mail: mrec@dllr.state.md.us
Web: www.dllr.state.md.us/license/occprof/
recomm.html

Rate filing statute: Prior approval
Customary fee splits:
Owner's policy: Buyer
Lender's policy: Buyer
Transfer taxes: Seller, may be negotiable
Closing costs: Negotiable
Recording fees: Buyer
Real estate transfer disclosure required? Yes
Agency relationship disclosure required? No

Massachusetts

Attorneys handle closings. Conveyance is by warranty deed in the western part of the state and by quitclaim deed in the eastern part. Mortgages with private power of sale are the customary security instruments. Creditors forced to foreclose generally take advantage of the private power of sale, but they may foreclose through peaceable entry (entering unopposed in the presence of two witnesses and taking possession for three years) or through the rarely used judicial writ of entry. Frequently, cautious creditors will foreclose through both power of sale and peaceable entry. People in Massachusetts use ALTA owner's and lender's title insurance policies and endorsements. Buyers pay closing costs and title insurance fees, except in Worcester, where sellers pay. Sellers pay the documentary taxes. Property taxes are payable in two installments, November 1 and May 1.

Consumer Complaints:
Consumer Assistance Section
Division of Banks
1 South Station, 3rd Floor
Boston, MA 02110
Toll-free in MA: 800-495-2265, 617-956-1500,
   TDD: 617-956-1577
Fax: 617-956-1599
Web: www.state.ma.us/dob/consum1.htm
Office of Consumer Affairs and Business
   Regulation
Division of Insurance
1 South Station, 5th Floor
Boston, MA 02110-2208
617-521-7794, 617-521-7777, TTY: 617-521-
   7490
Fax: 617-521-7772, 617-521-7575
Web: www.state.ma.us/doi
Board of Registration of Real Estate Brokers
   and Salespersons
Real Estate Board
239 Causeway Street, Suite 500
Boston, MA 02114
617-727-2372, TTY: 617-727-2099
Fax: 617-727-2197
Web: www.state.ma.us/reg/boards/re

Rate filing statute: No direct rate filing provisions
Customary fee splits:
Owner's policy: Buyer
Lender's policy: Buyer
Title search: Buyer
Transfer taxes: Seller
Closing fees: Negotiable
Recording fees: Buyer
Real estate transfer disclosure required? No, agents may be required to disclosure any known facts
Agency relationship disclosure required? Yes

Michigan

Title companies, lenders, real estate agents, and attorneys may conduct closings. Conveyance is by warranty deed, which must give the full consideration involved or be accompanied by an affidavit that does. Many transactions involve land contracts. Mortgages are the security instruments. Private foreclosure is permitted; it requires advertising for four consecutive weeks and a sale at least 28 days following the date of first publication. The redemption period ranges from one to 12 months. Michiganders use ALTA policies and endorsements. Buyers generally pay closing costs and the lender's title insurance premium; sellers pay the state transfer tax and the owner's title insurance premium. Property taxes that pay for city and school expenses fall due July 1; others (county taxes, township taxes, and some school taxes) fall due December 1. In many tax jurisdictions, taxpayers may opt to pay their taxes in two equal installments without penalty.

Consumer Complaints:
Office of Financial and Insurance Services
P.O. Box 30224
Lansing, MI 48909-7724
333 S. Capitol Avenue, Suite A
Lansing, MI 48933-2022
Toll-free: 877-999-6442, 517-373-3460
Fax: 517-335-0908
E-mail: ofis-fin-info@cis.state.mi.us
Web: www.cis.state.mi.us/ofis
Office of Financial and Insurance Services
P.O. Box 30220
Lansing, MI 48933-7220
Ottawa Building, 2nd Floor
611 W. Ottawa Street
Lansing, MI 48933-1070
Toll-free: 877-999-6442, 517-373-0220
Fax: 517-335-4978
Web: www.cis.state.mi.us/ins
Department of Consumer and Industry Services
Bureau of Commercial Services
Board of Real Estate Brokers and Salespersons,
    Compliance Section
P.O. Box 30243
Lansing, MI 48909
2501 Woodlake Circle
Okemos, MI 48864
517-241-9267
Fax: (517) 241-9296
E-mail: bcsinfo@cis.state.mi.us
Web: www.cis.state.mi.us/bcs/re/home.htm

Rate filing statute: File and use
Customary fee splits:
Owner's policy: Seller
Lender's policy: Buyer
Title search: Included in premium
Transfer taxes: Seller
Closing fees: Divided equally
Recording fees: Buyer
Real estate transfer disclosure required? Yes
Agency relationship disclosure required? Yes

Minnesota

Title companies, lenders, real estate agents, and attorneys may conduct closings. Conveyance is by warranty deed. Although deeds of trust are authorized, mortgages are the customary security instruments. The redemption period following a foreclosure is six months in most cases; it is 12 months if the property is larger than 10 acres or the amount claimed to be due is less than two-thirds of the original debt. This is a strong abstract state. Typically a buyer will accept an abstract and an attorney's opinion as evidence of title, even though the lender may require title insurance. People in the Minneapolis-St. Paul area use the Torrens system. Minnesotans use ALTA policies. Buyers pay the lender's and owner's title insurance premiums and the mortgage tax. Sellers usually pay the closing fees and the transfer taxes. Property taxes are due on May 15 and October 15.

Consumer Complaints:
Division of Financial Examinations
Department of Commerce
85 7th Place East, Suite 500
St. Paul, MN 55101-2198
651-296-2135
E-mail: financial.commerce@state.mn.us
Web: www.commerce.state.mn.us/pages/
    FinancialServicesMain.htm

Rate filing statute: File and use
Customary fee splits:
Owner's policy: Negotiable
Lender's policy: Buyer
Title search: Shares, seller often pays for abstract
Transfer taxes: Seller
Closing fees: Shared by parties
Recording fees: Buyer
Real estate transfer disclosure required? No, except wells and septic system disclosures
Agency relationship disclosure required? Yes

Mississippi

Attorneys conduct real estate closings. Conveyance is by warranty deed. Deeds of trust are the customary security instruments. Foreclosure involves a non-judicial process that takes 21-45 days. Mississippians use ALTA policies and endorsements. Buyers and sellers negotiate the payment of title insurance premiums and closing costs. There are no documentary, mortgage, or transfer taxes. Property taxes are payable on an annual basis and become delinquent February 1.

Consumer Complaints:
Department of Banking and Consumer
   Financing
501 N. West Street, 901 Woolfolk Building,
   Suite A
P.O. Box 23729
Jackson, MS 39225-3729
601-359-1031
Fax: 601-359-3557
Web: www.dbcf.state.ms.us
Mississippi Real Estate Commission
P.O. Box 12685
Jackson, MS 39236
2506 Lakeland Drive, Suite 300
Jackson, MS 39232
601-932-9191
Fax: 601-932-2990
E-mail: mrec@mrec.state.ms.us
Web: www.mrec.state.ms.us
Consumer Services Division
Department of Insurance
P.O. Box 79
Jackson, MS 39205
501 N. West Street, Woolfolk State Office
   Building, 10th Floor
Jackson, MS 39201
Toll-free in MS: 800-562-2957, 601-359-2453,
   601-359-3569
Fax: 601-359-2474
Web: www.doi.state.ms.us

Rate filing statute: File and use
Customary fee splits:
Owner's policy: Seller
Lender's policy: Buyer
Title exam: Seller
Closing fees: Divided equally
Recording fees: Buyer
Real estate transfer disclosure required? Yes
Agency relationship disclosure required? Yes

Missouri

Title companies, lenders, real estate agents, and attorneys may conduct closings. In the St. Louis area, title company closings predominate. In the Kansas City area, an escrow company or a title company generally conducts the closing. Conveyance is by warranty deed. Deeds of trust are the customary security instruments and allow private power of sale. The trustee must be named in the deed of trust and must be a Missouri resident. Foreclosure involves publication of a sale notice for 21 days, during which time the debtor may redeem the property or file a notice of redemption. The foreclosure sale buyer receives a trustee's deed. Missourians use ALTA policies and endorsements. Buyers and sellers generally split the closing costs. Sellers in western Missouri usually pay for the title insurance polices; elsewhere the buyers pay. There are no documentary, mortgage, or transfer taxes. Property taxes are payable annually and become delinquent January 1 for the previous year.

Consumer Complaints:
Division of Finance
P.O. Box 716
Jefferson City, MO 65101
Harry S Truman State Office Building, Room
   630
Jefferson City, MO 65102
573-751-3242
Fax: 573-751-9192
E-mail: finance@mail.state.mo.us
Web: www.ecodev.state.mo.us/finance
Division of Consumer Affairs
Department of Insurance
P.O. Box 690
301 W. High Street, Room 630
Jefferson City, MO 65102
573-751-2640, 573-751-4126, TDD: 573-526-
   4536
Fax: 573-526-4898, 573-751-1165
E-mail: mdicons@mail.state.mo.us
Web: www.insurance.state.mo.us
Real Estate Commission
P.O. Box 1339
Jefferson City, MO 65102-1339
3605 Missouri Boulevard
Jefferson City, MO 65109
573-751-4352, TTY: 800-735-2966
Fax: 573-751-2777
E-mail: realesta@mail.state.mo.us
Web: www.ecodev.state.mo.us/pr/restate/

Rate filing statute: File and use
Customary fee splits:
Owner's policy: Varies from county to county
Lender's policy: Buyer
Title search: Varies from county to county
Closing fees: Divided equally
Recording fees: Buyer

Real estate transfer disclosure required? No
Agency relationship disclosure required Yes

Montana

Real estate closings are handled through escrow. Conveyance is by warranty deed, corporate deed, or grant deed. Mortgages, deeds of trust, and unrecorded contracts of sale are the security instruments. Mortgages require judicial foreclosure, and there's a six- to 12-month redemption period following sale. Foreclosure on deeds of trust involves filing a notice of default and then holding a trustee sale 120 days later. Montanans use ALTA policies and endorsements. Buyers and sellers split the escrow and closing costs; sellers usually pay for the title insurance policies. There are no documentary, mortgage, or transfer taxes. Montanans may pay their property taxes annually by November 30 or semi-annually by November 30 and May 31.

Consumer Complaints:
Department of Commerce, Banking and
    Financial Institutions Division
846 Front Street
Helena, MT 59620
406-444-2091
Web: commerce.state.mt.us/bnk&fin/index.html
Department of Insurance
840 Helena Avenue
P.O. Box 4009
Helena, MT 59601
406-444-2040
Fax: 406-444-3497
Web: www.state.mt.us/sao
Department of Labor and Industry
Business Standards Division
Board of Realty Regulation
P.O. Box 200513
Helena, MT 59620
301 S. Park
Helena, MT 59602
406-444-2961
Fax: 406-841-2323
Web: discoveringmontana.com/dli/bsd/license
    /bsd_boards/rre_board/board_page.htm

Rate filing statute: File and use
Customary fee splits:
Owner's policy: Seller
Lender's policy: Buyer
Title exam: Included in premium
Closing fees: Divided equally

Recording fees: Buyer
Real estate transfer disclosure required? No
Agency relationship disclosure required? Yes

Nebraska

Title companies, lenders, real estate agents, and attorneys all conduct closings. Conveyance is by warranty deed. Mortgages and deeds of trust are the security instruments. Mortgage foreclosures require judicial proceedings and take about six months from the date of the first notice when they're uncontested. Deeds of trust do not require judicial proceedings and take about 90 days. Nebraskans use ALTA policies and endorsements. Buyers and sellers split escrow and closing costs; sellers pay the state's documentary taxes. Property taxes fall due April 1 and August 1.

Consumer Complaints:
Financial Institutions Division
Department of Banking and Finance
The Atrium, 1200 N Street, Suite 311
P.O. Box 95006
Lincoln, NE 68509-5006
402-471-2171
Web: www.ndbf.org
Consumer Affairs Division
Department of Insurance
941 O Street, Suite 400
Lincoln, NE 68508-3639
402-471-2201, TDD: 800-833-7352
Fax: 402-471-4610
E-mail: consumer_affairs@doi.state.ne.us
Web: www.nol.org/home/ndoi
Real Estate Commission
1200 N Street, Suite 402
P.O. Box 94667
Lincoln, NE 68509-4667
402-471-2004
Fax: 402-471-4492
E-mail: DDEnf@nrec.state.ne.us
Web: www.nrec.state.ne.us

Rate filing statute: Prior Approval
Customary fee splits:
Owner's policy: Divided equally
Lender's policy: Divided equally
Title search: Included in premium
Transfer taxes: Seller
Closing fees: Divided equally
Recording fees: Buyer
Real estate transfer disclosure required? Yes
Agency relationship disclosure required? Yes

Nevada

Escrow similar to California's is used for closings. Conveyance is by grant deed, bargain-and-sale deed, or quitclaim deed. Deeds of trust are the customary security instruments. Foreclosure involves recording a notice of default and mailing a copy within 10 days. Following the mailing there is a 35-day reinstatement period. After that, the beneficiary may accept partial payment or payment in full for a three-month period. Then come advertising the property for sale for three consecutive weeks and finally the sale itself. All of this takes about 4½ months. Nevadans use both ALTA and CLTA policies and endorsements. Buyers and sellers share escrow costs. Buyers pay the lender's title insurance premiums; sellers pay the owner's and the state's transfer tax. Property taxes are payable in one, two, or four payments, the first one being due July 1. Nevada is a community property state. There are no state income, inheritance, gift, or estate taxes.

Consumer Complaints:
Financial Institutions Division
Department of Business and Industry
406 E. 2nd Street, Suite 3
Carson City, NV 89701-4758
775-684-1830
Fax: 775-684-1845
2501 E. Sahara Avenue, Suite 300
Las Vegas, NV 89104
702-486-4120
Fax: 702-486-4563
E-mail: fid@govmail.state.nv.us
Web: fid.state.nv.us
Department of Business and Industry
Division of Insurance, Consumer Services
   Section
788 Fairview Drive #300
Carson City, NV 89701
775-687-4270, 800-992-0900
2501 E. Sahara Avenue #302
Las Vegas, NV 89104
702-486-4009, 800-992-0900
Web: www.doi.state.nv.us
Real Estate Division, Compliance Division
788 Fairview Drive, Suite 200
Carson City, NV 89701-5453
775-687-4280
Fax: 775-687-4868
2501 E. Sahara Avenue, Suite 102

Las Vegas, NV 89104-4137
702-486-4033
Fax: 702-486-4275
E-mail: realest@red.state.nv.us
Web: www.red.state.nv.us/

Rate filing statute: Prior approval
Customary fee splits:
Owner's policy: Seller
Lender's policy: Buyer
Title search: Included in premium
Transfer tax: Seller
Closing fees: Divided equally
Real estate transfer disclosure required? No
Agency relationship disclosure required? Yes

New Hampshire

Attorneys conduct real estate closings. Conveyance is by warranty or quitclaim deed. Mortgages are the customary security instruments. Lenders may foreclosure through judicial action or through whatever power of sale was written into the mortgage originally. Entry, either by legal action or by taking possession peaceably in the presence of two witnesses, is possible under certain legally stated conditions. There is a one-year right-of-redemption period. The people of New Hampshire use ALTA owner's and lender's policies. Buyers pay all closing costs and title fees except for the documentary tax; that's shared with the sellers. Property tax payment dates vary across the state.

Consumer Complaints:
Banking Department
64 B Old Suncook Road
Concord, NH 03301-5151
603-271-3561
Fax: 603-271-1090, 603-271-0750
Web: webster.state.nh.us/banking
Department of Insurance
56 Old Suncook Road
Concord, NH 03301-7317
Toll-free: 800-852-3416, 603-271-2261
Fax: 603-271-0248, 603-271-1406
E-mail: requests@ins.state.nh.us
Web: webster.state.nh.us/insurance/
Real Estate Commission
State Annex House, Room 437, 4th Floor
25 Capitol Street
Concord, NH 03301
603-271-2701, TDD: 800-735-2964
Web: www.state.nh.us/nhrec

Rate filing statute: Prior approval
Customary fee splits:
Owner's policy: Buyer
Lender's policy: Buyer
Title search: Buyer
Transfer taxes: Divided equally
Closing fees: Negotiable
Recording fees: Buyer, seller pays for release of any liens
Real estate transfer disclosure required? No, except for disclosure for private water and septic systems and type of insulation in home
Agency relationship disclosure required? Yes

New Jersey

Attorneys handle closings in northern New Jersey; title agents customarily handle them elsewhere. Conveyance is by bargain-and-sale deed with covenants against grantors' acts (equivalent to a special warranty deed). Mortgages are the most common security instruments, though deeds of trust are authorized. Foreclosures require judicial action, which takes six to nine months if they're uncontested. New Jerseyites use ALTA owner's and lender's policies. Both buyer and seller pay the escrow and closing costs. The buyer pays the title insurance fees, and the seller pays the transfer tax. Property taxes are payable quarterly on April 1, July 1, October 1, and January 1.

Consumer Complaints:
Department of Banking and Insurance, Division of Banking
P.O. Box 40
Trenton, NJ 08625-0040
20 W. State Street
Trenton, NJ 08625
609-984-2777
Fax: 609-777-0107
Web: www.state.nj.us/dobi
Department of Banking and Insurance, Division of Insurance
20 W. State Street
P.O. Box 329
Trenton, NJ 08625-0329
Toll-free in NJ: 800-446-7467, 609-292-5316
Fax: 609-292-3144
Web: www.state.nj.us/dobi
Department of Banking and Insurance, Real Estate Commission
P.O. Box 328
Trenton, NJ 08625-0328

609-292-8300
Fax: 609-292-0944
E-mail: realestate@dobi.state.nj.us
Web: www.state.nj.us/dobi/remnu.htm

Rate filing statute: Prior approval
Customary fee splits:
Owner's policy: Buyer
Lender's policy: Buyer
Title search: Buyer
Transfer taxes: Seller
Closing fees: Buyer
Recording fees: Buyer
Real estate transfer disclosure required? No
Agency relationship disclosure required? Yes

New Mexico

Real estate closings are conducted through escrows. Conveyance is by warranty or quit-claim deed. Deeds of trust and mortgages are the security instruments. Foreclosures require judicial proceedings, and there's a nine-month redemption period after judgment. New Mexicans use ALTA owner's policies, lender's policies, and construction and leasehold policies; they also use endorsements. Buyers and sellers share escrow costs equally; sellers pay the title insurance premiums. There are no documentary, mortgage, or transfer taxes. Property taxes are payable November 5 and April 5. New Mexico is a community property state.

Consumer Complaints:
Regulation and Licensing Department, Financial Institutions Division
725 St. Michael's Drive
Santa Fe, NM 87501
505-827-7100
Web: state.nm.us/rld/fid/fidhome.htm
Department of Insurance
P.O. Box 1269
Santa Fe, NM 87504-1269
505-827-4601
Fax: 505-827-4734
Web: www.nmprc.state.nm.us
Real Estate Commission
1650 University Drive, NE, Suite 490
Albuquerque, NM 87102
505-841-9120, 800-801-7505
Fax: 505-246-0725
E-mail: NMREC@state.nm.us
Web: www.state.nm.us/nmrec

Rate filing statute: Promulgate
Customary fee splits:
Lender's policy: Seller
Lender's policy: Buyer
Title search: Included in premium
Closing fees: Divided equally
Real estate transfer disclosure required? No,
except if an agent is involved
Agency relationship disclosure required? Yes

New York

All parties to a transaction appear with their attorneys for closing. Conveyance is by bargain-and-sale deed. Mortgages are the security instruments in this lien-theory state. Foreclosures require judicial action and take several months if uncontested or longer if contested. New Yorkers use policies of the New York Board of Title Underwriters almost exclusively, though some use the New York State 1946 ALTA Loan Policy. Buyers generally pay most closing costs, including all title insurance fees and mortgage taxes. Sellers pay the state and city transfer taxes. Property tax payment dates vary across the state.

Consumer Complaints:
Banking Department
2 Rector Street, 18th Floor
New York, NY 10006-1894
212-618-6951, 800-522-3330, 800-334-3360
Fax: 212-618-6440, 212-618-6570
Web: www.banking.state.ny.us/
Consumer Services Bureau, Insurance
  Department
Empire State Plaza, Agency Building 1
Albany, NY 12257
518-474-6600
Fax: 518-474-6630
E-mail: consumers@ins.state.ny.us
Web: www.ins.state.ny.us
Department of State, Division of Licensing
  Services
84 Holland Avenue
Albany, NY 12208-3490
518-474-4429, 518-473-2728
Fax: 518-473-6648
E-mail: licensing@dos.state.ny.us
Web: www.dos.state.ny.us/lcns/licensing.html

Rate filing statute: File and use
Customary fee splits:
Buyer pays almost all closing costs, including
title insurance

North Carolina

Attorneys or lenders may handle closings, and corporate agents issue title insurance. Conveyance is by warranty deed. Deeds of trust with private power of sale are the customary security instruments. Foreclosures are non-judicial, with a 10-day redemption period following the sale. The entire process takes between 45 and 60 days. North Carolinians use ALTA policies, but these require an attorney's opinion before they're issued. Buyers and sellers negotiate the closing costs, except that buyers pay the recording costs, and sellers pay the document preparation and transfer tax costs. Property taxes fall due annually on the last day of the year.

Consumer Complaints:
Commissioner of Banks
316 W. Edenton Street
Raleigh, NC 27603
4309 Mail Service Center
Raleigh, NC 27699-4309
919-733-3016
Fax: (919) 733-6918
Web: www.banking.state.nc.us/
Department of Insurance, Consumer Services
Dobbs Building
430 North Salisbury Street
P.O. Box 26387
Raleigh, NC 27611
919-733-2032, 919-733-7349, 800-546-5664
Fax: 919-733-6495
E-mail: consumer@ncdoi.net
Web: www.ncdoi.com/
Real Estate Commission
P.O. Box 17100
Raleigh, NC 27619-7100
1313 Navaho Drive
Raleigh, NC 27609-7461
919-875-3700
E-mail: ai@ncrec.state.nc.us
Web: www.ncrec.state.nc.us/

Rate filing statute: Modified file and use
Customary fee splits:
Owner's policy: Buyer
Lender's policy: Buyer
Title search: Buyer
Transfer taxes: Seller
Closing fees: Negotiable
Recording fees: Buyer
Real estate transfer disclosure required? No
Agency relationship disclosure required? Yes

North Dakota

Lenders, together with attorneys, conduct closings. Conveyance is by warranty deed. Mortgages are the security instruments. Foreclosures require about six months, including the redemption period. North Dakotans base their title insurance on abstracts and attorneys' opinions. Buyers usually pay for the closing, the attorney's opinion, and the title insurance; sellers pay for the abstract. There are no documentary or transfer taxes. Property taxes are due March 15 and October 15.

Consumer Complaints:
Department of Financial Institutions
2000 Schafer Street, Suite G
Bismarck, ND 58501-1204
701-328-9933
E-mail: dfi@state.nd.us
Web: www.state.nd.us/bank/
Department of Insurance
600 E. Boulevard Avenue, 5th Floor
Bismarck, ND 58505-0320
701-328-2440, toll-free: 800-247-0560
Fax: 701-328-4880
E-mail: insuranc@state.nd.us
Web: www.state.nd.us/ndins
Real Estate Commission
314 E. Thayer Avenue
Bismarck, ND 58501
P.O. Box 727
Bismarck, ND 58502-0727
701-328-9749, 701-328-9739
Fax: 701-328-9750

Rate filing statute: File and use
Customary fee splits:
Owner's policy: Buyer
Lender's policy: Buyer
Title search: Seller
Closing fees; Buyer
Recording fees: Buyer
Real estate transfer disclosure required? No
Agency relationship disclosure required? Yes

Ohio

Title companies and lenders handle closings. Conveyance is by warranty deed. Dower rights require that all documents involving a married person be executed by both spouses. Mortgages are the security instruments. Judicial foreclosures, the only kind allowed, require about six to 12 months. People in Ohio use ALTA policies; they get a commitment at closing and a policy following the recording of documents. Buyers and sellers negotiate who's going to pay closing costs and title insurance premiums, but sellers pay the transfer taxes. Property tax payment dates vary throughout the state.

Consumer Complaints:
Division of Financial Institutions
Department of Commerce
77 S. High Street, 21st Floor
Columbus, OH 43215-0121
614-728-8400
E-mail: webdfi@dfi.com.state.oh.us
Web: www.com.state.oh.us/ODOC/dfi/
Consumer Advocate/Assistant Director
Department of Insurance
Office of Consumer Services
2100 Stella Court
Columbus, OH 43215-1067
614-644-2658, 614-644-3378, 800-686-1526,
   614-644-2673, TDD/TTY: 614-644-3745
Fax: 614-644-3743, 614-752-0740, 614-644-
   3744
Web: www.ins.state.oh.us/
Department of Commerce
Division of Real Estate and Professional
   Licensing
77 S. High Street, 20th Floor
Columbus, OH 43215-6133
614-466-4100
Fax: 614-644-0584
E-mail: webreal@com.state.oh.us
Web: www.com.state.oh.us/ODOC/real/

Rate filing statute: File and use
Customary fee splits:
Owner's policy: Seller
Lender's policy: Buyer
Title search: Seller
Transfer taxes: Buyer
Closing fees: Negotiable
Recording fees: Buyer
Real estate transfer disclosure required? Yes
Agency relationship disclosure required? Yes

Oklahoma

Title companies, lenders, real estate agents, and attorneys may conduct closings. Conveyance is by warranty deed. Mortgages are the usual security instruments. Foreclosures may be by judicial action or by power of sale if properly allowed for in the security instrument. Oklahomans use

ALTA policies and endorsements. Buyers and sellers share the closing costs, except that the buyer pays the lender's policy premium, the seller pays the documentary transfer tax, and the lender pays the mortgage tax. Property taxes may be paid annually on or before the last day of the year or semi-annually by December 31 and March 31.

Consumer Complaints:
State Banking Department
4545 N. Lincoln Boulevard, Suite 164
Oklahoma City, OK 73105-3427
405-521-3653, 405-521-2782
Fax: 405-522-2993
5800 S. Lewis Avenue, Suite 173
Tulsa, OK 74105-7120
918-743-4763
Fax: 918-743-4775
Web: www.state.ok.us/~osbd/
Insurance Department
P.O. Box 53408
Oklahoma City, OK 73152-3408
2401 N.W. 23rd Street, Suite 28 (Shepherd Mall)
Oklahoma City, OK 73107-2442
405-521-2828, toll-free in OK: 800-522-0071
Fax: 405-521-6652
E-mail: okinsdpt@telepath.com
Web: www.oid.state.ok.us
Real Estate Commission
2401 N.W. 23rd Street, Suite 18 (Shepherd Mall)
Oklahoma City, OK 73107
405-521-3387
Fax: 405-521-2189
E-mail: orec.help@orec.state.ok.us
Web: www.state.ok.us/~orec/

Rate filing statute: No direct rate filing provisions
Customary fee splits:
Owner's policy: Buyer
Lender's policy: Buyer
Title search: Seller
Closing fees: Negotiable
Recording fees: Buyer records deed of trust, seller pays for documents to convey title
Real estate transfer disclosure required? Yes, if an agent is involved or is requested by buyer
Agency relationship disclosure required? Yes

Oregon

Closings are handled through escrow. Conveyance is by warranty or bargain-and-sale deed, but land sales contracts are common. Mortgage deeds and deeds of trust are the security instruments. Oregon attorneys usually act as trustees in non-judicial trust-deed foreclosures. Such foreclosures take five months from the date of the sale notice; defaults may be cured as late as five days prior to sale. Judicial foreclosures on either mortgages or trust deeds allow for a one-year redemption period following sale. Oregonians use ALTA and Oregon Land Title Association policies. Buyers and sellers split escrow costs and transfer taxes; the buyer pays for the lender's title insurance policy and the seller pays for the owner's policy. Property taxes are payable November 15, February 15, and May 15; owners receive a 3% reduction if they pay in full by November 15.

Consumer Complaints:
Department of Consumer and Business Services
Division of Finance and Corporate Securities
350 Winter Street, NE, Room 410
Salem, OR 97310-3881
503-378-4140, TTY: 503-378-7387
Fax: 503-947-7862
E-mail: dcbs.dfcsmail@state.or.us
Web: www.cbs.state.or.us/dfcs/
Insurance Division
350 Winter Street, NE, Room 440-2
Salem, OR 97310-3883
503-947-7980, toll-free in OR: 888-877-4894, TTY: 503-947-7280
Fax: 503-378-4351
E-mail: dcbs.insmail@state.or.us
Web: www.cbs.state.or.us/ins
Real Estate Agency
1177 Center Street, NE
Salem, OR 97301-2505
503-378-4170
Fax: 503-373-7153
Web: www.rea.state.or.us/

Rate filing statute: File and use
Customary fee splits:
Owner's policy: Seller
Lender's policy: Buyer
Title search: Included in premium
Closing fees: Divided equally

Recording fees: Buyer
Real estate transfer disclosure required? Yes
Agency relationship disclosure required? Yes

Pennsylvania

Title companies, real estate agents, and approved attorneys may handle closings. Conveyance is by special or general warranty deed. Mortgages are the security instruments. Foreclosures take one to six months from filing through judgment plus another two months or more from judgment through sale. State law restricts aliens in owning real property with respect to acreage and income and includes special restrictions affecting farmland. Pennsylvanians use ALTA owner's, lender's, and leasehold policies. Buyers pay closing costs and title insurance fees; buyers and sellers split the transfer taxes. Property tax payment dates differ across the state.

Consumer Complaints:
Department of Banking
333 Market Street, 16th Floor
Harrisburg, PA 17101-2290
Toll-free in PA: 800-PA BANKS, 717-787-1854,
    TDD: 800-679-5070
Fax: 717-787-8773
E-mail: ra-pabanking@state.pa.us
Web: www.banking.state.pa.us/
Bureau of Consumer Service
Insurance Department
1321 Strawberry Square, 13th Floor
Harrisburg, PA 17120
Toll-free: 877-881-6388, 717-787-2317
Fax: 717-787-8585
E-mail: consumer@ins.state.pa.us
Web: www.insurance.state.pa.us
Real Estate Commission
P.O. Box 2649
Harrisburg, PA 17105-2649
717-783-3658
Fax: 717-787-0250
E-mail: realesta@pados.dos.state.pa.us
Web: www.dos.state.pa.us/bpoa/recomm/main-
    page.htm

Rate filing statute: File and use
Customary fee splits:
Owner's policy: Buyer
Lender's policy: Buyer
Title search: Buyer
Transfer taxes: Divided equally
Closing fees: Included in premium

Recording fees: Buyer
Real estate transfer disclosure required? No
Agency relationship disclosure required? No

Rhode Island

Attorneys usually conduct closings, but banks and title companies may also conduct them. Conveyance is by warranty or quitclaim deed. Mortgages are the usual security instruments. Foreclosures follow the power-of-sale provisions contained in mortgage agreements and take about 45 days. Power-of-sale foreclosures offer no redemption provisions, whereas any other foreclosure method carries a three-year right of redemption. Rhode Islanders use ALTA policies and endorsements. Buyers pay title insurance premiums and closing costs; sellers pay documentary taxes. The custom is that monies are not disbursed at the closing table. Checks are normally mailed or wired to your bank account. Property taxes are payable annually, semi-annually, or quarterly with the first payment due in July.

Consumer Complaints:
Banking Division
Department of Business Regulation
233 Richmond Street, Suite 231
Providence, RI 02903-4231
401-222-2495, 401-222-2246, TDD: 401-222-2999
Fax: 401-222-6098
E-mail: BankInquiry@dbr.state.ri.us
Web: www.dbr.state.ri.us/banking.html
Commercial Licensing and Regulation
    Division, Real Estate
Department of Business Regulation
233 Richmond Street, Suite 230
Providence, RI 02903-4230
401-222-2255, TDD: 401-222-2999
Fax: 401-222-6654
Web: www.dbr.state.ri.us/real_estate.html
Insurance Division
Department of Business Regulation
233 Richmond Street, Suite 233
Providence, RI 02903-4233
401-222-2223, TDD: 401-222-2999
Fax: 401-222-5475
E-mail: InsuranceInquiry@dbr.state.ri.us
Web: www.dbr.state.ri.us/insurance.html

Rate filing statute: File and use
Customary fee splits:
Owner's policy: Buyer

Lender's policy: Buyer
Title search: Buyer
Transfer taxes: Seller
Closing fees: Buyer
Real estate transfer disclosure required? Yes
Agency relationship disclosure required? Yes.

South Carolina

Attorneys customarily handle closings. Conveyance is by warranty deed. Mortgages are most often the security instruments. Foreclosures are judicial and take three to five months, depending on court schedules. Foreclosure sales take place on the first Monday of every month following publication of notice once a week for three consecutive weeks. South Carolinians use owner's and lender's ALTA policies and endorsements. Buyers pay closing costs, title insurance premiums, and state mortgage taxes; sellers pay the transfer taxes. Property tax payment dates vary across the state from September 15 to December 31.

Consumer Complaints:
Department of Consumer Affairs
P.O. Box 5757
Columbia, SC 28250-5757
3600 Forest Drive, 3rd Floor
Columbia, SC 29250
Toll-free in SC: 803-734-4200, 800-922-1594, 803-
  734-9450
Fax: 803-734-4286
Web: www.state.sc.us/consumer/home.htm
Department of Insurance
Consumer Services
300 Arbor Lake Drive, Suite 1200
Columbia, SC 29223
Toll-free in SC: 800-768-3467, 803-737-6180
Fax: 803-737-6231
E-mail: cnsmmail@doi.state.sc.us
Web: www.state.sc.us/doi/Consumer.html
Department of Labor, Licensing, and Regulation
Real Estate Commission
Synergy Business Park, Kingstree Building
110 Centerview Drive
Columbia, SC 29210
P.O. Box 11847
Columbia, SC 29211-1847
803-896-4400
Fax: 803-896-4404
Web: www.llr.state.sc.us/POL/RealEstateCom-
  mission/

Rate filing statute: Deemer period
Customary fee splits:
Owner's policy: Buyer
Lender's policy: Buyer
Title search: Buyer
Transfer taxes: Seller
Closing fees: Buyer
Recording fees: Buyer
Real estate transfer disclosure required? No
Agency relationship disclosure required? Yes

South Dakota

Title companies, lenders, real estate agents, and attorneys may handle closings. Conveyance is by warranty deed. Mortgages are the usual security instruments. Foreclosures may occur through judicial proceedings or through the power-of-sale provisions contained in certain mortgage agreements. Sheriff's sales follow publication of notice by 30 days. The redemption period allowed after sale of parcels smaller than 40 acres and encumbered by mortgages containing power of sale is 180 days; in all other cases, it's a year. There's a unique statute that stipulates that all land must be plotted in lots or described by sectional references rather than by metes and bounds unless it involves property described in documents recorded prior to 1945. There's another unique statute called the Affidavit of Possession Statute. Certain exceptions aside, it provides that any person having an unbroken chain of title for 22 years thereafter has a marketable title free of any defects occurring prior to that 22-year period. South Dakotans use ALTA policies and endorsements. Sellers pay the transfer taxes and split the other closing costs, fees, and premiums with the buyers. Property taxes come due May 1 and November 1.

Consumer Complaints:
Division of Banking
Department of Commerce and Regulation
217½ W. Missouri
Pierre, SD 57501-4590
605-773-3421
Fax: 605-773-5367
E-mail: bankinfo@state.sd.us
Web: www.state.sd.us/dcr/bank/
Division of Insurance
Department of Commerce and Regulation
118 W. Capitol
Pierre, SD 57501-2000
605-773-3563

Fax: 605-773-5369
Web: www.state.sd.us/insurance
Real Estate Commission
118 W. Capitol
Pierre, SD 57501
605-773-3600
Fax: 605-773-4356
E-mail: DCR-REALESTATE@state.sd.us
Web: www.state.sd.us/dcr/realestate/Real-
  hom.htm

Rate filing statute: Prior approval
Customary fee splits:
Owner's policy: Divided equally
Lender's policy: Buyer
Title exam: Included in premium or paid by
buyer
Transfer taxes: Seller
Closing fees: Divided equally
Recording fees: Buyer
Real estate transfer disclosure required? Yes
Agency relationship disclosure required? Yes

Tennessee

A title company attorney, a party to the contract, a lender's representative, or an outside attorney may conduct a closing. Conveyance is by warranty or quitclaim deed. Deeds of trust are the customary security instruments. Foreclosures, which are handled according to trustee sale provisions, are swift, that is, 22 days from the first publication of the notice until the public sale, and there is normally no right of redemption after that. Tennesseans use ALTA policies and endorsements. The payment of title insurance premiums, closing costs, mortgage taxes, and transfer taxes varies according to local practice. Property taxes are payable annually on the first Monday in October.

Consumer Complaints:
Division of Consumer Affairs
500 James Robertson Parkway, 5th Floor
Nashville, TN 37243-0600
Toll-free in TN: 800-342-8385, 615-741-4737
  Fax: 615-532-4994
Web: www.state.tn.us/consumer
Department of Commerce and Insurance
500 James Robertson Parkway, Davy Crockett
  Tower
Nashville, TN 37243-0565
Toll-free in TN: 800-342-4029, 615-741-2241
Fax: 615-532-6934

Web: www.state.tn.us/commerce
Real Estate Commission
Department of Commerce and Insurance
500 James Robertson Parkway, Suite 180
Nashville, TN 37243-1151
Toll-free: 800-342-4031, 615-741-2273
Fax: 615-741-0313
E-mail: trec@mail.state.tn.us
Web: www.state.tn.us/commerce/trec/

Rate filing statute: File and use
Customary fee splits:
Owner's policy: Seller
Lender's policy: Buyer
Title exam: Seller. In most counties there is a charge in addition to the premium for the exam, based on the amount of work performed by examining attorney.
Transfer taxes: Buyer
Closing fees: Divided equally
Recording fees: Buyer

Texas

Title companies normally handle closings. Conveyance is by warranty deed. Deeds of trust are the most common security instruments. Following the posting of foreclosure sales at the local courthouse for at least 21 days, the sales themselves take place at the courthouse on the first Tuesday of the month. Texans use only Texas standard policy forms of title insurance. Buyers and sellers negotiate closing costs. There aren't any documentary, transfer, or mortgage taxes. Property taxes are due October 1. Texas is a community property state.

Consumer Complaints:
State Finance Commission
2601 N. Lamar Boulevard
Austin, TX 78705-4294
Toll-free: 877-276-5554, 512-475-1300
Fax: 512-474-1313
Web: www.fc.state.tx.us/
Department of Insurance
P.O. Box 149104
Austin, TX 78714-9104
333 Guadalupe Street
Austin, TX 78701
Toll-free in TX: 800-252-3439, 800-578-4677,
  512-463-6169
Fax: 512-475-2005, 512-475-1771
E-mail: ConsumerProtection@tdi.state.tx.us
Web: www.tdi.state.tx.us

Real Estate Commission
P.O. Box 12188
Austin, TX 78711-2188
1101 Camino La Costa
Austin, TX 78752
512-459-6544 or 800-250-TREC (8732)
Fax: (512) 465-3962
E-mail: enforce@trec.state.tx.us
Web: www.trec.state.tx.us

Rate filing statute: Promulgate
Customary fee splits:
Owner's policy: Seller
Lender's policy: buyer
Title exam: included in premium
Transfer taxes: N/A
Closing fees: Negotiable
Recording fees: Buyer, except seller pays for recording documents to release encumbrances

Utah

Lenders handle about 60% of the escrows; title companies handle the rest. Conveyance is by warranty deed. Mortgages and deeds of trust with private power of sale are the security instruments. Mortgage foreclosures require judicial proceedings, which take about a year; deed-of-trust foreclosures take advantage of private power-of-sale provisions and take about four months. Utahans use ALTA owner's and lender's policies and endorsements. Buyers and sellers split escrow fees, and sellers pay the title insurance premiums. There are no documentary, transfer, or mortgage taxes. Property taxes are payable November 30.

Consumer Complaints:
Department of Commerce
Division of Corporations and Commercial Code
P.O. Box 146701
Salt Lake City, UT 84114-6701
160 E. 300 South
Salt Lake City, UT 84111
Toll-free in UT: 877-526-3994, 801-530-4849
E-mail: corpucc@utah.gov
Web: www.commerce.utah.gov/cor/index.html
Insurance Department
State Office Building Room 3110
Salt Lake City, UT 84114-6901
Toll-free in UT: 800-439-3805, 801-538-3805,
    TDD: 801-538-3826
Fax: 801-538-3829
Web: www.insurance.state.ut.us

Department of Commerce
Division of Real Estate
Box 146711
Salt Lake City, UT 84114-6711
160 E. 300 South
Salt Lake City, UT 84111
801-530-6747
Fax: 801-530-6749
E-mail: realest@e-mail.state.ut.us
Web: www.commerce.utah.gov/dre/index.html

Rate filing statute: File and use
Customary fee splits:
Owner's policy: Seller
Lender's policy: Buyer
Title exam: Included in premium
Transfer taxes: N/A
Closing fees: Divided equally
Recording Fees: Buyer

Vermont

Attorneys take care of closings. Conveyance is by warranty or quitclaim deed. Mortgages are the customary security instruments, but large commercial transactions often employ deeds of trust. Mortgage foreclosures require judicial proceedings for "strict foreclosure"; after sale, there is a redemption period of one year for mortgages dated prior to April 1, 1968, and six months for all others. Vermonters use ALTA owner's and lender's policies and endorsements. Buyers pay recording fees, title insurance premiums, and transfer taxes. Property tax payment dates vary across the state.

Consumer Complaints:
Department of Banking, Insurance, Securities,
    and Health Care Administration
89 Main Street, Drawer 20
Montpelier, VT 05620-3101
Toll-free in VT: 800-964-1784, 802-828-3307,
    802-828-3302
Fax: 802-828-3301
Web: www.bishca.state.vt.us/
Office of Professional Regulation
Real Estate Commission
26 Terrace Street, Drawer 09
Montpelier, VT 05609-1106
802-828-2363, 802-828-3228
E-mail: opr@sec.state.vt.us
Web: vtprofessionals.org/opr1/real_estate/

Rate filing statute: Use and file
Customary fee splits:

Owner's policy: Buyer
Lender's policy: Buyer
Title exam: Buyer
Transfer taxes: Buyer
Closing fees: Negotiable, closing normally handled by attorney performing the title exam
Recording fees: Buyer
Real estate transfer disclosure required? No, but voluntary disclosure is common
Agency relationship disclosure required? Yes, by closing

Virginia

Attorneys and title companies conduct real estate closings. Conveyance is by bargain-and-sale deed. Deeds of trust are the customary security instruments. Foreclosure takes about two months. Virginians use ALTA policies and endorsements. Buyers pay the title insurance premiums and the various taxes. Property tax payment dates vary.

Consumer Complaints:
State Corporation Commission
Bureau of Financial Institutions
1300 E. Main Street, Suite 800
P.O. Box 640
Richmond, VA 23218-0640
804-371-9705, 804/371-9657, TDD: 804-371-9206
Fax: 804-371-9416
E-mail: bfiquestions@scc.state.va.us
Web: www.state.va.us/scc/division/banking/index.htm
State Corporation Commission
Bureau of Insurance
P.O. Box 1157
Richmond, VA 23218
1300 E. Main Street
Richmond, VA 23219
Toll-free in VA: 800-552-7945, 804-371-9741, TDD: 804-371-9206
E-mail: bureauofinsurance@scc.state.va.us
Web: www.state.va.us/scc/division/boi/index.htm
Department of Professional and Occupational Regulation
3600 W. Broad Street
Richmond, VA 23230
804-367-8500, TDD: 804-367-9753
Fax: 804-367-2475
E-mail: dpor@dpor.state.va.us
Web: www.state.va.us/dpor/indexie.html

Rate filing statute: File and use
Customary fee splits:
Owner's policy: Buyer
Lender's policy: Buyer
Title exam: Buyer
Transfer taxes: Varies—buyer normally pays state and local taxes, seller pays grantor's tax
Closing fees: Negotiable—title exam and attorney's fees are not regulated
Recording fees: Buyer
Real estate transfer disclosure required? Yes, or seller may execute a residential property disclaimer statement
Agency relationship disclosure required? Yes

Washington

Title companies, independent escrow companies, lenders, and attorneys may handle escrows. An attorney must prepare real estate documents, but there is a "limited practice rule" that lets licensed non-attorneys prepare most of the commonly used real estate documents. Conveyance is by warranty deed. Both deeds of trust with private power of sale and mortgages are used as security instruments. Mortgages require judicial foreclosure. Deeds of trust require that a notice of default be sent first and 30 days later a notice of sale. The notice of sale must be recorded, posted, and mailed at least 90 days before the sale, and the sale cannot take place any earlier than 190 days after the actual default. Sellers generally pay the title insurance premiums and the "revenue" tax; buyers and sellers split everything else. Property taxes are payable April 30 and October 31. Washington is a community property state.

Consumer Complaints:
Department of Financial Institutions
P.O. Box 41200
Olympia, WA 98504-1200
210 11th Avenue, SW, Room 300
Olympia, WA 98501
360-902-8700 or 800-372-8303
Fax: 360-586-5068
Web: www.dfi.wa.gov/
Office of the Commissioner of Insurance
Consumer Advocacy
P.O. Box 40256
Olympia, WA 98504-0256
Rowesix, Building 4
4224 Sixth Avenue, SE
Lacey, WA 98503

Toll-free in WA: 800-562-6900, 360-753-3613,
   TDD: 360-407-0409 or 360-664-3154
Fax: 360-407-0186, 360-586-3535
E-mail: cad@oic.wa.gov
Web: www.insurance.wa.gov
Department of Licensing, Business and
   Professions Division
Real Estate Program
P.O. Box 9015
Olympia, WA 98507-9015
2000 4th Avenue, W, 2nd Floor
Olympia, WA 98507
360-586-4602
Fax: 360-586-0998
Web: www.wa.gov/dol/bpd/refront.htm

Rate filing statute: File and use
Customary fee splits:
Owner's policy: Seller
Lender's policy: Buyer
Title exam: Included in premium
Transfer taxes: Seller
Closing fees: Divided equally
Recording fees: Buyer
Real estate transfer disclosure required? Yes
Agency relationship disclosure required? Yes

West Virginia

Attorneys conduct escrow closings, although lenders and real estate agents do them occasionally. Conveyance is by warranty deed, bargain-and-sale deed, or grant deed. Deeds of trust are the customary security instruments. Foreclosures are great for lenders; when uncontested, they take only a month. West Virginians use ALTA policies and endorsements. Buyers pay the title insurance premiums and sellers pay the documentary taxes; they divide the other closing costs. Property taxes may be paid in a lump sum after July 6th or in two installments on September 1 and March 1.

Consumer Complaints:
Division of Banking
1900 Kanawha Boulevard E, Building #3,
   Room 311
Charleston, WV 25305-0240
304-558-2294
Fax: 304-558-0442
Web: www.wvdob.org/
Insurance Commission
1124 Smith Street
Charleston, WV 25301

P.O. Box 50540
Charleston, WV 25305-0540
Toll-free in WV: 800-642-9004, 304-558-3354
Fax: 304-558-0412
E-mail: wvinscs@mail.wvnet.edu
Web: www.state.wv.us/insurance
Real Estate Commission
1033 Quarrier Street, Suite 400
Charleston, WV 25301-2315
304-558-3555
Fax: 304-558-6442
E-mail: wvrec@wvrec.state.wv.us
Web: www.state.wv.us/wvrec/
No mandatory property condition disclosure requirement

Rate filing statute: File and use
Customary fee splits:
Owner's policy: Buyer
Lender's policy: Buyer
Title exam: Buyer (All title insurance is written by attorney-agents. Exam fees and costs usually established at attorney-agent discretion.)
Transfer taxes: Seller
Closing fees: Negotiable
Recording fees: Buyer

Wisconsin

Lenders and title companies conduct what are called "table closings" throughout the state, except in the Milwaukee area, where attorneys conduct the closings. Conveyance is by warranty deed, but installment land contracts are used extensively, too. Mortgages are the customary security instruments. Within limits, the actual mortgage wording determines foreclosure requirements; redemption varies from two months for abandoned property to a full year in some cases. Lenders generally waive their right to a deficiency judgment in order to reduce the redemption period to six months. Wisconsinites use ALTA policies and endorsements. Buyers generally pay closing costs and the lender's policy fees; sellers pay the owner's policy fees and the transfer taxes. In transactions involving homesteads, conveyances may be void if not joined into by the spouse. Property taxes may be paid in full on February 28 or half on January 31 and half on July 31. Wisconsin is a quasi community property state.

Consumer Complaints:
Department of Regulation and Licensing

Division of Enforcement
P.O. Box 8935
Madison, WI 53708-8935
1400 E. Washington Avenue, Room 173
Madison, WI 53703
608-266-2112
E-mail: web@drl.state.wi.us
Web: www.drl.state.wi.us/
Office of the Commissioner of Insurance
121 E. Wilson Street
Madison, WI 53702
Toll-free in WI: 800-236-8517, 608-266-3585,
    TDD toll-free: 800-947-3529 (ask for 608-
    266-3586)
Fax: 608-266-9935
E-mail: information@oci.state.wi.us
Web: oci.wi.gov/

Rate filing statute: File and Use
Customary fee splits:
Owner's policy: Seller
Lender's policy: Buyer
Title exam: Included in premium
Transfer taxes: Seller
Closing fees: Seller pays for deed closing,
buyer pays for loan closing
Recording fees: Buyer, except seller pays for
recording documents to release encumbrances
Real estate transfer disclosure required? Yes
Agency relationship disclosure required? Yes

Wyoming

Real estate agents generally conduct closings. Conveyance is by warranty deed. Mortgages are the usual security instruments. Foreclosures may follow judicial or power-of-sale proceedings. Residential foreclosures take around 120 days; agricultural foreclosures take around 13 months. Wyomingites use ALTA owner's and lender's policies and endorsements. Buyer and seller negotiate who's going to pay the various closing costs and title insurance fees. There are no documentary, mortgage, or transfer taxes.

Property taxes may be paid annually December 31 or semi-annually September 1 and March 1. There are no state income taxes in Wyoming.

Consumer Complaints:
Department of Audit, Division of Banking
Herschler Building, 3rd Floor East
122 W. 25th Street
Cheyenne, WY 82002
307-777-7797
Fax: 307-777-3555
Web: audit.state.wy.us/banking/default.htm
Wyoming Department of Insurance
Herschler Building, 3rd Floor East
122 W. 25th Street
Cheyenne, WY 82002-0440
Toll-free in WY: 800-438-5768, 307-777-7401
Fax: 307-777-5895
E-mail: wyinsdep@state.wy.us
Web: insurance.state.wy.us
Real Estate Commission
2020 Carey Avenue, Suite 100
Cheyenne, WY 82002-0180
307-777-7141
E-mail: cander2@missc.state.wy.us
Web: realestate.state.wy.us/index.htm

Rate filing statute: Prior approval
Customary fee splits:
Owner's policy: Seller
Lender's policy: Buyer
Title exam: Included in premium
Transfer taxes: N/A
Closing fees: Divided equally
Recording fees: Buyer
Real estate transfer disclosure required? No
Agency relationship disclosure required? Yes

Directory of Escrow and Closing Resources on the Web

Companion Web Site: www.escrowhelp.com

This valuable resource will supplement the information found in the book. Click on "Ask Sandy" to ask your closing or escrow questions. Read articles written by Sandy Gadow on real estate related and closing topics. Also found on Sandy's Web site are helpful resource links for buyers, sellers, and real estate professionals, including links to state title associations, recommended reading lists, and a mortgage calculator. Keep up to date on new developments in escrow and closing practices.

Appraisals

The Appraisal Institute
www.appraisalinstitute.org
Click on "Find an Appraiser" to find an appraiser in your area.

National Appraisal Network, Inc.
www.appealit.com
Information on making appeals related to appraisers, cancellation of private mortgage insurance.

Complaints

Complaints Against Banks
Office of the Comptroller of the Currency
www.occ.treas.gov
Regulates national banks.
The Board of Governors works with the 12 Federal Reserve Banks to make sure that commercial banks abide by their laws.

Office of Thrift Supervision
www.ots.treas.gov
Regulates all federal and many state-chartered thrift institutions, including savings banks and savings and loan associations. There are five regional offices, located in Jersey City, Atlanta, Chicago, Dallas, and San Francisco.

Complaints Against a Federal Savings Association Insurance Fund or a Federally Chartered Savings Bank
Federal Reserve Board: banks
www.federalreserve.gov/pubs/complaints/complain2.htm

Complaints Against Contractors
Contact your local State Building License Division.

RESPA Violations: Complaint Letter
www.hud.gov/offices/hsg/sfh/res/reslettr.cfm

Credit Reports

Look at your credit report prior to submitting your loan application. Correct any errors you may find.

Equifax
www.equifax.com
Credit profile report.

Experian
www.experian.com
You can add a profile search, "Credit Profile Report." $8 per report.

Understanding FICO scores
www.myfico.com
Improve your credit score.

ConsumerInfo.com
www.consumerinfo.com

My Vesta.com Financial Health Center
www.myvesta.com
Credit coaches, free publications.
Look at "Credit Scoring: How it works and actions you can take to improve your score and get approved for credit."

National Foundation for Consumer Credit
www.nfcc.org

Qspace (formerly icreditreport.com)
www.qspace.com
One-line credit source. Merged form from all three credit-reporting bureaus.

Government Sites

These Web sites offer solid background information for your home purchase or sale. They will give you a good general overview of loan programs, RESPA regulations, tips to understand your closing, and tax information.

FHA Loans
www.fhatoday.com
FHA vs. conventional financing, FHA rates, apply online, maximum mortgage limits for your area.

Federal Mortgage Programs
www.hud.gov/buying/mortprog.cfm
www.hud.gov/offices/hsg/comp/refunds/index.cfm
How to find out if you are owed a refund on your FHA loan.

Fair Credit Reporting Act
www.fair-credit-reporting-act.com

Federal Trade Commission
www.ftc.gov
Click "consumer protection,"
then "credit,"
then "Fair Credit Reporting Act."

Freddie Mac
www.freddiemac.com
Information on the homeownership process.
Includes advice on how to avoid predatory lending practices.

First-Time Homebuyer Loan Programs
www.homepath.com

HUD-1 Closing Statement Costs Explained
www.hud.gov
From Homes menu, click "Buying"
then under "Settlement or Closing" click "Settlement Cost and Helpful Information," to get text of the book, *Buying Your Home: Settlement Costs and Information.*

RESPA Disclosures
www.hud.gov/offices/hsg/sfh/res/sc2sectg.cfm

State and Local Government Web Sites
www.statelocalgov.net

Internal Revenue Service
hwww.irs.gov/pub/irs-pdf/p530.pdf
Look at the online booklet, Publication 530, "Tax Information for First-Time Homeowners."

Federal Consumer Information Center
www.pueblo.gsa.gov/housing.htm
Look at the online manual "Buying Your Home: Settlements Costs and Helpful Information."

VA Loans
www.vba.va.gov
Click on "Home Loan Guaranty Benefits."
FAQ, regional loan centers, VA approved lenders, free pamphlets.

FHA & VA Home Loans Online
www.fha-va-home-loans-online.com
www.homeloans.va.gov/veteran.htm

Home Inspections

For information on how to hire a home inspector.

American Society of Home Inspectors
www.ashi.com

National Association of Home Inspectors, Inc.
www.nahi.org

Insight Professional Home Inspection
www.inspectit.com/insight
List of questions to ask when selecting a home inspector.

American Society of Home Inspectors
www.ashi.com
Provides a list of home inspectors, tips for homebuyers, and home sellers.

ServiceMaster/American Home Shield

www.servicemaster.com

InspectAmerica Home Inspection SuperSite
www.inspectamerica.com
Find information on the home inspection process. Dedicated to homebuyers.

Homeowner Associations

Condo Management Online
www.condomgmt.com
Resource for community associations.

Insurance

Compare insurance rates early on. Rates can vary greatly from one agency to another.

Insurance Information Institute
www.iii.org

Insurance.com (Fidelity Investments)
www.insurance.com

Legal Forms

USlegalforms.com
www.uslegalforms.com

For Sale By Owner Forms
LegalKitStore.com
www.legalkitstore.com

Professional Computer Forms
www.formsrus.com

AllLaw.com
www.alllaw.com

Kaktus.com
www.kaktus.com
Purchase agreements, rental forms, lease option forms.

Loans

Caveat Emptor: Be careful of giving these loan Web sites your Social Security number, unless you are serious about applying for a loan with that particular lender. The lender may run a credit check to verify your credit. Many lenders look at frequent and recent credit inquiries as a negative on your credit profile.

While the Internet provides a great way to search for loan rates and programs and to pre-qualify for a loan, once you narrow down your search, you may want to contact your preferred lender by telephone or in person, to apply for the loan and get loan advice from a loan mortgage professional. Oftentimes establishing a relationship with the loan officer or mortgage broker will prove invaluable in helping you to obtain the best loan program for you and your financial needs. The loan officer often will help you prepare your documentation and give you advice on how to speed up your loan process. After all, the loan officer knows the underwriting requirements best for that lending institution and knows the internal protocol to get you the best loan, with the best possible terms.

Most of these loan Web sites have a toll-free number that you can call to talk to a loan representative.

Bankrate.com bank rate monitor
www.bankrate.com
Check interest rates, find a lender, apply online.

E-Loan
www.eloan.com
Check current rates.

General Mortgage Information
mortgage.com
www.mortgage.com

Consumer Loan Information

HSH Associates
www.hsh.com
Includes current interest rates, how to find a loan, how to protect your credit rating, chart of average closings costs.

iOwn.com
www.iown.com
An independent lender that has good "find an agent" and "shop mortgage rates" features. Claims to represent 15,000 mortgage brokers.

Mortgage Bankers Association of America
www.mbaa.org/consumer

Quicken.com
www.quicken.com

Mortgage Insurance Companies of America
www.privatemi.com
Private mortgage insurance.

VA Loans

Home Loan Guaranty Services
www.homeloans.va.gov/veteran.htm
FAQ, regional loan centers, VA approved
lenders, free pamphlets.

Homepath.com
www.homepath.com/calcs.htm
Calculate your maximum mortgage amount.

Moving

Moving.com
www.moving.com
Storage, real estate, neighborhood, insurance
quote system.

monstermoving.com
movecentral.com
Mortgage quotes, movers, repairs, pest control,
storage.

Allied Van Lines
alliedvan.net
Find local agents, free estimates, relocation
services.

Bekins Company
www.bekins.com
Get estimates and find locations.

MoveQuest.com
www.movequest.com
Street maps, homes, comparables, calculator
for moving.

MoversGuide.com
www.moversguide.com
Moving tips.

Pest Inspection Reports

Orkin Pest Control
www.orkin.com

Public Records

DataQuick Information Systems
www.dataquick.com

Private Mortgage Insurance

Mortgage Insurance Companies of America
www.privatemi.com
Private mortgage insurance.

GE Mortgage Insurance
www.ge-mi.com

Property Valuation

Domania
www.domania.com
Find out what a property sold for in your area
(not all areas, not all states). Includes a "Home
Price Check" calculator.

Relocation Services

Employee Relocation Council
www.erc.org
Includes job search and job listings.

MoversGuide.com
www.moversguide.com
Change of address service, moving tips.

Tax-Deferred Exchanges

National Exchange Service Group
www.exchangeservice.com
Offers exchange services nationwide.

IRS
www.irs.gov/pub/irs-pdf/p544.pdf
IRS Publication 544, "Sales and Other
Dispositions of Assets."

Section 1031 Services, Inc.
www.1031services.com
Good question-and-answer page with
Frequently Asked Questions.

Realty Exchangers, Inc.
www.1031help.com
Publishes a taxation newsletter. Offers a free
question-and-answer forum at askrich@1031uni-
versity.com.

Title Companies

For the sake of convenience, I will list the
large, nationwide title companies. There may
be local and independent title companies in
your area that may provide excellent closing
services. Check with your state department of
insurance or state department of corporations
for a list of title companies in your area.

Chicago Title Company
www.ctic.com

Fidelity National Title Insurance Company
www.fntic.com

The First American Corporation
www.firstam.com

LandAmerica
www.landam.com
Parent company of: Commonwealth Land Title Insurance Company, Lawyers Title Insurance Coporation, Transnation Title Insurance Company (formerly Transamerica Title Company).

The Web is constantly changing. If you find any links that are out-of-date or you would like to recommend links, please let me know. I will make every effort to add the new site to our companion Web site, www.escrowhelp.com.

Thank you for your suggestions!

Glossary of Real Estate Terms

These are basic explanations of escrow terms. They are not intended to be strict, legal definitions.

abstract of title A listing of all documents affecting title to any particular real property; used in some areas instead of a preliminary title report.

acceleration clause A provision added to a note or deed of trust causing it to become due and payable under certain conditions, such as in the event of the sale of the property; also called a *dueonsale clause*.

accommodator An intermediary who holds funds in a delayed exchange.

accrue To increase or accumulate; interest on loans is said to accrue daily.

acknowledgment A formal declaration before a notary public or qualified officer that the person signing a document is doing so voluntarily and using his or her legal name and signature; popularly called *notarizing*.

addendum An attachment to a purchase agreement or to escrow instructions. Used to modify or make changes.

adjustable rate mortgage A mortgage with an interest rate subject to change during the term of the loan.

ad valorem A Latin expression that means "according to the value"; an ad valorem tax or fee is assessed according to the value of the property.

adverse possession Acquisition of title to real property through continued occupation over a period of time (usually five years); title acquired in this way is not considered marketable until established by court proceedings against the owner of record.

affidavit A written statement or declaration that is sworn to or affirmed before somebody who has the authority to administer an oath or affirmation.

agency disclosure A disclosure made by real estate agents to buyer and seller that describes real estate agents' roles and responsibilities.

agreement of sale See *land contract*.

alienation clause A clause that calls for the entire loan balance to be paid upon the sale, loan, or transfer of title; an acceleration clause.

all inclusive deed of trust A deed of trust that includes within its terms the obligations owing under a prior deed of trust; used in wraparound loans.

ALTA American Land Title Association.

ALTA Title Insurance Policy American Land Title Association combination of various policies and endorsements that lenders usually require when making a loan; expands normal coverage to include unrecorded mechanic's liens, unrecorded physical easements, facts not revealed by a physical survey, water and mineral rights, and the rights of parties in possession such as buyers who have unrecorded claims and tenants.

amendment A change made to correct an error or to alter or augment part of an agreement without changing its principal idea or essence.

amortization The paying down of the loan balance with each payment.

amortize Pay off a debt in installments.

amortized loan, fully A loan paid off in installments; part of each installment pays down the principal and part pays the current interest owed; a fully amortized loan over 10 years would have 120 equal monthly payments; after making these payments every month, the borrow would owe nothing.

annual percentage rate (APR) The annual yearly rate of interest on a loan.

appraisal Value of a property determined usually by someone knowledgeable about the sales of similar properties.

appurtenance Anything incidental or belonging to land that might be considered part of the property, such as an improvement or an easement for ingress and egress.

appurtenant Belonging to.

ARM See *adjustable rate mortgage*.

arrears That which is behind; used when describing payment of past due interest and loan payments.

assessed value Value placed on property by the county assessor; used as a basis for computing property taxes; California law states that the assessor must value property for tax purposes at 25% of the fair market value; assessments are made a matter of record on March 1.

assessment bond An obligation to pay for costs of local improvements such as sidewalks, sewers, or street lighting.

assignment A transfer in writing of one's interest in something, as to assign an interest in a promissory note and deed of trust.

assumption Taking over another person's financial obligation; taking title to a property with the buyer assuming liability for paying an existing note secured by a deed of trust against the property.

attorney-in-fact A person given the power to act in a place of another; that person is said to have the power of attorney; written authorization of this power should always be recorded in the county where the power is to be used.

balloon payment The final payment that pays a note in full; much larger than the preceding payments.

bargain-and-sale deed A deed that includes the consideration together with the necessary language for conveying real property; depending on the state involved, it may or may not imply warranties.

beneficiary The recipient of benefits, often from a deed of trust; usually the lender of a sum of money.

beneficiary statement A report from the lender that sets forth the terms and conditions of a loan already on record, such as the remaining loan balance, interest rate, and monthly payment.

bilateral escrow instructions A single set of escrow instructions signed by both the buyer and seller (as practiced in Southern California); often signed at the opening of escrow, not at the end. Cf. *unilateral escrow instructions*.

bill of sale Signed document which transfers ownership of personal property from the seller to the buyer.

binder Written confirmation of insurance coverage provided by an insurer prior to issuance of the actual policy.

boot Profit realized in a tax-deferred exchange upon which income is not deferred; may be in either cash or paper.

borrower's statement to the lender Document prepared by the lender and signed by the borrower authorizing the lender to perform certain acts (complete a loan, etc.); usually included in the loan package.

breach Failure to fulfill a specific promise or obligation or to perform a specified duty.

cancel escrow To terminate escrow by mutual written instructions.

cap A ceiling on interest rate increases.

CC&R's Covenants, conditions, and restrictions that control the owner's rights to the use of owned and common areas in a condominium subdivision or planned unit development.

certificate of reasonable value (CRV) An appraisal commitment of property value made by the Department of Veterans Affairs.

certificate of title Written opinion by an attorney that ownership of a particular property is as stated in his or her certificate.

chain of title The history of ownership of a parcel of real estate; each deed or other instrument transferring the title is called a *link* and all of these links make up the chain of title.

chattel Personal property.

chattel mortgage A lien or security instrument against personal property.

close of escrow (COE) The date when documents are recorded and title passes from seller to buyer; on this date buyer becomes the legal owner and title insurance becomes effective.

closing costs Costs, apart from the purchase price, that are payable at the close of escrow; they include loan fees, title insurance fees, escrow fees, recording fees, notary fees, prorated items, etc.

closing statement A final accounting of the closed escrow showing the actual figures used to compute the completed escrow; may be filled out on a RESPA or HUD form.

cloud on title A claim appearing in some legal form on the title, but that is likely invalid; adversely affects a title's marketability until cleared.

CLTA California Land Title Association.

COE See *close of escrow*.

collateral Marketable real or personal property pledged by a borrower as security for a loan.

commission A real estate agent's earnings for handling a property transaction; usually computed as a percentage of the selling price and negotiable between the seller and the agent.

commitment of title Similar to a preliminary title report; guarantees that a title company will issue title insurance.

common areas All the spaces in a condominium or planned unit development that are not specifically reserved to the individual owners; include walkways, parking lots, and yards.

community property A way to hold title that exists in community property states and is presumed unless property is acquired by husband or wife specifically as separate property; neither spouse may sell community property without the consent of the other.

competent Legally qualified.

concurrent escrow A real estate transaction procedure in which the closing of one escrow is dependent upon the closing of another one; also called a *double escrow*; commonly used in exchanges and in instances where the buyer depends on funds he expects to get from the sale of another property.

concurrently Occurring simultaneously, at the same time; real estate exchanges often must be recorded concurrently.

condemnation The taking of private property for public use.

conditions Specifications detailed in a deed; they may cover such things as setbacks, types of dwellings, etc.

condominiums Apartments or other types of property in which the owner has fee title to the part actually occupied, with a proportionate interest in areas used by all occupants, such as walkways and parking areas.

conforming loan A loan that does not exceed Fannie Mae/Freddie Mac limits. This limit changes annually.

consideration Amount of money a buyer is willing to give a seller to purchase property.

construction loan A temporary loan to the home buyer by the lender to pay the building contractor, either in installments or in one lump sum at the end of construction.

constructive notice Notice given to the general public by the county records.

constructive receipt Control of the cash proceeds in a *delayed exchange* without actual physical possession by exchanger or his or her agent.

contingency A condition that must be met or an event that must happen before a purchase contract becomes binding between the parties.

contract Agreement to perform certain acts; may be legally binding.

contract of sale Agreement to purchase property wherein legal title is retained by the seller until the buyer has paid the purchase price in accordance with the terms of the contract.

convey To transfer title in property from one person to another.

cooperative Multiple family housing with each occupant being entitled to perpetual use of his own unit and receiving a share certificate giving him a proportionate interest in the entire property.

cotenancy Ownership shared by more than one person; tenacy in common and joint tenancy are both cotenancy arrangements.

county records A system for recording documents in permanent books at the county court house; maintained by each county and provided by law; open to public examination.

covenant A written agreement to control the use of property by future owners.

credit An item in your favor; what is owed to you; also, your financial ability to borrow money.

credit application A statement provided by a borrower for a prospective lender in order to establish or exhibit financial stability.

CRV See *certificate of reasonable value.*

debit A charge; an item you must pay for; what you owe.

deed A written document that transfers title to property; there are several different types: a *grant deed*, the most common, is simply used to convey property; a *gift deed* is used to make a gift of property; a *quitclaim* deed is used to transfer an interest owned in a property and, incidentally, contains no warranties; a *tax deed* is used to convey title held by the state; and a *deed of reconveyance* is used to convey legal title back to the borrower from the trustee.

deed of reconveyance A legal instrument that conveys title from a trustee back to the borrower under a mortgage once the mortgage has been paid out.

deed of trust Security for a property loan; deeds the property to a third party (trustee) to hold until the loan is paid.

deemer period Refers to the way this state regulates rate filing by title companies, in other words, how approval is obtained for rate filings by the regulatory authorities.

default Failure to make good on a promise, such as failure to make payments on a note or to live up to the terms of a contract.

deficiency judgment A personal judgment in a foreclosure action for whatever amount remains owing after the foreclosure sale of an encumbered property.

demand Specification by a lender as to what will cause them to call a loan balance due.

demise A transfer of an estate to another person for a specified period of years, for life, or at will.

Department of Veterans Affairs See *DVA.*

deposit A sum of money usually given to bind an agreement or an offer on a property.

description A reference to certain maps, plats, and other instruments that are recorded with the county and serve to make a positive property identification.

devise To give property by will; a *devisee* is the beneficiary to whom the property is willed and the *devisor* (more commonly called the *testator*) is the deceased person through whom the property is devised.

disbursement The release of monies held in an escrow account; usually on the day when escrow closes.

documentary stamps Tax applicable to property transfers and affixed to the grant deed; varies from county to county, city to city; sometimes called a *transfer tax.*

double escrow A real estate transaction procedure in which the closing of one escrow is dependent upon the closing of another one; also called a *concurrent escrow*; commonly used in exchanges and in instances where the buyer depends on funds he expects to get from the sale of another property.

dual agent A real estate agent representing both buyer and seller in a transaction. Also referred to as a *transactional broker.*

due-on-sale clause A clause that calls for an obligation to become due upon the sale of a property previously put up as collateral for a promissory note; frequently broadened to become a *due-on-transfer clause*; also called an *acceleration clause.*

DVA Department of Veterans Affairs, established on March 15, 1989 to succeed the

Veterans Administration; the DVA guarantees loans to qualified veterans; like the FHA loan, a DVA loan guarantees payment to the lender if the borrower should default.

earnest money A deposit made to bind an agreement between buyer and seller.

easement A right of one person to make limited use of another's property; for example, the right to cross a property and maintain a road or right-of-way or the right to install and maintain public utility services.

easement appurtenant An easement created for the benefit of a parcel of land; belongs with the land.

easement in gross An easement created for the benefit of an individual apart from the ownership of the land; a public utility easement is one example.

egress A means for departing from one's own property without trespassing on another person's property, as applied to an easement.

eminent domain The government's right to acquire private property for public or quasipublic use through condemnation; requires full compensation.

encroachment Extension of an improvement onto the land of another person.

encumbrance A general term for something that restricts the title of real property; encumbrances may be liens, leases, mortgages, judgments, deeds of trust, or easements.

endorsement An addition to a California Land Title Association (CLTA) or American Land Title Association (ALTA) Policy of Title Insurance that either expands or lessens the standard coverage; special coverages for specified concerns, such as mechanic's liens, that may be obtained for an additional fee.

equity The difference between fair market value of a property and the debts owing on it; the owner's interest in a property.

escrow The depositing of papers and funds with a third party along with instructions to carry out an agreement; the entire transaction of depositing items with an impartial party.

escrow agent See *escrow officer*.

escrow instructions Instructions from a buyer, seller, or lender to the escrow company as to what conditions must be met before escrow can close.

escrow number The file number assigned to an escrow by the escrow officer for identification purposes.

escrow officer Also known as an *escrow agent*; someone qualified to perform all the steps necessary to prepare and carry out escrow instructions, which might involve such tasks as obtaining title insurance; securing payoff demands; prorating taxes, interest, rents, etc.; and disbursing the funds held in escrow.

estate The degree, quantity, nature, and extent of a person's interest in property.

exceptions Conditional items listed on a preliminary title report and affecting the title; would be excluded from coverage by a title insurance policy.

execute To give validity by signing documents so that an intention may be completed.

Fannie Mae Federal National Mortgage Association, a federally sponsored private corporation that provides a secondary market for housing mortgages.

Federal Home Loan Mortgage Corporation An affiliate of the Federal Home Loan Bank that creates a secondary market in conventional residential loans and in FHA and VA loans by purchasing mortgages; also called *Freddie Mac.*

Federal National Mortgage Association A federally sponsored private corporation that provides a secondary market for housing mortgages; also called *Fannie Mae.*

fee simple estate The greatest interest one may hold in real property; usually means ordinary ownership of real estate and is sometimes called *fee title.*

FHA Federal Housing Administration, a federal agency that insures institutional lenders against losses resulting from defaults on loans that are made according to the agency's requirements.

FHLMC Federal Home Loan Mortgage Corporation (also called *Freddie Mac*), an affiliate of the Federal Home Loan Bank that creates a secondary market in conventional residential loans and in FHA and VA loans by purchasing mortgages from members of the Federal Reserve System and the Federal Home Loan Bank System.

fiduciary Someone entrusted with financial responsibility in someone else's behalf.

file and use Title insurers in most states file rate schedules, policy forms, and endorsement forms with the state insurance department; they may then use those rates and forms after a specified waiting interval; rates so filed are mandatory.

finance charges All costs the borrower must pay directly or indirectly to obtain credit for a specific loan.

financing real estate Securing a loan by giving real property as collateral for payment of the debt.

fire insurance requirement form A form included in loan papers that a borrower must sign, in which the borrower agrees to obtain fire insurance coverage to protect the property and insure the lender.

fixed rate mortgage A mortgage with an interest rate that does not change over the life of the loan.

FNMA Federal National Mortgage Association (also called *Fannie Mae*), a federally sponsored private corporation that provides a secondary market for housing mortgages.

foreclosure A legal process that deprives a mortgagor of his or her interest in a property because he or she has failed to comply with the terms of the mortgage.

Freddie Mac Federal Home Loan Mortgage Corporation, an affiliate of the Federal Home Loan Bank that creates a secondary market in conventional residential loans and in FHA and VA loans by purchasing mortgages.

freehold An estate of indeterminable duration, such as a life estate or fee simple estate.

front-end ratio The ratio used by lenders to qualify a borrower for a loan, determined by adding the principal, interest, taxes, insurance, and mortgage insurance on the new loan and dividing by the borrower's gross monthly income.

FSBO (For Sale by Owner) Property offered for sale typically without the use of a real estate broker.

funding The release of loan funds from a lending institution to the escrow company, generally on the closing day of escrow or recordation.

funding letter Written request to a lender for release of loan funds; also called the *request for loan proceeds.*

gift deed A deed granted out of "love and affection" rather than any material consideration.

graduated payment mortgage (GPM) A land loan for which the periodic payments increase at a stated rate over a stated period of time and then level off for the remainder of the term of the loan.

grant To convey title of property by means of a deed; a *grantor* conveys a property to a *grantee.*

grantee One who acquires title to property by means of a grant deed; usually the buyer.

grantor One who transfers title of a property by means of a grant deed; usually the seller.

hazard insurance Fire insurance policy that often includes liability insurance and extended coverage insurance.

homeowner's association A nonprofit association created to own or lease common areas and make improvements in a condominium or planned unit development; serves as the administrative and legislative arm of the unit owners.

homeowner's endorsement An addition to a policy of title insurance that extends the normal policy to cover items other than those stated in the standard policy; may include such items as mineral rights and mechanic's liens.

HUD Department of Housing and Urban Development.

HUD form A final accounting of closing costs, itemizing buyer's and seller's closing costs separately; a consumer protection form.

impound account A trust account established by a lender for the accumulation of borrower's funds to meet periodic payment of taxes, FHA mortgage insurance premiums, and future insurance premiums required to protect the property acting as security for a loan; the borrower pays impounds with the loan payment.

indemnity A guarantee against loss; a building contractor may, for example, give a title company an indemnity agreement that renders the title company harmless against any liens that may arise due to the contractor's failure to pay his or her bills.

index A number used by a lender to measure interest rate changes over time; used as a guide for resetting interest rates of adjustable rate loans.

individual lender Seller, third party, or real estate agent; any person or group of persons other than institutional lenders.

inflation endorsement Coverage that may be added to the standard owner's policy of title insurance; it adjusts the amount of coverage according to the cost-of-living index.

ingress A means for entering one's own property without trespassing on another person's property, as applied to an easement.

installment note A promissory note with payments of principal and interest made at designated intervals.

institutional lenders Savings and loan associations, banks, life insurance companies, and mutual savings banks.

instrument A written legal document such as a contract, a promissory note, a deed, or a grant.

insurable title A property title that a title insurance company is willing to insure.

interest rate Cost of borrowing money expressed as a percentage of the amount borrowed; this percentage figure is the cost of borrowing for one year; for example, if the interest rate were 10%, the cost of borrowing $1,200 for a year would be $120 and the cost of borrowing $1,200 for a month would be $10.

intermediate theory state A state in which the security for the mortgage is based on the title theory or deed of trust, but that requires the lender to foreclose to obtain legal title.

inter vivos trust A living trust; *inter vivos* is a Latin expression meaning "among the living."

interval ownership See *time sharing*.

intestate Someone who has died with no will; the estate reverts to the next of kin.

joint protection policy A title insurance policy insuring the interest of both owner and lender.

joint tenancy One way for several persons to hold title; joint tenants own an undivided equal interest and have equal rights to use the entire property; they are said to have the *right of survivorship*, that is, they inherit the property automatically upon the death of the other joint tenant; this right is the principal distinction between a joint tenancy and a tenancy in common.

joint tenancy deed A deed that gives title to grantees as joint tenants.

joint trusteeship A trust created jointly by husband and wife.

judgment A court's final decree, generally resulting in a lien; may encumber the sale of a property and must be satisfied before it can be sold.

judicial foreclosure Type of foreclosure that requires court proceedings; mortgage foreclosure requires court proceedings while deed-of-trust foreclosures generally do not; state laws dictate.

jumbo loan A loan amount that exceeds the Fannie Mae/Freddie Mac guidelines for a conforming loan; the limit is adjusted annually; also known as a *non-conforming* loan.

junior mortgage A mortgage that is subordinate to another mortgage.

jurat Certificate of an officer, such as a notary public or magistrate, who has witnessed someone's signature to a sworn document; also, that part of an affidavit stating by whom, where, when, and before whom it was sworn.

land contract (land sale contract) An agreement providing that the seller retains legal title until the purchaser has made required payments.

lease option A lease in which the lessee is given the option to purchase the property at a specific price and under terms set out in the lease option agreement.

leasehold estate An estate created by a lease for a certain period of time; in contrast to a *fee simple estate*, it is a lesser interest.

legal description A description of land recognized by law and based on government surveys, spelling out the exact boundaries of the entire piece of land; should so thoroughly identify a parcel that it cannot be confused with any other.

lender's escrow instructions A lender's instructions to the escrow company giving specific conditions that must be met before escrow can close or the deed of trust can be recorded.

lien A legal claim upon property for the payment of a debt; a money encumbrance; there are numerous types, some of them overlapping: *general liens*, which affect all property of an owner; *involuntary liens*, which can be placed on a property without the necessity of the owner's consent, such as property taxes; *specific liens*, which affect specific property of an owner, such as a deed of trust; *voluntary liens*, which are placed on a property by the owner, such as a deed of trust; *tax liens*, which put a claim on property when its taxes are not paid; *judgment liens*, which are general liens resulting when a person suing another person wins a judgment from a court for the sum owing him or her; *mechanic's liens*, which are claims made by subcontractors, laborers, or materials suppliers who file with the county to obtain payment for their services.

lien theory states States in which the mortgagor (borrower) retains legal title to the property; lender (mortgagee) has a lien on the property as security for the debt.

life estate Use of property only during a person's lifetime; this interest may be sold, encumbered, or leased, but only for the term of the life estate.

link Each deed or other instrument transferring the title in the *chain of title*, the history of ownership of a parcel of real estate.

lis pendens Legal notice that litigation is pending on a certain property and that anyone obtaining an interest in the property after the notice date may be bound by the judgment.

littoral rights Rights to shoreline property on a large body of water, such as an ocean or lake.

loan application A lender's initial source of information on a borrower/applicant and the collateral involved; stipulates the amount of money requested and the repayment terms.

loan commitment A lender's agreement to lend a specified amount of money; must be exercised within a certain time limit.

loan fees Costs charged by a lender for giving out a loan; may include points, tax service fees, appraisal fee, etc.

loan-to-value ratio (LTV) Percentage of a loan to a property's appraised value; expressed in terms of how much a lender will lend; an LTV of 75% would be a loan equaling 75% of the property's value.

lot book report A short title company report providing the property owner's name, the vesting, the property's legal description, and a plat map.

maturity date The end of a loan repayment period; a specific date in the future when full payment for a loan becomes due.

mechanic's lien A lien that a subcontractor, laborer, or supplier of materials may put on a property after furnishing labor or materials to improve the property without being paid.

metes and bounds Boundary lines of land given in terminal points and angles.

mineral rights Ownership of minerals found on a property.

mortgage A two-part contract that pledges specific property as security for payment of a debt; commonly used to refer to a property loan.

mortgage insurance Insurance required to be paid for by the borrower to protect the lender in the event payments are not made on time; most often required when the loan amount exceeds 80% of the purchase price.

mutual consent Approval of both parties to terms of a contract.

negotiable Capable of being assigned or transferred by endorsement; checks, drafts, and notes are all negotiable.

non-conforming loan A loan for an amount that exceeds the Fannie Mae/Freddie Mac guidelines for a *conforming loan*. The limit is adjusted annually. Also known as a *jumbo loan*.

non-recurring closing costs Fees and costs that are paid only once, usually at closing, such as title insurance or points.

notary public Person who acknowledges oaths, such as the signing of a grant deed or deed of trust; must be duly appointed by the proper authorities.

note A written promise to pay; *straight* notes have payments that cover interest only and *installment* notes have payments that cover the interest plus some of the principal.

notice of completion Document recorded to give constructive notice that a building job has been completed.

notice of default A formal recorded declaration that a default has occurred; starts foreclosure proceedings.

official records A master set of books kept by the county recorder in which copies of all recorded documents in that county are stored; may be microfilmed.

offset statement A statement by an owner or a lien holder concerning the liens against a property.

opinion of title An attorney's written evaluation of the condition of title to real property, based upon a careful examination of the abstract of title.

origination fee Fee paid to the lender for originating and closing the loan; typically 1% of the loan amount.

paper Notes in lieu of cash; sellers frequently "take back paper" when they can't or don't wish to get all their equity out of a property in cash.

parcel Land fitting a single description.

partial reconveyance The release of part of someone's interest in real property secured by a mortgage or deed of trust.

payee One who receives money.

payoff check Final disbursement check to a lender to pay off a loan in full.

payor Person who pays the sum due on a note to the payee.

personal property That which is not real property; curtains, furniture, appliances, and other items not attached permanently to the property.

PITI payment The monthly payments necessary to cover principal, interest, taxes, and insurance.

planned unit development (PUD) A development consisting of private and common areas that provides for a sharing of responsibility for the common areas.

plant department Department in a title company where research materials and copies of official documents are kept.

plat map Map of a land subdivision or housing development.

PMI Private mortgage insurance. See *mortgage insurance*.

point In the context of a loan, a point is equal to 1% of the loan amount and would be included in loan costs.

portfolio lender A lender that keeps loans for its own portfolio, rather than selling the loan on the secondary money market to Freddie Mac or Fannie Mae.

possession date Day when the buyer actually moves onto the property; may be different from the close of escrow or recording date.

power of attorney The authority given one person by another to act on his or her behalf.

preliminary report A report showing the current status of a property and the condition under which a title company is willing to insure title as of a specified date.

prepayment penalty Fine charged by a lender when a borrower pays off a loan before the due date; sometimes called a *prepayment bonus* by those involved in creative financing.

prescription Doctrine by which easements are acquired through long, continuous, and exclusive use or possession of property.

price The amount of money or other consideration given for a property; agreed upon between buyer and seller; also called *purchase price* or *sales price*.

principal The amount borrowed or financed; the unpaid balance of a loan; also, a main party to a transaction or a party handling a property transaction on his own behalf.

priority Taking place in rank or order; taking precedence over; in real estate transactions, priority is established by the order in which documents affecting a property are recorded and also by the language contained in those documents.

private mortgage insurance See *mortgage insurance*.

probate The judicial process supervising transfer of a deceased's estate to the heirs and beneficiaries.

promissory note Document with a promise to pay a sum of money; may be an installment note or a straight note.

proration A method of dividing up taxes, interest, and other sums proportionately between buyer and seller according to a certain date (usually close of escrow).

public records Records that by law give constructive notice of matters relating to property.

purchase price See *price*.

quiet title Court action brought to establish undisputed title; removal of a cloud on the title; see *cloud on title*.

quitclaim deed A deed in which the grantor releases any claim he or she may have on a property; most commonly used between spouses and in partnerships; it contains no warranties.

real property Term used to describe land and that which is permanently attached to the land.

reconveyance Transfer of title from the trustee back to the real owner of property; occurs when a loan has been paid in full; releases the trustor (borrower) from any further liability for that debt.

recordation Process of placing a document on file with the county recorder for everyone to see; said to give constructive notice of the document's existence; claims against property usually are given a priority on the basis of the time and date when they are recorded.

recurring closing costs Costs and fees that will be paid monthly or annually, such as fire insurance, interest, property taxes and mortgage insurance.

redemption Reclaiming real property from someone who has taken legal title to it.

redemption period Period of time in which borrower may redeem his or her property.

refinance To renew, revise, or reorganize an existing loan by obtaining a new loan; usually pays off the existing loan.

Regulation Z An estimated breakdown of costs that will be incurred in obtaining a loan; given to borrower by an institutional lender before the loan is taken out; a consumer protection form.

release clause A stipulation allowing for the release of a specific piece of property from a blanket lien that covers it and other property in exchange for a specific payment.

remainder Future interest in a property.

remainderman Person who holds a future interest that exists in favor of a party other than the grantor or his or her successors, as in a life estate relationship.

rescission See *right of rescission.*

reservation A particular right withheld by a grantor when conveying property.

RESPA Real Estate Settlement Procedures Act.

RESPA statement Settlement statement showing the final closing figures used to complete an escrow; also called a *HUD statement.*

restriction A limit on the use of property, usually imposed by a previous owner.

rider An addition to a document.

right of rescission A borrower's right to cancel a credit contract within three business days from the day he or she entered into the loan contract.

right of survivorship A right created by joint tenancy that states that, upon the death of one owner, the other immediately becomes the owner of the property.

right of way The right to cross or pass over a parcel of land; may be a right to use a road or driveway, a right to construct power lines through the property, or a right to put pipes underground.

right, title, and interest Term used in deeds to denote that the grantor is conveying all claims to a property.

riparian rights The right to use water running through or beside a property.

sales price See *price.*

secondary financing A loan taken out in addition to a first loan; usually obtained from an individual lender.

security Property pledged to ensure payment of a debt; collateral.

separate property Property that is held singly by either a husband or wife, described on a deed as "sole and separate property."

setback The minimum distance a building or other improvement must stand from property lines, in accordance with local zoning ordinances or deed restrictions.

settlement Time at which property purchase is finalized, closing costs paid, deeds exchanged, and money disbursed; also called the *closing* and *close of escrow.*

settlor One who creates an inter vivos or living trust.

shared appreciation mortgage (SAM) A loan arrangement that allows the lender, in exchange for a reduced interest rate, to share in any gain in the value of the property against which the mortgage is secured.

short-term rate A reduced rate for title insurance applicable in cases where the owner of a property has been insured previously or where any lender has been insured somewhat recently on the property.

specific performance A legal doctrine that enables a court to compel someone to perform according to his or her agreement.

Starker A taxpayer who won an important U.S. Court of Appeals case in 1979 (*T.J. Starker v. U.S.)* dealing with a *delayed exchange* and whose name is synonymous with those exchanges; the Starker ruling has since been modified in IRS Code Section 1031.

statement of identity Form often required by title company from buyer and seller to ensure that items found in the title search apply to the individuals in question.

statute of limitations Law specifying time limits for initiating enforceable legal action.

straight note A promissory note whose interest is payable in specified payments at various intervals and whose principal (original sum) is payable in one lump sum.

subdivision A tract of land surveyed and divided into lots.

subject to To take title without paying off the existing loan or deed of trust; original borrower remains ultimately responsible for repaying the loan; the buyer (new borrower) does not make a formal agreement with the lender.

subordinate That which takes second place; to be of lesser priority, such as a newly created deed of trust being subordinate to an existing one.

subordination agreement A written agreement that changes the priority of documents, making, for example, one deed of trust subordinate to another.

swing loan A short-term loan to bridge the gap between the purchase of a new home and the subsequent sale of an old one.

takeout loan A loan arranged for a buyer by a seller or builder/ developer.

tax deed The instrument of conveyance when a government body sells a property to pay for arrears of taxes.

tax-deferred exchange A method for postponing capital gains when disposing of real property by trading one property for another of like kind.

tax sale number A number assigned to a property when property taxes are not paid on time; identifies that property on the delinquent tax roll.

tax service A reporting service that notifies the lender in the event the borrower does not keep the property taxes current.

tenancy in common A form for taking title when two or more people buy property and own it together with either equal or unequal shares; if any one of the tenants in common dies, his or her interest passes to his or her heirs, not to the remaining tenants.

time-sharing Partial interest in a property allowing exclusive use for a specific time period.

title Evidence of a person's right to property.

title company Company authorized to issue title insurance, as well as to serve escrow needs.

title insurance Insurance protecting a property owner against losses resulting from an imperfect title.

title theory state A state in which the borrower assigns title to the lender, typically in a deed of trust.

Torrens system A governmental title registration system that uses certificates of title issued by a public official (the registrar of title) as evidence of title.

transactional broker A real estate agent representing both buyer and seller in a transaction; also referred to as a *dual agent*.

transfer tax See *documentary stamps*.

trustee Person or corporation appointed to hold title for another until repayment of an obligation has been made; a trustee for a deed of trust holds title to the property until the amount owing has been paid.

trustor Person who executes a deed of trust; the borrower on a note.

truth-in-lending Name given to the federal statutes and regulations form (Regulation Z) provided to borrowers prior to entering into a loan contract.

underwriting The analysis completed by a lender to determine the worthiness of a requested loan.

undivided interest Unsegregated interest of a co-owner in a whole property owned in common.

unilateral escrow instructions Separate sets of escrow instructions, one for the buyer and one for the seller; normally drawn up after all the information is in and escrow is ready to close. Cf. *bilateral escrow instructions*.

unsecured note A loan granted solely on the strength of a borrower's signature; no security is pledged, and no deed of trust is recorded.

UPC Identification number for a specific property; also called *assessor's tax parcel number*, *account number*, or *folio number*.

usury Charging an interest rate above the maximum allowed by state law.

VA Veterans Administration, succeeded as of March 15, 1989 by the Department of Veterans Affairs; see *DVA*.

variable interest rate An interest rate that may fluctuate up or down over the life of a loan; changes occur generally at six-month intervals.

vendee The buyer.

vendor The seller, one who disposes of something.

vest To confer or bestow upon, as in the expression, "Title shall vest in...."

vestee Current recorded owner.

vesting The manner in which title to real property is held.

Veterans Administration Federal agency succeeded as of March 15, 1989 by the Department of Veterans Affairs; see *DVA*.

Veterans Affairs, Department of See *DVA*.

waiver The release of a right to require something to take place, such as the waiver of a contingency found in the purchase agreement.

warranty deed Deed with written guarantees of title.

wraparound loan A loan that is really a combination of loans, the existing loan(s) and a new second loan.

zoning City or county regulations governing the use of property.

Index